PIRONI

PIRONI

THE CHAMPION
THAT NEVER WAS

D A V I D   S E D G W I C K

First published by Pitch Publishing, 2018

Pitch Publishing
A2 Yeoman Gate
Yeoman Way
Worthing
Sussex
BN13 3QZ
www.pitchpublishing.co.uk
info@pitchpublishing.co.uk

A CIP catalogue record is available for this book
from the British Library.

ISBN 978-1-78531-349-3

Typesetting and origination by Pitch Publishing
Printed in the UK by TJ International, Padstow, Cornwall

Contents

Foreword

THE day I first came across the name 'Didier Pironi' is still clear in my memory. A 12-year-old schoolboy, I had just blown my entire week's pocket money of £1 on a sticker album intriguingly entitled *Formula 1*. Save for a sketchy idea that Formula 1 had something to do with car racing, I knew next to nothing about the sport. I did, however, know that I loved collecting stickers (5p per packet of 5) and above all else placing them carefully into the albums provided by the Italian company Figurine Panini. Usually such albums were dedicated to football. Everton and especially Liverpool football club stickers had particularly high currency at my Merseyside primary school. Breaktimes would invariably find a gaggle of schoolboys swapping and bartering stickers with as much fervour as if on the floor of the London Stock Exchange. But Formula 1? An unknown. I believe I was the only boy in our school to have this sticker album.

Villeneuve, Andretti, Reutemann... just seeing those names – strange, foreign, exotic – was enough to hook me. However, there was one name above all others that intrigued me: Didier Pironi. 'What a great name for a racing driver,' I thought. I would repeat those six syllables over to myself, *Di-dee-ay Pe-ro-nee.* I loved the sound of that name. To me it seemed to perfectly encapsulate this strange, faraway world and the dashing heroes who inhabited it.

Anxious to find out more about this new sport, in that same year of 1980 I broke open the piggy bank to purchase my first F1 book, *Grand Prix*, a huge, lavish publication, the illustrations of cars, drivers and circuits having left such an impression on my young mind that I can still see them today. Indeed, one particular line of text written by motorsport journalist Nigel Roebuck stood out: 'After a race has finished,' wrote Roebuck in his portrait of Didier, one of 20 such driver profiles, 'you will find Pironi, showered and relaxed, watching the razzmatazz around him with a faintly mocking smile…' A faintly mocking smile! This Pironi character sounded my type of hero – detached, ironic, cool. I liked the sound of him. I wanted to find out more.

In swift order, my hitherto blue bedroom plastered with all things Everton – mainly its star players – went red – not the red of rivals Liverpool FC I hasten to add, but Ferrari red. I had found myself some new heroes. Thanks to a consignment of back issues of the legendary *Grand Prix International* magazine (sourced from a local second-hand bookstore), I was able to decorate my bedroom with all things Ferrari. Nightly I imagined myself sat in the cockpit of one of these incredible machines, imagined myself as Didier Pironi or team-mate Gilles Villeneuve flying around Monza in my very own Ferrari.

When Didier crashed so horrifically at Hockenheim in August 1982, it signalled the end of not only his career but also my ability to follow him. In the pre-Internet age keeping up with news of Didier was all but impossible. Save for a few occasional lines in *Autosport*, British motorsport forgot all about the Ferrari daredevil who had come within touching distance of the world championship. How I ached for news. Even then as a 13-year-old, I felt a sense of injustice: if only he had not gone out on to the German circuit that treacherous morning. If only. I was, however, alone in my angst, football being the only topic of conversation among my school friends.

Instead, I cheered on Arnoux and Tambay – Ferrari's new drivers – during 1983 but it was not the same. Besides, I had started to become aware of another driver currently making waves in British Formula 3, another daredevil, of Brazilian extraction, Ayrton da Silva…

And so, gradually, Didier faded away. I still thought about him from time to time, wondered what he was doing, but in the absence of any media interest I had no alternative but to abandon any hope of hearing about him again. Until, that is, in August 1987. I can still remember that Sunday morning, a grey overcast day in Merseyside as I rode my bike through town. I also remember the shock upon picking up the newspaper in a friend's house the following morning. Didier was on the front page of the British tabloid the *Daily Express*. Didier? But why? Hardly daring to look, I read the account of the *Colibri* accident with a trembling hand. Until that moment, I had not even known that Didier had been pursuing a career in powerboating, let alone racing in the south of England that fateful weekend. I was numb. I suppose it is how one feels under such circumstances, a realisation that somehow, however irrational, you have lost a little part of yourself. Didier was gone. It seemed unfair, cruel. Somewhere in my adolescent brain I guess I had been holding out some hope one day of cheering him on once more in Formula 1, perhaps of even meeting him face to face. I felt inexplicably sad.

The years passed by. New heroes came and went in Formula 1. I followed the career of that British Formula 3 driver now going by the name of Ayrton Senna. Didier would sometimes appear in the musings of *Autosport's* Nigel Roebuck such as his 1986 book *Grand Prix Greats* in which the journalist penned some illuminating portraits of his favourite Grand Prix drivers. I was intrigued when Mr Roebuck mentioned that he had often been asked to write a fictional novel with a Formula 1 setting, and that if he ever did embark on such a project more than likely he would model the hero of his book on none other than the life of Didier Pironi. Not Senna? Lauda? Clearly, there was more to Didier than met the eye.

Like Mr Roebuck, I too have been hibernating an idea of my own. What if I could write Didier's actual biography? I would then be able to fill in the gaps so to speak, to satisfy the curiosity that has always lingered and first took hold of a 12-year-old schoolboy 30-odd years ago. Would it even be possible? In summer 2014 I decided to test the water. Thus, I was very heartened when an article I wrote about Didier ('August is the Cruellest Month') attracted a fair bit of interest when it was published by Motorsport.com. Feedback seemed to suggest that I was not the only one interested in this remarkable individual.

A few years on, hundreds of articles and almost as many interviews later (or so it seems) I have finally arrived at my destination: *Pironi: The Champion That Never Was*. It has been a long and arduous task, a detective story which as well as leading to some dead ends has, occasionally, led to some moments of pure serendipity. While far from exhaustive, my hope is that this current book manages to provide at least some insights into a man whose life was a rollercoaster ride of triumph and tragedy, a life lived on the very edge, a life always and forever lived at full throttle.

David Sedgwick
Liverpool
May 2017

Acknowledgements

MY SINCERE thanks go to members of the Pironi-Dolhem and Weffort families, without whose help and blessing this project would not have been possible: Gilles and Didier, Catherine, Laurence, Thibault, Marie-Annick and Moreno.

For kindly sharing their memories of Didier and those golden years I would like to thank all of the following: Jean-Pierre Jarier, Jean-Louis Schlesser, Derek Daly, Jean-Pierre Jaussaud, Jean-René Popot, Gianfranco Ricci, Eric Lucas, Gilles Klein, Piercarlo Ghinzani, Eleonora Vallone, Andrea de Adamich, Beppe Gabbiani, Ingo Hoffman, Jean-Louis Conré, Eric Bhat, Jean-Pierre and Philippe Paoli, Francine – partner to the late Dr Letournel, Christian Courtel, Philippe Streiff, Jacques Laffite, François Mazet, Steve Leyshon, Brian Lisles, Allan de la Plante, Stephane Fruitier, Aldo Cichero, Just Jaeckin, Eric Lemuet, Mario Hytten, Dario Calzavara, Philippe Lecouffle, Gilles Gaignault, Fred Opert, Allen Brown of OldRacingCars.com

Special thanks to John Walker, one of the UK's leading authorities on offshore powerboating, and upon whose work much of the chapters on offshore racing are based.

For kindly loaning their images to the project, special thanks are due to Pascal Auffrere, Emmanuel Zurini, Bernard Bakalian, Laurence Villaume-Dolhem, Bernard Asset, Denis Briot, *St Tropez* magazine, Jürgen Tap, Eric Lemuet, Christian Courtel, and Jeff Lehalle.

ACKNOWLEDGEMENTS

A special mention to Paul Reidy, secretary of The Royal Motor Yacht Club Poole, who kindly provided a copy of the official *Colibri* accident report.

The following list of publications were also invaluable: *Grand Prix International, Motoring News, Car and Driver, Autosprint, Auto Hebdo, Autosport, Motorsport, La Stampa, L'Équipe, L'Automobile, Sport-Auto, Le Parisien.* I am also indebted to *GEO* and *Paris Match* who granted permission to quote extensively from two superb articles, 'Le Risque et le Passion' and 'Pironi: Sauve par l'amour', respectively.

Front cover image: Bernard Bakalian
Back cover image: Nicolas Cancelier.

How dull it is to pause, to make an end,
To rust unburnish'd, not to shine in use!
As tho' to breathe were life!

Ulysses (Alfred Lord Tennyson)

One

The castle at Boissy

O UR story starts in rural Italy, to the north-east of the country to be exact, in the years that followed the First World War. In common with customs and beliefs of the time, the family of Antonio Weffort increased its number annually with the addition of yet another child to an already burgeoning brood. Eventually, the family would number 14 children in total, all boys! In common with other families in the region, the Wefforts eked out a living from the land, but with so many mouths to feed times were tough.

Italy in the early 1920s was a country characterised by austerity. In the aftermath of war, food rationing was just one of many hardships endured by a bruised and battered population. Inflation spiralling out of control, it had even been necessary for the government to set a fixed price for bread. This volatile economic situation would lead directly to the infamous 1922 March on Rome, a revolt that would catapult Mussolini's fledgling Fascist Party into power. For Italians, these were uncertain times.

Antonio's second-born son, Giuseppe was just one of hundreds of thousands of young Italians facing an uncertain future, more so for those inhabitants of rural areas like Friuli, the region of north-east Italy bordering present-day Slovenia and Austria, and which the Weffort family had called home for well over a century. Like his brothers, Pepi – as he was known – had been born under the flag of Austria during the period when the Austro-Hungarian Empire had been in the ascendancy. At the outbreak of war however, 18-year-old Pepi had fought on the Italian front against the might of that very empire.

Upon his return home, Giuseppe promptly married his sweetheart Santa. The birth of three daughters consolidated a marriage that would last the rest of the couple's lives. Eldest daughter Ilva was born in 1919, Imelda in 1923, while Maria (b. 1921) did not survive infancy. The joy of fatherhood was, however, tempered by the economic realities of the times. Italy's transformation from poor relative to leading economic powerhouse was still several decades away. For a man with a wife and young family to support, the chronic shortage of work in post-war Italy would have been of serious concern. Labouring and agricultural work, where it did exist, was invariably poorly paid, and anyway Pepi had always been ambitious. His thoughts thus turned to France, to Paris.

The prospect of steady, relatively well-paid work abroad had been luring Italians from their homeland for a century and more. The United States, Germany, France, Argentina, the natives of Virgil's golden land had never been afraid to seek a better life elsewhere. Stability, perhaps even prosperity awaited those willing to take the plunge. There was, however, a price to pay: the heartache of leaving loved ones behind. Indeed, by the time of Giuseppe's departure from Italy in the mid-1920s, several branches of the Weffort family were already established in faraway Brazil where they continue to prosper to this day. Leaving the tightly knit community of Villesse would be a wrench, but it was a price that Pepi and others must have thought worth paying.

Busily establishing itself as the cultural cradle of the modern world, the Paris of the roaring twenties was a city of innovation and creativity – an ideal location for a young émigré intent on making his way in the world. Post-war gloom shed, the city was blossoming. Writers such as Scott Fitzgerald and Hemingway had made the city their home. Picasso was also resident. Paris symbolised a new energy surging through the continent, a heady brew of optimism and opportunism that would continue throughout the decade right up to the Wall Street Crash of 1929. It was into this dynamic hub that Giuseppe and his young family arrived.

Initially, Pepi took work wherever he could find it. Paris in the 1920s was a city in the process of reinventing itself, many of its buildings and tenement blocks being in drastic need of refurbishment. This was also the era of Art Deco. Demand for labour – immigrant labour – was high.[1] Over time, the young Friulian worked hard. As their fortunes increased, the family was eventually able to move out to the suburbs where Pepi formed his own company, Sud Est Travaux (South East Building).

Around this time – towards the end of the Second World War – Ilva met a dashing young man by the name of Louis Dolhem. The couple fell in love and married. Soon enough Louis had joined the family business, bringing his own not inconsiderable talents to the table. Intelligent, resourceful and urbane, Louis's abilities combined with those of his father-in-law enabled Sud Est Travaux to expand ever more rapidly. In 1944 Louis and Ilva welcomed a son, Louis Joseph (José) into the world.

Louis's antecedents are somewhat obscure. Save for the fact he seems to have originated from northern France, his family background is indeed rather sketchy. For here was a young man who conducted his affairs with the utmost discretion. If he tended towards reserve – on occasion reticence – such dispositions were more than offset by action and endeavour. As far as Louis was concerned actions spoke louder than words, a tendency both his sons would come to share. In his youth, he had harboured ideas of racing cars, but strapped for cash had been unable to pursue his motor racing dreams. Instead, he had taken up long-distance cycling. Events such as the gruelling 156km Montceau-les-Mines race attracted not only amateurs such as Louis, but also the likes of Jean-Jacques Lamboley who would progress to national and world championship glory. Competing was in Louis's blood, another trait that he would pass on to both his sons.

Cycling achievements aside, he first comes to prominence during the Second World War when fighting for the French Resistance. After capture by the Nazis, the resourceful young man promptly escaped from Dachau concentration camp riding a bicycle, disguised as a German soldier! A little while later he became a prominent figure in the French Forces of the Interior (FFI), the resistance groups who did so much to aid the allies from 1944 onwards. Louis became commander of the Livry-Gargan group taking part in and organising espionage and sabotage activities that involved a high level of personal risk; bravery – yet another quality he would pass on to his progeny. While performing these critical duties he made contact with another young man of equally fierce independence and patriotism, Charles de Gaulle. The two men would remain connected long after war had ended. Later, as his political ambitions increased, Louis would become acquainted with the great and good of French politics including future president, Jacques Chirac. War hero, athlete and businessman, Louis undeniably oozed charisma. In post-war Paris, the name of Louis Dolhem was one to be reckoned with.

Post 1945, business was booming for the Franco-Italian enterprise. Amongst their many other gifts, Italian émigré and French freedom fighter were imbued with a definite entrepreneurial bent. Ably supported by the female half of the family, Louis and Pepi steered Sud Est to ever more prosperity. At its peak in the 1960s, the company would boast a workforce of several hundred, many of them, like Pepi, Italian expatriates to whom the firm were only too happy to offer employment.

Such was the success of the venture that the family was able to buy a plot of land in leafy Boissy-Saint Léger, a commune ten miles south-east of Paris. In former times, Boissy had been characterised by forests and lush countryside where wild boar and deer had freely roamed. By the 1940s, it had developed into a town of tranquil villas, yet to be fully engulfed by the metropolitan sprawl of Paris. When a photographer for *LIFE* magazine took a series of images of post-war Paris, he drew attention in imagery to what he referred to in words as the 'tragic beauty' of the city. Boissy then would have been a breath of fresh air, literally. A suitable plot of land purchased, Pepi could use all the tricks of his trade to design and build a family home to his exact requirements. Even for affluent Boissy, the house on the corner of Rue de Valenton and Rue de la Procession was a striking edifice, a labyrinth of multiple bedrooms and offices as well as outbuildings, which served as garages to the company's fleet of bulldozers, trucks and other commercial vehicles. Number 40 Rue de Valenton was a statement house, a celebration of hard work, endeavour and acumen.

By any standards, Louis Dolhem was a handsome man. A photograph taken in the 1940s, after he had become a father for the first time, depicts a poised, assured individual exuding confidence. It is no exaggeration to say there was surely a touch of star quality about this immaculate Parisian. Certainly, women succumbed all too easily to his charm and film star looks. Precisely what went on inside the castle in those post-war years will forever stay within its very commodious walls. Louis had an eye for a pretty woman, that much is certain, and by 1952 Imelda was carrying his second child. What Ilva thought about the union between her husband and younger sister is anyone's guess.

Fast forward to spring that year and at three o'clock on the afternoon of 26 March, Imelda[2] gave birth to a boy, Didier Joseph Louis. It was a time of great joy, but also some anxiety.

1950s Paris was a very different place to the cosmopolitan city of the 21st century. What may be considered as a mere trifle to modern sensibilities would have been a real dilemma in conservative post-war France: two sisters, two sons with just a single father. As pillars of the local community, Giuseppe and Louis would have been understandably keen to avoid even a whiff of scandal. Mud, as they say, has a habit of sticking. Prior to Didier's birth, the castle had echoed to the sound of endless discussions – many of them heated. How to avoid a scandal? Family honour was at stake.

Eventually Pepi, Louis and the sisters reached a solution, of sorts. A surrogate father needed to be found, one furthermore who would be prepared to marry the young girl. At this stage, love was not necessarily on the agenda. Step forward the shadowy figure of Valdi Pironi.

This mysterious individual was known to Giuseppe through a business associate. Of Friulian extraction himself, Pironi ticked many boxes. Imelda could now marry within her circle thus avoiding the stigma attached to childbirth out of wedlock. In the eyes of Monsieur and Madame Weffort, Valdi was the perfect solution to their problem. Elaborate as this plot now seems, in the context of the times, it must have seemed like an eminently sensible course of action, one that ensured the family's reputation would not be tarnished. Valdi accepted the conditions. Did the promise of becoming an integral part of this upwardly mobile family of émigrés with their booming construction business and shiny castle prove just a little too hard to resist? Not until he was a university student would Didier finally discover the identity of his real father. Until that time, Louis would always be 'mon oncle'.

Whatever the ins and outs of this complicated domestic situation, when the time came to register the birth in the nearby district of Villecresnes, it was not in the name of Dolhem that Didier's birth was registered, but rather in the name of 'Pironi'. The family secret was safe. With the arrival of Didier and his surrogate father, the population of the castle had expanded to eight: six adults and two children. Business continuing to expand, theirs was a busy house. Louis's involvement with both sisters made it an unconventional one as well.

Family secret notwithstanding, by the 1950s the family could rightly be proud of their achievements. Twenty-five years ago, Pepi had arrived in Paris with little else but a dream. In the ensuing decades, with his son-in-law's assistance not to mention connections, he had established one of the largest building companies in the whole of the city. Not only did he now drive a sleek Mercedes-Benz – a brand to which the family would always remain loyal – he would later acquire a Piper Navajo aeroplane, the same plane in which both his grandsons would one day learn to fly. Among the many family cars, Didier and José would vividly recall a Ford Vedette, a luxurious American sedan designed in Detroit and manufactured in Poissy. Family holidays were taken in the south of France in a sumptuous villa up in the St Tropez hills complete with stunning views over the Mediterranean. Skiing became another favourite pursuit. Winter holidays included trips to the fashionable resorts of the Auvergne-Rhône-Alpes region of the country. Life was good.

Despite his success, the businessman never forgot his Friulian roots. Such was his reputation among his kinsmen, trips back to Villesse had all the hallmarks of a state visit. Surrounded by a throng of excited villagers, the prodigal son would roll into the village in his gleaming sedan – invariably a shiny Mercedes. Though only a small boy at the time, Moreno Weffort still recalls the awe such occasions inspired: 'The whole village was in turmoil, it was a magical moment as we carried our best fruits and drink up to the family house in his honour. To this day, I can still remember the excitement those visits generated.' Moreno also warmly recalls the generosity of an uncle who believed in looking after the family he had left behind in Friuli. In later years, the businessman would thrill his family and neighbours by arriving in his private aeroplane.

Whether by chance or design neither of Pepi's daughters would give birth to any more children, by the standards of the time an unusual phenomenon. The same was not true of the dapper Louis, of which more later. It is hardly surprising therefore that Imelda formed a particularly strong bond to her only son. Didier literally became the centre of his mother's world. Adored, cosseted and yes, a trifle indulged.

Family wealth of course provided material benefits. In some quarters, it also provoked envy. Throughout his life, Didier's privileged upbringing would prove problematical for certain rivals who had not been similarly blessed and who clearly resented this urbane Parisian his somewhat pampered background. Money, both a blessing and a curse. Critics could and did claim that family money rather than talent had bought Didier a place at the top table of motorsport. 'A lot of people were jealous of Didier,' recalls an old school friend, 'jealous of his family and his background, jealous of the big house, the money.' The solution? To prove the critics wrong, repeatedly.

It was here within this somewhat eclectic Franco-Italian milieu, within the gilded walls of a fabulous Parisian castle, that José and his younger 'cousin' Didier grew up. It was undeniably a charmed existence, but one not devoid of the usual vicissitudes of family life, perhaps more so considering the somewhat unorthodox domestic arrangements. As a member of the Parisian bourgeoisie, a life of comfort and relative ease lay ahead. Along with José, Didier would surely one day take over the reins of the family business, expand its horizons, increase its fortunes further.

Not so Didier. Since his earliest years, the pleasure he derived from playing with his collection of toy cars had been apparent for all to see. These models captured little Didier's imagination like nothing else. Cars, cars, cars. At the dinner table soup bowls would transform into temporary steering wheels, cutlery would take the place of a gearstick. At the sort of tender age when infants are intent on exploring the world around them and discovering its secrets, young master Pironi was already well on the way to finding a nirvana all his own.

Two
Wild thing

EIGHT o'clock on a peaceful morning in Boissy. The town is just waking up. One or two shutters are coming up in the Rue de Paris, the main shopping road of this tranquil suburb. A few blocks away, the residents of Rue de la Procession are going about their morning routines, taking a sip of coffee, buttering a roll or two before the day's work begins. All is quiet on the streets outside save for a familiar clatter.

The little boy flies down the road as if his very life depends upon it. Balanced on the handlebars of his prized mini racing bicycle sits 'Jam', his favourite teddy bear, a mascot that accompanies him everywhere he goes. Determination is etched all over the rider's face. Preoccupied with some imaginary childish quest, it is hard not to smile as the youngster from the big corner house streaks past at breakneck speed. Pedalling furiously, he reaches the junction with Hottinguer Avenue. He lurches precariously to the left, leaning into the curve in the style of a racing hotshot. But for a slight kink, it is a straight run down to the end of this elegant tree-lined boulevard. The young cyclist hurtles along. Ahead lies a steep uphill run to school. The five-year-old steels himself. If he wishes to beat his record time, he will need to summon up every ounce of strength in his tiny frame.

Twenty minutes later he charges into the school gates, sweat dripping from his freckled face. A crowd of children gather round.

'Did you beat your record?' As ever, Didier's arrival is greeted with a flurry of excitement. 'I did it!' Didier mouths between gasps for breath. 'I smashed it!' His classmates roar their approval while casting admiring glances at the little bicycle. How dearly they would love to possess such a bike for themselves. Green with envy, the Valet brothers petition their father the Mayor of Boissy for a similar bicycle – without success.

He might not yet have been out of short trousers, but even as a five-year-old Didier was already developing a love of speed, a desire to set and surpass targets that would come to define the mature adult. Those daily dashes between home and school, juvenile, trivial and bemusing, were also the building blocks upon which a young man was moulding a character.

And never far away, the shrewd eye of an ever-watchful mother. As an integral part of the family business as well as doting parent, Imelda Pironi certainly had her hands full during these formative years. Those who knew Didier's mother describe a shrewd, capable woman. Perhaps there was an element of control too, a natural disposition to influence the behaviour of those around her. While elder sister Ilva contented herself in the domestic sphere, Imelda it was who busied herself with matters of company administration. Here was a woman with very clear ideas of what was right and wrong. The two sisters could not have been less alike.

Much activity centred on the yard of 40 Rue de Valenton. From here, the company's trucks would emerge each day before heading off all over Paris. With Imelda overseeing the paperwork, and Joseph (Giuseppe having adopted a more Franco-friendly moniker) and Louis running the contracts, Sud Est Travaux was a real family concern.

Didier would spend much time in the company's garages and workshops. Things mechanical seemed to fascinate the young boy from an early age. Armed with a toy hammer, the youngster would carry out imaginary repairs on his own play cars. When it came time to eat, uproar often descended upon the castle.

'Where are you? Didier! It is time to eat!' Imelda could shout herself hoarse. Often his parents would discover the pint-sized boy sat at the wheel of some truck or other, lost in a world of his own, legs dangling unable to reach the pedals. It would take a sharp rebuke from grandfather Joseph (aka 'Nonno') to tear the young boy away from this fascinating world of clutches, steering wheels and gear levers.

This charmed existence was briefly disturbed one autumnal afternoon of 1960. Didier's mother was sitting in the office when she heard a commotion in the yard, a cacophony of screams and shouts.

'Mum! Come at once! Thieves!' Imelda flung open the window to see, through a cloud of dust, Didier and some friends scrambling around the yard on their bicycles. Ignoring what she thought were childish games, she returned to her work.

'I'm busy! Go off and play somewhere else!'

A while later Didier and his gang returned, this time with more urgency. 'Call the police!' yelled Didier. 'Quickly! Tell them to come! We catch the thieves! Hurry!' Hesitatingly, Imelda did as instructed.

Didier and his friends had been playing out on their bicycles when they had heard cries for help. A gang of thieves had targeted the home of a female neighbour, bounding and gagging the unfortunate woman while ransacking her house. The chums had heard her calls. Before tearing back to the castle, the friends had had the presence of mind to note the registration details of a grey pick-up truck parked outside the house. Consequently, the police located and arrested the perpetrators. Press and television descended upon Boissy to cover the story. Didier and his friends were the heroes of the moment.

In typical Didier fashion, the hero of the hour would never so much as even allude to this incident that so captured the news headlines that day. 'I am not sure what displeased Didier, for I am sure I never heard him mention this episode again,' notes Imelda in her memoirs, with just a hint of puzzlement. Taciturnity. A Pironi trademark.

It is no exaggeration to say that in the ensuing years Didier would achieve a certain amount of notoriety in and around the environs of this quiet corner of Paris – and not always entirely for acts of altruism.

One such episode occurred shortly after the amateur sleuth had helped to rid the streets of Boissy of at least a few of its more undesirable elements. On this occasion, the good folk of the commune simply could not believe their eyes: a driverless car! Sure enough, a car was making its way steadily through the streets of the town, up and down, a vehicle conspicuously lacking in any form of chauffeur... *Mon Dieu!*

'Mrs Pironi! But this is completely unacceptable!' The local police were understandably exasperated. 'Do you comprehend, Madame, the enormity of the situation?'

Poor Imelda could only apologise. The young scamp had slipped out behind his mother's back, making his way across the courtyard to the garage where he had slipped into the driver's seat of one of the company's trucks. Moments later the very same truck had emerged onto the streets of Boissy, its driver not tall enough to see above the dashboard. Taking Didier firmly by the scruff of the neck, his mother marched the young boy all the way home. It would not be the first nor last time Mrs Pironi would find herself apologising profusely on behalf of the young miscreant.

'You'll get sent to prison! You're crazy!'

Beloved son or not, back at the castle it was time for a furious mother to dole out some tough love. In her memoirs, Imelda vividly recalls the incident and the little urchin's response, or lack of it: 'Didier looked at me fixedly, bolt upright, without a word, without flinching for a single moment from the spanking he so richly deserved.' At certain times, Didier it seemed could exert an almost preternatural control over his emotions.

Imelda might have been forgiven for thinking there the matter might rest. Not a jot. No sooner had one crisis been averted than another one would begin. With his long, blonde hair and freckled face, he might have looked the archetypal choirboy, but this angelic creature had a distinctly wild, untamed side to his nature.

'Mrs Pironi, Didier is going too far, really it has to stop.' The telephone call had come unexpectedly. 'Today we mistook his antics for those of a fugitive. We almost shot him...' On hearing those words Imelda froze, *shot him...!*

As a tremulous mother registered these words, a car door opened and slammed shut in the courtyard. Didier came skipping into the house. 'Yes, yes. I promise I will do whatever is necessary. Thank you, Inspector.' Even as an agitated mother put the receiver down, her son had dismissed the incident. Meanwhile, the sound of gushing water indicated that the young rogue was taking a cold shower, a favourite way to unwind.

'Hey! Get out of there. Now!' shouted Imelda, banging on the bathroom door.

Wrapped in a towel, moments later Didier appeared, unconcerned, cool as you like.

'Yes? What's going on?' he asked calmly.

'You know what!'

And with that, Imelda gave her son a slap to the cheek that almost knocked him flying. No reaction. Shaking with anger and pangs of regret, Imelda reports how her son didn't flinch, but stood before her, 'quiet, solid as a rock, with the beginnings of a smile upon his lips... '

Earlier in the day gangsters had stolen a blue car, in response to which the police had set up armed roadblocks throughout the borough. It just so happened that on the same day Didier had decided to 'borrow' his cousin's blue Gordini. Engine howling, the youngster had soon attracted the attention of the Gendarmerie, who naturally assumed that the blue car driving as if possessed by the devil was the one they were hoping to apprehend. Hotly pursued, Didier had led the constabulary a merry dance through the streets of Boissy.

And boy, could this kid drive! Many were the times when José, fatigued after a day of hunting or flying, had entrusted the steering wheel to a cousin only too eager to take the wheel. Illegal yes, risky no; José had every confidence in the ability of his little cousin. The police had never stood a chance.

There can be little doubt that the family's exalted position helped to mitigate any possible repercussions such escapades might have been expected to attract. The Dolhem-Pironis assuredly had friends in high places, some of whom wore the badge of justice.

While the little 'urchin' was seemingly intent on raising hell on the streets of Boissy, cousin José was discovering the joys of speed in a more conventional arena – that of the racetrack. With the likes of François Cevert, Jean-Pierre Beltoise, Johnny Servoz-Gavin and Patrick Depailler coming through the ranks, a golden era of French motorsport had begun. Dormant for far too long, France was once more finding its motor racing feet. Just down the road in Villecresnes, José had become friendly with Etienne Vigoureux, another up-and-coming driver. The young men had much in common: they both shared a love of speed – four wheels or two – and both could depend on the munificence of wealthy parents to indulge their whims. In the case of Etienne, his family were said to cultivate the finest roses in the whole of France, roses which they supplied to the city elite – to celebrities and even royalty.

On one occasion, José arrived in Villecresnes with his cherubic little cousin in tow. Inevitably, as is often the way with siblings, the younger boy was extravagantly fond of the older one. Though ostensibly cousins, the relationship between the two had always been more akin to that between little and big brother, with the junior brother eager to impress his older sibling, sometimes a little too much.

On this particular day, a hot June afternoon, José and Didier arrived at the Villecresnes home of their friend to be met by a sight that dazzled their eyes: Etienne's brand new racing car with which he intended to contest the French Formula 3 championships. Gleaming in the warm summer sunshine and framed by a rose garden from heaven, this was a scene to ravish the senses. The brother-cousins fell silent. Here was the most beautiful machine they had ever clapped eyes on. Young Didier could not take his eyes off the machine. Avidly discussing the intricacies of handling and aerodynamics, José and Etienne briefly retired indoors. It was all too much for the youngster. Jumping into the cockpit, he wasted no time in firing the machine up. He may have just entered his teenage years but here was a kid who knew exactly how to handle a racing car capable of attaining speeds up to 150mph.

Vroom! Vroom! José and Etienne rushed outside only to see the rear end of a gleaming F3 thoroughbred disappearing out of the drive… The good folk of Villecresnes had never seen – or heard – anything like it! Just what was going on inside the head of this young man? When questioned, Didier would say in that cool, detached way of his that he had simply been unable to resist the chance of sampling the machine first-hand. Boys will be boys, so goes the old saying. Seen from another viewpoint, this was a young man out of control, in need of a firm hand.

The time had come to seek guidance from higher authority. As noted, the family had plenty of friends in just such high places.

'If you continue in these ways, you will seriously harm your future,' declared the president of Créteil's Criminal Court, summoning up the sternest face he could manage. 'You are only 14 years old and already you have several charges of driving without a licence!' Didier looked glum.

'This is a very serious matter!' Observing what he detected to be the young man's contrition, the president softened his tone: 'What do you think about this?' A pause.

'I want to be a champion of motorsport!'

All of which was news to Imelda, who never would reconcile herself to her son's chosen path, not even at the height of his fame. A few more judicious words from the official appeared to have worked the oracle. A period of relative calm ensued. Around the same time, the reformed hellraiser would have his first introduction to organised motor racing.

In conjunction with Ford France, in 1964 fledgling racing magazine *Sport-Auto* had helped launch an entry-level motorsport category, the aim of which was to provide a stepping-stone for French racing talent into categories such as Formula 3. These were the days before Formula Renault and its structured nursery programme where aspiring drivers could earn their spurs. Using Lotus Sevens, the format pitted regions of France against one another. Potential drivers were invited to write in to *Sport-Auto* outlining why they deserved a seat in the category. José was one of a lucky few selected to represent Île-de-France. Rivals included Patrick Depailler (Auvergne) and Henri Pescarolo (Paris). Cheering on his older cousin, Didier would have witnessed some real wheel-to-wheel racing at circuits such as Montlhéry. José's career would, however, prove to be short-lived. University was calling. It would be another five years before he would be able to resume his career. Nonetheless, his younger cousin had been bitten by a bug, a bite so deep it penetrated his youthful imagination to the point where cars – racing cars – filled his waking as well as his sleeping hours.

Three
The golden child

ADOLESCENCE, the bridge between child and adulthood, can be a difficult time for those obliged to navigate its uneven waters, more so perhaps when the child in question has been blessed with precocity. Wherever he went, whatever he chose to do, Didier always seemed earmarked to succeed. A golden child blessed with an array of gifts, the teenager always stood out from the crowd.

Following his legendary brushes with the local police, the young hothead seems to have finally knuckled down into his studies once more. University had always been the goal, at least as far as Imelda was concerned. Securing a good education was a priority.

A pal who attended the prestigious College Mount Thabor at the same time as Didier and whom he had first met in autumn 1965, recalls a friend who exuded his own special aura: 'He was a brilliant student, calm and poised, always in the top three in tests.' In particular Didier excelled in maths and science. According to the same friend, had he chosen to, Didier could have easily been a scholar of some repute.

However, his real passion – speed – was never far from his thoughts. For the debonair boy about Paris there really was just a single way to travel – par Vespa. By the mid-sixties, these Italian style icons were all the rage in the French capital. Despite her apparent indignation over her son's antics, there must have been at least some complicity from an adoring mother, who for better or worse, allowed her son to take possession of one of these little flying machines before he had finished his studies. Engine revving hard, stones flying and dust clouds forming, there was never a moment's peace at the castle as Didier flew in and out of its courtyard. Delighted friends would gather to cheer the young gallant on. Quiet by inclination, when in control of a car (or motorbike) Didier was just the opposite: flamboyant, daring, a natural-born showman.

Relief that the obsession for four wheels had seemingly subsided was tempered by the realisation that the fixation had merely shifted to two wheels. The long-suffering Imelda would have cause to grumble anew. It was not long before the local constabulary were knocking once more on the castle door.

Imelda was going about her duties on a Thursday afternoon when the unmistakable sound of the Vespa's 50cc engine broke the peace. Silence. Didier had returned home from school.

'If anyone asks, I have not moved since school!'

Imelda stopped what she was doing. Looking into the hall, she just caught sight of her son vaulting up the large staircase. Somewhat bewildered, she followed the boy upstairs. Whatever could he mean? Moments later, she found Didier lying on his bed poring over some school textbook or other just as downstairs someone began hammering at the front door. Her son did not so much as even flinch. Imelda hurried downstairs.

'Yes gentlemen, how can I help you?' Even as she spoke, she quelled a horrible feeling in the pit of her stomach.

'Ah, Madame. I don't suppose you have seen a kid riding a motorbike like an alien?' The two visitors wore the insignia of the motorcycle division of the area police. 'Impossible to catch! He seemed to turn here…'

The cop peered past the hostess into the interior of the castle. If Imelda had ever hankered after a career on stage now was the time to test her abilities. The villain had turned into *this* house? Could the detective not have been mistaken? The lady of the house was adamant: she had not seen or heard a thing. All the while, the poor woman was praying the detectives would not wander over to the garage where she knew they must inevitably find the scooter.

Meanwhile, Didier had forged a friendship with the younger Vigoureux brothers, Andre and Antoine. The 'band of three' as they were known soon became the talk of the school. Whether it was pulling wheelies or holding impromptu races around the block on their motorcycles, entertainment was never far away from the school gates. A Honda 125cc in rakish black soon replaced the Vespa; more power, more speed.

'These three were the darlings of the school and their auras grew by the day. But even then it was clear to see that Didier was the most talented of all,' recalls a contemporary who was just one of many school friends who daily marvelled at these exploits.

Inevitably, the school authorities did not take kindly to the antics of this young daredevil and his cronies. After a series of warnings, Didier was 'advised' to find an alternative school. It would not be the first nor last time. How to explain such transgressions? Teenage exuberance? Whatever the reasons, it cannot have been easy for Imelda, having to walk a thin line between discipline and a natural inclination to indulge this, her only child, a precocious one at that. Had it not been for motorsport, and with it the opportunity to curb some of these wilder instincts, who knows where it might all have led?[3]

Wherever there was trouble, the leader of the gang was never far away. That much seemed assured. A move to Saint-Aspais de Melun, an exclusive Catholic college on the southern outskirts of Paris, however, did little in the way of checking a nature that seemed innately rebellious.

On one occasion, Imelda found herself driving to the new school at the behest of a very irate headmaster. What had the young rebel done *now*? A range of possible scenarios rushed through her head. Upon arrival at the school, the anxious lady was greeted by a severe head teacher and a 'smirking' Didier. It transpired that the school vending machine had been accepting money but failing to despatch the anticipated fizzy drinks. The disgruntled young customers had turned to Didier. It was not long before the young gallant had discovered how to breach the security of the machine and, in the best traditions of Robin Hood, was soon distributing free drinks to the entire school! Poetic justice or not, suffice to say that the headmaster saw things very differently.

Yet despite these clashes with authority, Didier seemed peculiarly immune to the consequences of his worst excesses. Approaching 16 years of age, with his choirboy looks, his bold and daring exploits on a range of ever more powerful motorbikes, this liberator of school vending machines, a fighter for truth and justice, had all the attributes of a very popular figure within the environs of his new college. With its bent towards technical subjects, Didier was flourishing too in the Melun classroom. By now, the Honda had been replaced with the latest craze from Japan, the Suzuki T20, a six-speed rocket capable of nudging nearly 100mph. Ever the trailblazer, Didier was the first student in the school to own a motorcycle.

Tennis, rowing, swimming – Didier's sporting prowess was also gaining him admirers. In an interview several years later, he would acknowledge a definite preference for individual over team sports. In the swimming pool, he reigned supreme, recording a best time of just over 57 seconds for the 100m freestyle, the French junior record at the time.

Sixteen years of age, wealthy, handsome and with the admiration (and envy) of his peers, the golden child was sailing through life.

Adulation from one's peers often has the effect of increasing the perceived attractiveness of an individual, popularity being an aphrodisiac as potent as any other. Could this help to explain the turn of events in Didier's last year at Melun? Until now, his escapades had been predictable: pushing the limits, discovering whether he had it within himself to not only approach, but go beyond those limits. Roaring through the streets of south-east Paris, police in tow, sirens flashing, had been a trial run, a prequel to a future yet vaguely glimpsed.

Decades have passed since the young guy from Boissy set the streets on fire with his T20, but one or two people still remember those epic runs southwards from Boissy to Melun. Driving at an average speed the journey takes approximately 30 minutes. Didier's record? Eight minutes…

If Imelda thought that her wayward son was at last settling down into some sort of routine she was alas mistaken.

A telephone call from the head teacher, though unwanted, was not entirely unexpected. Imelda dropped what she was doing and headed straight for her car. On the drive down to Melun there had been plenty of time to speculate. Why had the head declined to tell her the reason for the summons? Didier must surely have done something serious. Anxiety gnawing her, it was a nervous mother tremulously knocking on the door of the headmaster's study some 30-odd minutes after she had left Boissy.

'Ha! Madame Pironi! I have been expecting you!'

The anxious mother entered the study relieved at least to find no harm had come to her son who stood to one side of the room, every inch the naughty schoolboy. Met by an indifferent look from the young man, Imelda looked expectantly to the head.

'Your son has surpassed even himself on this occasion,' announced the teacher through gritted teeth. Imelda felt her heart flutter. 'Imagine the scandal! Your son, Madame, has become involved with a married woman, here within this high school! The very thought!'

Shaking with rage, the headmaster seemed to be on the verge of a seizure.

Mrs Pironi was stunned. Had she heard that correctly? She looked to Didier for a reaction. Nonchalant as well as indifferent, the mischief-maker shrugged. This she had *not* expected. For heaven's sake, her son was just 16 years old! Now she was being told that her Didier – her little man – was conducting an affair with a married woman! It was too much to bear. Choked, Imelda needed to sit down.

For a moment silence reigned, until…

'Mr Headmaster, really you are worrying my mother too much. Observe!' As a student 'in disgrace', Didier's interjection had not exactly been expected nor was it particularly welcome. Unconcerned, the young man addressed himself to a very indignant head. 'It's no big deal. I behave like a normal boarder. I'll try to arrange it differently in future.'

Dumbstruck, both adults could only look on as this utterly audacious young buck continued: 'As for you, Mr Principal, you would be advised to monitor the actions of your staff regarding certain pupils. You haven't noticed? You, our guardian angel!'

Thus, another educational chapter ended, his dismissal from the school coyly attributed to 'too much maturity…'

Didier had indeed caught the eye of a member of staff, a certain Madame K, an older, married woman who had, by all accounts, initiated the relationship. The affair had been going on for some time – right under the noses of the school hierarchy. She was not the only teacher either to fall under the golden child's spell. When Madame Pironi met with Didier's maths teacher she was disconcerted to find a young lady who could not hide her admiration for a student whom she insisted on describing as 'awesome...'

It wasn't only the desires of beautiful women and how to manage them that preoccupied Didier in the dying embers of the 1960s. Another passion was developing during these years, one that took the teenager high into the skies above the city of light.

At the tender age of 16 (on his birthday), Didier obtained his pilot's licence, becoming at the time France's youngest registered pilot. The cousins spent many a happy hour at Aérodrome de Lognes, a private airfield a 30-minute drive from Boissy where the family aeroplane was often kept. Flying became a way of life. From light aeroplanes to helicopters, both cousins loved to be airborne and despite their relatively tender years, could both rightly claim to be pilots of some accomplishment.

Having finally finished his studies in economics and engineering, in 1969 José entered the Volant Shell competition, by now a rite of passage for France's wannabe racers. A picture snapped just moments before José left the pits depicts Didier crouching by the side of his cousin's car, hands tucked into his bomber jacket, a wistful, contemplative figure. While all around panic ensued, the cousins remained unfazed. Indeed, José's preparations were a masterclass of self-control. The contrast between him and his rivals that day was remarkable. After all, as days went, they did not get much bigger than Volant Shell, where victory could lead to a ticket to the big time.

Since its inception in 1963, the likes of Jean-Pierre Jaussaud and François Cevert had scooped this much-coveted title, the winner able to count on a full year's financial backing from the petroleum giant in a suitable category of motorsport. Old pal Etienne Vigoureux had participated in the 1966 event, finishing just behind Cevert and Depailler in what must have been one of the hottest nursery competitions ever.

José's moment had arrived. Fast and lavishly talented himself, the 25-year-old won the 1969 competition running in fine style. Formula 3 now beckoned.

And watching the progress of his cousin, drinking in the ambience of this exciting, high-octane world, itching to gain entry to it himself, the blonde, freckle-faced rebel who had not so long ago declared his own ambition to be a 'champion of motorsport'. Thanks to José's connections, Didier had been acting as mechanic to the legendary motorcycle ace Claude Vigreux, himself a former winner of Volant Shell.

This multi-talented young racer would die in a tragic accident in April 1967. What effect Vigreux's death had on Didier is unclear, but it did not prevent the youngster from agreeing to partner his pal, Jean-Claude Guénard in the 1970 Bol d'Or, a motorcycle race that lasted 24 hours and magnet to the brave, the reckless and just the plain crazy. Until his mother said 'non' Didier and GueGue had been raring to go. Thwarted in this ambition, he yearned to compete more than ever.

Before he could pursue this aim, the thorny question of education arose. Had not José completed his baccalaureate? For their parts, the sisters were adamant: education came first. José had complied with the wishes of Ilva, hence Didier was fully expected to follow suit. Thus, as a new decade dawned Didier's trajectory, far from lying on the racetracks of France – at Reims, at Clermont-Ferrand – lay rather in the lecture theatres and workshops of the University of Paris. Didier duly signed up to study a course in public works engineering. A mix of practical and theoretical challenges lay ahead, but as he was to admit some years later, he had always been a reluctant student, his heart never really in it.

As a new era dawned – the 1970s – Didier in fact longed to join his cousin on the racetracks of France. Instead, he found himself back in the classroom. For now at least, he had to content himself with playing a part in José's motorsport ambitions, usually in the role of mechanic-cum-travelling companion as his cousin's F3 career gained momentum. On the Grands Prix circuits, he cheered on the swaggering Lotus F1 star Jochen Rindt who had become a firm favourite. It was not enough. Didier had a raging thirst to *do*; to compete.

As it stood, a career in motorsport was uncertain, unless of course he could emulate his cousin, unless he too could show his mettle, unless he too could go on and win a competition such as Volant Shell. Could he?

There was only one way to find out…

Four

Leader of the pack

OBTAINING a driver's licence is part of every youngster's path to maturity and independence. As ridiculous as it might seem, as far as passing his own driving test was concerned, Didier would struggle to achieve this maturation landmark. Had the self-taught young driver developed some bad habits during his 'bandit' years? Probably. After all, he had been driving – at considerable speeds – on the highways of south-east Paris for many years prior to taking the test. Reining it all in would prove problematical.

The test day arrived, a cold January morning. Snow falling steadily on the streets of Boissy, Didier set off for this, his second attempt to gain his licence.

Initially, all was well. Joining a faster stretch of road on the outskirts of town, the car quickly accelerated until approaching a set of traffic lights. Anticipating that the lights were about to change to red, Didier applied the brakes, but discovered to his great consternation his instructor about to do the same via his dual controls. Lock up. The car skidded precariously. For a moment disaster loomed. Despite the treacherously slippery conditions, Didier was somehow able to bring the vehicle under control – no mean feat. The colour all but drained from his face and the instructor eventually opened his eyes.

'Are you OK?' enquired the pupil, completely unfazed at what had been a very narrow escape. 'Did you want us to go in the river?'

'Get out of the car, Pironi! I never want to see you again!'

Shrugging, Didier did as instructed. Had he not, through his own instincts and sharp reflexes, just saved the day? This was some way to show gratitude.

All's well that ends well; the shaken instructor later relented. Didier got his licence but on the understanding that, 'he remembers that the public highways are not racetracks!'

Driving licence obtained, the young hustler wasted no time in acquiring a Ford Capri 2600 RS with which he 'dazzled' virtually the entire female population of south-east Paris! Didier was back on four wheels.

When not flying around the south-eastern suburbs of Paris on two or four wheels, Didier and José continued to lark around in the skies above the city in the family aeroplane. Flying was another passion the brother-cousins also shared. And where José led, Didier was sure to follow. Indeed, the younger cousin had become used to hearing of his older sibling's escapades. Naturally, he aspired to follow his example. Perhaps this is where the younger man's appetite for adventure – danger – began, in the castle's lounge, listening wide-eyed as José related another audacious tale.

One such story involved an emergency landing in the wilds of Greenland. In February 1971, José and Etienne had been flying a Cessna 310 from Miami along America's east coast: Atlanta, New York, Labrador, the journey had been going well enough. From Goose Bay in Canada, their next destination was Narsarsuaq, a tiny settlement in southern Greenland. However, the 1,600km journey across Baffin Bay would stretch the endurance of their craft to its maximum capacity. Landing in Greenland would also depend on the capriciousness of the weather in that desolate land. The men set off. It was an adventure, right? Besides, meteorological forecasts checked out.

As the plane approached the Greenland coast however, the men were greeted by the sudden kind of violent storm common to this region. Caught in a snowstorm, the plane was forced to take a detour. Fuel now running precariously low, and faced with thousands of kilometres of inhospitable terrain, the situation was becoming serious. Eventually, José was forced to land the plane amid snow and ice. Thanks to his expertise, the manoeuvre succeeded.

The French friends and their two American passengers spent a couple of very cold days and nights stranded in the wilderness until help arrived.

Hearing such stories fired Didier's imagination. He longed for his own adventures. Soon enough the urge to compete became too much to bear. By spring 1972, Mrs Pironi found herself coming under ever more pressure from an increasingly dissatisfied scholar: could he not accompany his friend Jacques in the Grand National race as navigator? Imelda baulked, and with good reason.

The Grand National Tour Auto was an event still in its infancy. Taking place over five days, it consisted of various track and road stages around France culminating at the Paul Ricard circuit in the south. Open to anyone in possession of a national licence, the event attracted a large and eclectic field of competitors. At the top end, professional drivers such as rally ace Bernard Darniche, towards the bottom end an array of amateurs and chancers. Quite a cocktail.

Didier pleaded with a wary mother without whose authorisation he would not be able to compete. So too did Jacques, an older head who promised to do all the driving. Not without misgivings, Imelda finally gave her blessing. The race was on!

Much to Didier's frustration his older friend turned out to be somewhat of a pedestrian in terms of race driving, caution his watchword. In no time at all the Capri fell down the order. The teenager's exasperation finally boiled over. Readying themselves for the final stage to Circuit Paul Ricard the youngster took Jacques by the arm.

'Listen, let me take the wheel for the final stage...'

'But Didier, I promised your mother.'

'Or I quit!'

On the final leg, the Capri started to claw its way back through the field. Way down the rankings and in a seemingly hopeless position, Didier was determined nonetheless to end with a flourish. Sure enough, the Capri entered Circuit Paul Ricard in first place! Even more remarkable, thanks to five days of wear and tear, this was a car without brakes! As impressive as this performance was, it was not good enough to worry the leaders, placings calculated on aggregate times accumulated over the entire five days. No matter.

This stage belonged to the Ford Capri and its unofficial, baby-faced driver.

Buoyed by his taste of competitive driving, Didier started to seriously consider a crack at the Pilot-Elf competition coincidentally also held at Paul Ricard – a lucky omen perhaps. Demonstrating remarkable assurance and foresight, he chose to ignore the advice of cousin José, who recommended Volant Shell, the same competition in which he had triumphed three years earlier. Correctly, as it transpired, Didier opted for Elf. Volant Shell was already running out of steam and would cease completely just one year later. By contrast, Elf would play a leading role in French motorsport for decades to come, pumping millions of francs into F1 and many other categories besides. Good call.

There just remained a final, formidable obstacle: Imelda.

One Sunday evening Didier decided to broach the subject. Now in his second year at university, the young man was rightly concerned that his mother would reject the idea out of hand. It was not just a question of money either, as the hefty course fees of 3,000 francs (about £3,000 as of 2017) could easily be met; no, it was the sport itself with its inherent dangers that truly haunted an over-protective mother.

'Mum, I have to talk to you,' said Didier quietly.

Imelda sensed what was coming. Mother and son sat down together in the lounge in front of the large, stone fireplace.

'I know you wish me to be an engineer, but it is not my passion. What I want is to compete. I want to register at Le Castellet driving school.' Mrs Pironi listened in silence. How could she possibly prevent her son from pursuing his ambition?

'I promise if I do not succeed I will focus on my studies. Mum, please agree.' Such was the sincerity of her son's words, so earnest his countenance, the lady of the house had no option but to acquiesce.

'Very well. But if you do not win, then you go back to your studies and you never talk about motor racing again. Understand?'

Didier nodded. Imelda could console herself with the thought that Pilot-Elf was a protracted process at the end of which just one racer could claim the title. The winner would invariably be an immensely gifted individual. What odds her son being that man?

The appearance of François Cevert at the castle one morning rather disconcerted Imelda, quite the opposite effect the tall, blue-eyed Adonis usually had upon the female sex. France's top F1 star dropping by for breakfast was not by any means an unusual occurrence either. Next time it might easily be Jean-Pierre Beltoise popping by for coffee. Thanks to José, French motor racing royalty was already making its way to the castle. How could a young man fail to be enamoured in such an environment?

The topic turned to Pilot-Elf. During the conversation, the Tyrrell star expressed his opinion that Didier had a real chance of taking the title. Imelda immediately paled. Pilot-Elf was a diversion, an opportunity for Didier to finally get this motor racing bug out of his system. *But winning? Out of the question!* François smiled and bade his hosts 'adieu' before heading off to the airport in company with José, where he was due to fly to the United States for a Tyrrell test session.

'I was particularly troubled,' writes Imelda, 'that this opinion had come from a champion of Formula 1, who doesn't mention his own brother, "Little Charles", who is also involved in the competition...'

First run in 1971, Pilot-Elf had already garnered a reputation for the quality of its courses. *The school is open to all automotive enthusiasts, those who believe driving is a pleasure and those who want to become a racing driver.* Thus ran the marketing blurb of the now legendary Winfield race driving school, the organisation charged with running the courses. Although ostensibly aimed at beginners, in truth the competition attracted a broad spectrum of drivers from novices to drivers such as Didier already familiar with a range of racing cars including José's F3.

Rolling up for the course in his Mercedes created an instant level of distrust among his peers. This kid was just a little too slick, a little too urbane. All of which might have been pardonable of course had the baby-faced Parisian also not been blessed with more than his fair share of talent. One of several hundred hopefuls at the outset, Didier progressed smoothly enough through the peripheral stages of the course.

Interviewed for Martine Camus' *La Flèche Brisée*, course tutor Antoine Raffaelli recalled a diligent student, one certainly not prone to flaunting his wealth. In particular, the instructor referred to what he termed the young racer's 'incredible casualness… as if his heart beat slower than the others'.

And so the process began: theory and practice. As well as the promise of learning 'how to take corners at the limit…' the eagle-eyed Raffaelli and a team of assistants monitored every student. Those who made the grade continued, while for those who did not it was 'au revoir'.

After each stage, Didier would report to his mother. Usually these calls consisted of proclamations to the effect of how he was already setting the fastest times, that the prize of Pilot-Elf would surely be his. How Imelda must have grimaced.

Come the day of the finals just six hotshots remained out of a field of 200 who had originally registered. Unable to maintain the blistering pace, some drivers such as little Charles Cevert had given up halfway through the course.

The decisive moment had arrived.

Ever the pragmatist, for Didier there were two – and only two – possible outcomes of this day: either he had the talent or he did not. Winning the competition would indicate the former, failure to win clear evidence of the latter. It was a characteristically cool assess-ment. Should he fail to scoop the top prize this composed student of public works was ready to walk away from motorsport for good. Taking part for its own sake – for fun – was never an option.

And so on a hot October weekend Didier arrived at the circuit for the shootout that would decide his future. It was a beautiful, cloudless day in and around the environs of Le Castellet, home to Circuit Paul Ricard some 28 miles east of Marseille. At just 20 years of age, he was the youngest driver to have made the finals, another factor that had not exactly endeared him to his fellow competitors. This Pironi kid seemed just a little too sure of himself.

Confusion reigned on Saturday when several members of the judging panel failed to materialise. As well as racing against the clock, the Pilot-Elf format included input from a panel of judges whose purpose was not only to effectively rubber stamp the results of the time trials, but also to arbitrate if required. More pointedly, their presence added clout and not a little pizzazz. Reigning Formula 1 world champion Jackie Stewart would be a member of a judging panel that included inaugural winner Patrick Tambay, journalist Jabby Crombac and F1 team boss Ken Tyrrell.

When three of the school's fleet of Renault-Alpine A362 race cars began to be dogged with engine gremlins on a windy Friday afternoon, it signalled the end of an inconclusive day's work. Pilot-Elf would be decided on Sunday's results alone.

On Saturday evening, the six finalists retired to the nearby Cadiére Riviera hotel. As well as Didier, five other hopefuls had made it this far, hoping that Pilot-Elf would ignite their own motor racing dreams. Weekdays would find Bernard Mandonato hard at work in the family bakery in Marseille; Pilot-Elf was the 27-year-old's chance to leave the ovens behind forever. Fellow Marseille resident Gerard Bacle was back for a second crack at the title having been very impressive in the 1971 event. Meanwhile, Gerard Saint-Aubin and Jean-Marc Brunel had literally never so much as even sat in a racing car prior to the competition. The latter had enrolled on a whim, 'to see how far I could get'. Frédéric Vialle, a 26-year-old accountant from Paris, completed the line-up.

After dinner, the would-be racers took coffee. Tomorrow only one of them would take the prize. What of the others? A life devoted to baking croissants, calculating balance sheets…

While the hopefuls politely chatted amongst themselves something inexplicable occurred. A dark, swarthy figure approached the group. This mysterious form – a 'mage' – reputedly possessed of mystical powers including the gift of foresight, was known to haunt the environs of Le Castellet. Pointing a withered finger at young Pironi, the witch fell into a stupor. At the sight of this unholy apparition, one or two competitors sniggered. Some recoiled.

'It's you! Tomorrow you will be the winner! You will go on to have a great career, but will never be world champion!' The mage fixed Didier with a penetrating eye. Typically, the young man did not flinch.

'One day you will die in competition, by fire!'

With that, the vision left a highly bemused group of young drivers. As haunting as this prophecy had been, it had not unduly disturbed Didier who dismissed the episode as quickly as it had happened.[4]

By next morning, focus had shifted to the final. Another lovely day had brought out the crowds who packed themselves into Paul Ricard's grandstands. Patrick Tambay, winner of this competition in 1971, was on hand to offer advice. Little could he have realised the circumstances under which his own path and that of the young blonde guy would one day cross. Clad in trademark cap, scarf and leather coat, Jackie Stewart had been signing autographs non-stop since his own arrival. Another judge, François Guiter, head of Elf's motorsport division, thumbed through the programme, his gaze eventually coming to rest on the short biography and picture of one of the finalists, Didier Pironi. Guiter contemplated the image. Something about this young man captured his imagination. Taking his place on the panel, this Svengali of French motor racing had chosen his winner before an engine had even fired up.

Meanwhile, five anxious pilots (plus Didier) awaited. Scheduled to drive ten laps of the 3.3km circuit, the winner would be the driver with the lowest aggregate time. Pilot-Elf had been designed to reward consistency as well as speed.

Under skies of azure blue, Didier drove with characteristic assurance. The judges were impressed, more so when they spied the disarmingly boyish features of this grinning, sun-kissed creature once his helmet had come off. His total time of 15'20.10 (15 minutes and 20.1 seconds) good enough to edge out Gerard Saint-Aubin by just under a second![5] Phew! It had been too close. On his tenth and final lap, the young Parisian had made an extra special effort, making the fastest lap of the day with a superb 1'31.1 – half a second faster than Saint-Aubin's fastest time. Just as he had predicted he would do to his mother, Didier had saved his best until last.

Photographs of the winning ceremony reveal a jubilant winner. Stewart, Tambay, Crombac and Tyrrell are all assembled squinting in the hot afternoon sun, posing with a young champion whose face is flushed, and hair dishevelled. In the background Mandonato, Bacle, Saint-Aubin and the rest look ruefully on, their own dreams of motor racing stardom now hanging by the proverbial thread.

On this languid, sun-drenched afternoon Didier had not only won Pilot-Elf, he had prevailed in a psychological battle with himself and just as importantly – more perhaps – with his mother.

In lieu of their agreement, hereafter Imelda had no other choice but to allow her son to pursue his motor racing ambition, though this most formidable of women would never reconcile herself to a sport that brought her nothing but trepidation, worry and anxiety.

Didier Pironi had just taken his first step on a flight that would take him to places he could never have imagined.

Five

Enter the American

ALONG with the prestige of winning Pilot-Elf, becoming its official 'laureate', came the more tangible reward of a season's racing in 1973 at the petrol giant's expense. On offer was a fully funded year in Formula Renault, a tough, junior category of motorsport, which provided highly competitive racing. It was an ideal series for a budding champion to serve an apprenticeship. As 1971 laureate, Patrick Tambay had enjoyed just such benefits the year following his triumph, admittedly with mixed results.

Didier had already met and been somewhat in awe of Tico Martini, the eponymous racing car builder based at the Magny-Cours circuit. So when it came time to choosing between an Alpine or a Martini chassis for the season ahead, he had no hesitation in opting for a Martini MK11, because 'Tico's cars win all the races'. Faultless logic.

Having just celebrated his 21st birthday, Didier could now call himself a professional racing driver. For the 1973 season, he would be allocated a seat at Ecurie Elf, in one of the company's two factory outfits.

The baby of the team, Didier became the third driver in a line-up also comprising Maxime Bochet, an experienced older hand, and Yannick Auxéméry, who was dropping back a category after an unsatisfactory crack at F3. Tambay, meanwhile, would be lining up for a second season under the Elf banner.

More competition would come in the shape of rival petroleum company Shell and their own laureate of 1972, the little Grenoblois, René Arnoux. Although Formula Renault attracted plenty of plucky privateers, the petrol conglomerates sliced up the sharp end of the grid during these years. Along with Shell and Elf, BP and Motul also fielded strong teams.

A long season lay ahead, with 20 races at circuits the length and breadth of France including overseas visits to Britain, Spain, Belgium, Germany and Italy. Races came thick and fast. For example, on 1 May, the Magny-Cours circuit in central France played host to the series, followed a week later with a 700km trek southwards to the Pau circuit, stamina and resolve tested to breaking point thereafter with a trip to the UK to race on the 13th of the month, followed immediately by a return to mid-France for a race at La Châtre on 20 May. Four races in four weekends and 3,000 kilometres clocked up!

Consisting of large fields of young and relatively inexperienced racers, Formula Renault was a fast and very furious category of racing.

While Arnoux and Tambay hit the ground running, Didier's career began on a more circumspect note. Not until the series crossed the English Channel, arriving at a wet and windy Snetterton for the sixth round of the championship, did the young man finally manage to show his talent with a steady fourth-place finish. It was progress, but hardly the blaze of glory the Pilot-Elf champion had envisaged. However, the factory team was underperforming. Team manager Roland Trollé duly came under increasing pressure from Elf top brass, who naturally expected to see their investment in the team rewarded with success.

The anticipated glory, however, was not forthcoming. Even the team's senior drivers struggled. Irony of ironies, it appears that the synthetic oil supplied by team sponsors Elf was having a detrimental effect on engine performance! High operating temperatures was just one of several problems plaguing the team. Mechanical breakdown became a depressingly common feature of the season for Didier and his team-mates.

However, the problems did not end there. Although very much the junior member of the squad, Trollé's conservative approach to the business of team management frustrated Didier. In particular, the rookie voiced concerns regarding how Elf's generous budget was being handled. In between F3 commitments of his own, cousin José also involved himself in some frank discussions on this topic.

'Didier was very young and very impulsive,' recalled Bochet, the team's lead driver. True enough; the Parisian was indeed a young man in a hurry. It was this mix of inexperience and impetuosity allied with mechanical fragility that was proving his undoing. Halfway into the season, the laureate had accumulated a paltry 16 points and was still waiting to climb the steps to his first podium.

Despite plenty of setbacks, Didier's spirit never wavered, a quality that impressed Elf as well as Bochet: 'He never gave up; he remained positive, showing intelligence, foresight and courage.' Another member of the team recalled a 'super-motivated' young man.

For the two senior drivers the outlook was even gloomier. Although he had scored what transpired to be the team's sole victory of the year at Pau, Bochet was under pressure; so too Auxéméry, whose best results had been two fourth-placed finishes at Nogaro and Monaco. As summer passed to autumn and results stubbornly refused to materialise, both men found themselves in the ignominious position of being 'surplus to requirements'. In their wisdom, Elf had chosen to terminate both drivers' contracts.

Christian Courtel was a new motorsport journalist back in 1972 whose career just happened to be coinciding with that of an aspiring racer fresh from his Pilot-Elf triumph. 'I was immediately seduced by his approach. He was then 22 years old, and despite a youthful face, one discerned a certain maturity in his eyes and speech.' Courtel observed the young man's progress through Formula Renault with interest. What impressed him most during these formative years was the young racer's pragmatism, especially in that often fraught 1973 rookie season: 'While his team-mates remained stuck in difficulties, Didier, more methodical, knew how to respond more effectively despite his lack of experience. Never once panicking, he developed a rigorous and constructive approach to problems.'

Didier thus became the team's sole representative. Far from being daunted, the youngster relished this new-found responsibility. Closing ranks around their remaining driver, the team could now lavish their full attention on the rookie. Almost immediately, his results improved. Not for the first time in his career, once out of the shadow of a team-mate, Didier experienced an upturn in fortunes.

Although it was far too late to challenge championship pacesetters Arnoux and Tambay, the Elf pilot finished the season with a flourish. The long-awaited first podium finally arrived thanks to a fine second place behind Alain Couderc in Nivelles.

By the time the circus arrived on the outskirts of Madrid for the final race of an exhilarating season, Didier's confidence was sky high. Qualifying his MK11 on the front row of the grid, the youngster gatecrashed what had become a thrilling three-way fight for the title between Arnoux, Tambay and Couderc. Forty-five minutes later, he was rewarded with yet another podium finish. Just as he had done at the Pilot-Elf finals, Didier had reserved his best performances for when it really mattered: at the business end of proceedings. After a tentative start to his season, one in which both his team-mates had been sacked, he had ended the season on an upward curve. His final haul of 75 points resulted in a solid if unspectacular sixth place in the overall standings.

1973 had been a tumultuous season. Without that late run of form, which had yielded three podium finishes in the last four races of the season, who knows in which direction the young man's future might have gone. Of the many lessons learnt, one stood out above all: a driver is only as good as his team. The rookie had a lot of thinking to do.

It was during this apprenticeship year that Didier had first made the acquaintance of a pretty 18-year-old who moved in much the same circles. While he busied himself with engines, tyres and whatnot, she might be engaged in a spot of promotional work, photography and the like. They hit it off immediately. Petite and vivacious, Catherine Goux was just the type of girl that Didier appreciated. When the pair met up on circuit or at the house of a mutual friend, the chemistry was obvious. The classic slow burner, a decade would elapse before the pair would finally come together.

Romance aside, of more concern at this stage of his career loomed the question of 1974. Didier was acutely aware that his debut season had somewhat underwhelmed – himself much more than the motor racing press or Elf. Could he afford another season of unfulfilment? Short answer: no. Motor racing talent abounded in France. To avoid the very real risk of becoming yet another lost prospect, Didier needed to think out of the box.

Which is precisely what he did. After a great deal of agonising, a thought occurred: *What if I could run my own team? What if I could control the budget, make my own decisions?* Always supremely confident in his abilities, taking control over his own destiny seemed an obvious solution.

Yet as ideas go, it seemed outlandish – even ridiculous. After all, at 22 years of age and with just a single lacklustre season of competitive racing under his belt, Didier was hardly in a position to make any sort of demands. Nevertheless, his mind was made up. If he wished to progress to Formula Renault Europe, the next stage up the racing ladder – which he did – his next move would be crucial. The power laid in the hands of Elf. Would the petroleum giant entertain him?

Enthused with the idea of going it alone, the would-be team boss sat down in the lounge at Boissy where he started to draw up plans with customary precision. Didier would need to convince Elf top brass to entrust him – a relative novice – with a whole year's budget. Considerable effort went into the business plan. Finally, it was time to test the water. Didier telephoned the company's head office in Rue Jean Nicot in central Paris to set up a meeting.

François Guiter, Elf's head of competition, was already a somewhat legendary figure in France and beyond. It is no exaggeration to claim that this gentle giant of a man had single-handedly created the conditions under which French motorsport had become a world leader, in F1, sports cars, rallying and many other junior formulae besides. Through his efforts, Elf had formed a very fruitful partnership with Ken Tyrrell's Formula 1 team and its triple world champion driver, Jackie Stewart. He had also been instrumental in setting up the Pilot-Elf competition, one of whose star graduates happened to be sitting opposite him in his office this very day.

'So, Pironi, how can I assist you today?' Guiter had a way of making eye contact that intimidated some, encouraged others.

Shifting his bulk, the 'Godfather' sat back in his executive leather chair.

Always the coolest of customers, the youngster presented his file, the fruit of several weeks' labour. Guiter was impressed. The young man had done his homework.

Something about this freckle-faced lad appealed to the ex-soldier who, when away from the office, liked nothing more than to dive into the dark, subterranean world of underground caves. A friend of the celebrated diver Jacques Cousteau, Guiter had learned to trust his instincts.

Didier explained his plan: he would find a suitable location in Magny-Cours near Tico Martini's workshop to serve as HQ, source a team of mechanics, negotiate with engine suppliers, prepare his own cars and manage all aspects of the budget and administration. In short, he would, with Elf's backing, create a successful Formula Renault enterprise.

Bemused, Guiter listened. The young man outlined his plan with a clarity and composure that belied his years. The motor racing mogul could not help but be impressed.

Guiter considered; at stake, a motor racing career.

'OK, baby Pironi, I am willing to trust you with the budget for 1974, on one condition…'

Didier could hardly believe his ears.

'You must win the title for us.'

'Monsieur Guiter, I promise I will win the title!' The two men shook hands. Didier left the office in a daze.

He had just secured a budget of some 300,000 francs![6] It would be a mistake, however, to think of this largesse as anything other than an investment. Elf's sponsorship of French motor racing and its drivers amounted entirely to a commercial proposition.

A little under 12 months ago he had rocked up at Paul Ricard to try his luck at Pilot-Elf, a blonde aristocrat who some had assumed (wrongly) would soon return to the Parisian suburbs once he'd had his fill of motor racing thrills 'n' spills. Underestimate Pironi at your peril. The young man had just taken a gigantic step forward on the road to his chosen goal.

There was no time to lose. Didier immediately set off for Magny-Cours, a small town of some 1,500 inhabitants, many of whose fortunes were inextricably linked to that of the nearby Nevers race circuit. At his side, Agnes, a young lady of elfin-like appearance he had met while on a Christmas skiing holiday in Les Gets some years earlier, and whom Didier at this time referred to as 'my fiancée'. A former butcher's shop located on the corner of the town's main square caught the couple's eye. Badly in need of refurbishment and some TLC, this grand old building seemed the perfect location from which to launch an adventure.

New town, new venture, new life. Exciting times laid ahead.

First things first: the building needed to be adapted to the requirements of a budding racing team. Using his skills gained in studying public building works, Didier hired and personally supervised a team of craftsmen to undertake the work. Agnes, meanwhile, got out the broom and dedicated herself to decorating the new house, the crowning glory of which would be a tasteful lounge featuring a Formula Renault steering-wheel-themed chandelier.

Fifty metres further down La Rue du Pré Morand, the team requisitioned a garage, which also received a major makeover. Benches, tools and drills installed, Team Pironi had acquired a base. Work often continued well into the evening.

In the midst of all this activity, Didier started to gather a trusted team of mechanics who had previously worked for José and who readily agreed to join the enterprise. A deal was soon thrashed out with the Bozian brothers to prepare engines. If all this was not enough, the baby-faced boss spent oodles of time over at Tico's workshops, a short walk from the main square through the town's narrow, winding streets. Didier could not wait to get his hands on his mentor's latest creation, the MK14, the only chassis to have in Formula Renault. With the arrival later in the year of future Renault F1 chief mechanic, Daniel Champion, another piece of the jigsaw would fall into place. Champion had worked previously with Patrick Tambay and Jean-Pierre Jabouille. The ex-house electrician from Normandy certainly knew his way around a Formula Renault car.

'Team Pironi' was starting to take shape.

Thus began a three-year sojourn in this sleepy part of mid-France. The gang lived, worked and played together. The new tenants wasted little time in shaping this old property to their requirements. Upstairs in the loft overlooking the sleepy square, they installed fitness and gym equipment. If the residents of number 1 La Rue du Pré Morand had not had their fill of motorsport on any given day, the huge Scalextric race track that occupied a part of the lounge would ease the transition from real race track to home.

'A total madhouse...' remarked Imelda upon visiting soon after the youngsters had commandeered the premises. 'Young, passionate, warm and friendly.' Theirs was a commune redolent with synergy.

1973 had been a chaotic year, but it had not been entirely wasted. Some valuable lessons had been learnt along the way. Drawing upon a maturity and a resolve that must have seemed incongruous for one of such a boyish appearance, right from the start Didier approached the job with utter professionalism. Awash with francs, young, independent, living a dream, less focused individuals might well have squandered a similar opportunity. Not Pironi. Elf, and in particular François Guiter, had shown enormous trust and Didier was determined to repay their faith in him.

When the French government suspended all forms of motorsport due to the OPEC oil crisis late that year, for one dreadful moment the dream looked shaky. Fuel rationing became a serious possibility. For the people who made their living in motorsport, uncertainty was never far away during the winter of 1973/74. Would there even be a Formula Renault championship in 1974? Indeed, Shell decided to close their racing operation down completely. Reigning champion and Shell's 1972 laureate, René Arnoux found himself out of a team and out of work, further vindication of Didier's decision to choose Elf over their rivals. Thankfully, the situation resolved itself before January's frosts had thawed.

It was full speed ahead at Team Didier: Pilot-Elf's 1973 laureate, Richard Dallest, joined the team and when Martini delivered the MK14 ahead of time – the result of endless pestering – the team immediately set about testing their new car. Even before the season's Paul Ricard curtain raiser scheduled for 7 April, the team had clocked up hundreds of miles of testing. Advantage Didier.

Despite Arnoux's enforced sabbatical, competition would be stiffer than ever for the season ahead. Driving in the colours of BP, and following his narrow miss in '73, Alain Couderc could rightly claim to be one of the category's brightest stars during this era. The talented duo of Marc Sourd and Dany Snobeck headed up a four-pronged attack for UFP (Union of French Petroleum). The total number of entrants for the competition swelled to over 120, making the fears inspired by the oil crisis of just a few months earlier seem absurd. Didier would certainly not have things all his own way – far from it.

The only snag as far the organisers were concerned turned out to be the paucity of entrants from outside La Republic. In an attempt to widen the series' appeal, the organisers offered a 1,000-franc start bonus per race to competitors racing outside their home country. It would take a brave man to take the French on at their own game.

A classic season of racing lay ahead.

Plenty of heads turned as the impressive Team Pironi transporter rolled up in the Paul Ricard paddock in early April, the logos of Renault and Elf prominently displayed. Dressed in their crisp blue overalls, Alain, Benito and Daniel – the team's mechanics – certainly looked the business. The same was true of Agnes, who assumed the role of timekeeper in addition to administrative duties. Slick and corporate, this was Didier all over.

What the other drivers must have thought of this show of strength can readily be guessed. When the team unloaded a pair of gleaming MK14s from the trailer, astonishment turned to dismay. It was not long before the green-eyed monster raised its ugly head: *Pironi! A rich kid! Spoilt!* The arrival of Le Patron in his powerful Mercedes-Benz 450 can hardly have helped matters.

They would come in time to call him 'the American', a sobriquet not entirely used as a term of endearment …

Nonetheless, all that pre-season hard work paid off handsomely. Didier swept to victory at Ricard, and repeated the feat a week later at Nogaro. Team-mate Richard Dallest caused a minor sensation when grabbing pole in his maiden outing at Ricard, but thereafter Didier usually had the measure of the man from Marseille.

'I couldn't believe how professional some of the oil-sponsored teams were,' recalls Gianfranco Ricci, one of just three non-French drivers to take part in the championship that year.

Ricci had arrived at Ricard having driven all the way down from his native Italy alone, pulling his race car behind on a rickety cart! Glimpsing the immaculate trailer and its equally immaculately attired mechanics of Team Pironi, not to mention the bountiful resources (a spare race car!) the Italian's heart sank.

How to possibly compete against such largesse? A difficult year lay ahead: 'I had no budget and I always struggled to qualify for the final. That was my first and last year in single seaters!'

One incident stood out in this baptism of fire year. On home soil at Monza later that season, the Italian privateer's resources finally ran dry. In sharp contrast to what some people have written over the years, Didier immediately stepped in. 'OK, so I wasn't a problem for him – not like some of the other drivers – but I remember that he did not hesitate to get me the parts I needed – brake pads and two front springs.' After a bruising year under fire from the full artillery of the French musketeers, Ricci returned home to Italy to compete in GT sports car series.

There were no such constraints for Didier of course. While the likes of Ricci were required to patch up their battered cars as best they could, those at the top end of the pyramid had the luxury of hopping into spare race cars. Night and day, haves and have-nots, but that is how it goes. Since the moment he had first glimpsed his baby-faced features in that Pilot-Elf brochure, François Guiter had taken a shine to the earnest young racer. It would prove to be a crucial slice of luck. In the not-too-distant future, Monsieur Guiter would again make a telling intervention on behalf of 'baby' Pironi, this time smoothing the path to the summit of his chosen profession. Indeed, as Didier himself later observed, 'Without the support of Elf there would have been no career in motorsport.' As far as international motorsport is concerned, money has always talked, loudly so.

The set-up at Team Pironi certainly impressed his childhood friend Eric Lucas who flew down to Magny-Cours via the family aeroplane in company with Louis Dolhem in early May. Met at Nevers-Fourchambault airfield by Agnes who, amongst her many other duties, also appears to have been acting as team chauffeur, the party drove the short journey to the former butcher's shop in the centre of town, headquarters now to a thriving motorsport team and a championship leading driver.

'We made a detailed visit of the premises and I was impressed by the magnitude of the situation. Everything had changed. For example, the team had five or six spare engines available, as many gearboxes and two spare chassis.' A little while later Team Pironi, along with Lucas and 'uncle' Louis, were lunching in the hospitality lounge of the Magny-Cours circuit. In just over an hour Didier would be attempting to secure a hat-trick of victories following his triumphs in the opening two races of the season. The mood was buoyant. Enjoying a meal of pasta, salad, cheese and Evian water, it was at this moment that Eric discerned that his friend's life had changed irrevocably. 'It was then I realised life would never be the same again.' Upwards and onwards, Didier was a man on the move.

In the race itself, Didier and Couderc engaged in a no-holds-barred dice for victory. Attempting to go down the inside of his rival however, the Elf driver found the door slammed firmly shut in his face. The resulting contact pierced the radiator of Didier's MK14. To avoid overheating there was no other choice but to back off. Didier eventually finished third, five seconds behind winner Couderc and two seconds in arrears of second-placed man Snobeck.

After the race, Eric encountered a disconsolate friend: 'Hey, it's not so bad, you learnt how to handle a particularly difficult situation today, it will serve you well.' Didier immediately brightened:

'Yeah, and I'll win all the others…'

Although the predicted domination did not unfold quite as the pilot might have hoped, by mid-season Didier was a hot favourite to win the championship. The key to success was consistency. While Couderc, Sourd and Snobeck enjoyed their own purple patches during the year, they could not quite match the relentless points-scoring of the younger man. A summer spell which yielded three further victories and two runner-up spots brought the longed-for title ever closer.

'In the long term I want to go as far as possible,' replied Didier when asked about his ambitions by the motorsport weekly *Sport-Auto*. 'The dream is Formula 1.'

Meanwhile, Couderc was proving to be a very dogged opponent. Following a thrilling duel at Nivelles on the undercard of the Belgian Grand Prix, a few weeks later the pair engaged in another full-blooded battle at Charade, a sweeping circuit set within the spectacular backdrop of the Auvergne Mountains. On a circuit made slippery by one of the region's heavy rainfalls, Couderc's leading Martini suddenly snapped out of control. An oil-spattered visor restricting his visibility, it was too late for Didier to take avoiding action. Crunch! The second-placed car slid off into the guardrail. Race over.

Bad luck at the Bugatti circuit where a fire destroyed Couderc's car and trailer signalled the end not only of a spirited season, but effectively a whole career.

Victory at Brands Hatch in early October finally clinched the title for the 22-year-old Parisian. Didier had made good his promise. More significantly, Guiter's gamble had paid off. Naturally, the champion now set his sights on the next rung of the motor racing ladder: Formula Renault Europe. Guiter, of course, said 'Oui.'

There was just time to seal a strong championship year with a final hurrah in Barcelona, venue for the 20th and last round of the year. As autumn arrived on its doorstep, the city's Montjuïc circuit was drowning under an avalanche of dead leaves. Many cars overheated as the leaves snuck into radiators and cooling systems. Notwithstanding, as several of his rivals floundered, Didier picked his way through the debris to take his seventh win of the year. Such was the attrition rate, Gianfranco Ricci took fifth place and with it, his only points of a long, arduous Formula Renault campaign.

Promotion and relegation; such are the vagaries of motorsport. Ricci was headed home to Italy, Didier to Formula Renault Europe.

Mission accomplished.

Six

Didi et René

I N a column written in 1982 at the height of his fame for *Auto Hebdo,* Didier would make passing reference to a quirk that had obviously not escaped his attention. Throughout his motor racing career, he noted, his own trajectory and that of his rival René Arnoux had run in parallel; both men had won their respective driving school championships in 1972 – René with Shell, Didier with Elf. The writer then briefly mused about a pattern that had since emerged: while Arnoux's successes had occurred in years ending with an odd number, his own had occurred in years ending in even numbers. Thus, René had become Formula Renault champion in 1973, while his own season had floundered. Conversely, the year 1974 had yielded a championship for Didier while his rival from Grenoble had endured a miserable time. This on-off pattern had continued up until the present day, wryly observed Didier in the summer of that fateful year.

If such was indeed the case, 1975 was set to be an Arnoux year. What fate then Didier? The auspices were not looking good when the reigning Formula Renault champion received an invitation to join the French military early in the year. La Republic was calling. National Service was a requirement of French citizenship and as such a call that could not be ignored.

Didier was aghast. Fresh from his championship-winning year the champ was relishing taking part in Formula Renault Europe, the new format created to supplant the national category. Not wishing to lose the momentum built over the past 12 months, Didier railed against what he perceived to be the injustice of his situation. What about Magny? The team? Elf? Above all, what about his career?

'The subject can't even be approached with him. He does not accept this mandatory obligation. His bitterness is great and his revolt disturbing,' notes Imelda in her diary.

At 23 years of age, the time was exactly ripe for military service. A year away from the sport though was an intolerable thought. No amount of pleading or family influence, however, could avoid the reality of the situation. Salvation arrived in the form of Le Bataillon de Joinville, a special unit reserved for athletes and sportsmen and where future stars such as footballer Zinedine Zidane would undertake their own obligations. Reluctantly, Didier agreed to join up. Under special dispensations granted to those of a sporting prowess, he would only be required to attend training one day per week. Though far from ideal, it was surely preferable than full-time conscription.

1975 would thus prove to be a busy year all round. In addition to consolidating his position as one of France's rising track stars, precious time would be spent marching on the parade ground or shooting on the rifle range – a discipline in which the racer excelled.

As far as the motor racing competition was concerned, the year ahead would be a reprise of the usual suspects with two intriguing additions. Lining up with Sourd, Snobeck and co would be rally ace Jean Ragnotti and the returning Arnoux. The field had just got that little bit stronger, and consequently the chances of retaining his crown as Formula Renault champion, that much harder. After a year in the wilderness chasing F2 drives and Lotus F1 testing contracts over in England, Elf had thrown René a lifeline in the shape of a small budget to enable him to compete in the new formula. Little René was ecstatic. Ragnotti on the other hand had already established himself as a class act. Movie stunt driver for the likes of Alain Delon, 'the Acrobat' – as Ragnotti was known – could arguably claim to be France's greatest all-round driver. A dip into single-seater racing seemed a good way to cement that reputation. Remaining with Team Pironi for a second season, great things were also expected of Richard Dallest. Competition without and within.

Life at the old butcher's shop, meanwhile, was as hectic as ever. When not testing or hanging out at Tico's place, Didier and the gang liked nothing better than to watch a movie under the bright lights of the steering-wheel chandelier – a constant reminder of their purpose. With Daniel Champion's wife and young child in situ since late 1974, conviviality and friendship were the order of the day chez Didier.

Disqualification at the opening race at Nogaro for Didier (2nd) and Richard (3rd) did not augur well. In a year when all the top contenders were using the Martini MK15 chassis, the scramble to modify and innovate in the hope of gaining a competitive advantage became something of a Holy Grail. Adjustments to the height of the back wing of the team's cars had consequently fallen foul of the regulations. For Didier, it was 12 vital points lost.

By the end of April, the season had settled down. Five races in and the squadron leader was still searching for his first victory. Although he was picking up podium finishes, the team were falling just short of resuming their place as regular winners. If Team Pironi had assumed they would continue in 1975 where they had left off the previous year, just a handful of races into the new season, that idea had been well and truly quashed as a glance at the championship table revealed:

Arnoux	54 pts
Ragnotti	46
Sourd	41
Pironi	40
Snobeck	38

Any one of five drivers could conceivably win the title. His meagre budget subsequently augmented by Elf, Arnoux was proving to be a tenacious opponent. A hat-trick of wins at Croix en Ternois, Ricard and Magny-Cours had propelled René to the top of the championship. If Didier felt a trifle overshadowed by his rival it is easy to see why. Not only had the little man migrated from Shell to Elf, racking up victory after victory, he was also forging a strong relationship with Tico Martini, the man Didier had adopted as his guru. A couple of ardent admirers, Didier and René vied for Tico's affections.

Keeping a secret in the tightly knit world of Formula Renault was no easy task. Rumours the championship leader had hit upon an innovative ventilated braking system soon had Daniel Champion sniffing around for clues. Given that René and Didier were both driving under the Elf banner, a compromise was reached: in the interests of team spirit, the young chargers warily agreed to exchange technical information. In this cut and thrust environment, gaining even the slightest of technical advantages could prove crucial. René and Didier were, after all, comrades of sorts, albeit ones who watched each other's moves with the keenness of eagles.

It was not until the sixth round at Monaco that Didier's season truly began. The playground of the rich and famous had always been a happy hunting ground in past seasons. On a wet and slippery May afternoon, Didier shadowed Snobeck's leading car in the colours of UFP for 22 laps of a race scheduled to run for 25. It was a race he desperately wanted to win. Three laps remaining and with the spray from the leading car playing havoc with his ignition, at the old Gasworks hairpin, Didier lunged inside the leader...

With the Monaco Grand Prix due off in a couple of hours' time, here was an irresistible opportunity to impress F1's movers and shakers. Inevitably, the two cars touched. Hampered by gearbox issues, Snobeck conceded the corner and the race. A much-needed 15 points secured, the victor would later reflect on how he had only 'lightly tapped' the leader in order to pass... With the win, Didier roared back into championship contention.

Victory in Monaco, however, could not mask a fundamental problem for the team: lack of raw power. While Didier's split-times revealed nothing shabby with his cornering speeds, such was not the case on straights, that part of a circuit where top-end grunt mattered most and where he was losing out significantly to championship pacesetters Arnoux and Ragnotti. Tico and Didier looked to Bozian, the company responsible for preparing the team's engines, not to mention those of Arnoux.

A change of engine tuners halfway through the season worked the oracle. In early June, Didier won at Hockenheim, pausing in the pit to collect Daniel and the rest of the guys who clung on to the hood of the car as the winner drove his victory lap. Success was always a team game. Later, as was his custom, Didier would treat his faithful mechanics to a slap-up meal. Drunk on success, the gang would arrive back late at Magny's quiet town square in the small hours, exhausted but happy, what Daniel Champion referred to as 'unforgettable times'.

As the heat of summer settled over France, Arnoux and Ragnotti were now in Private Pironi's sights. However, faulty spark plugs and a puncture denied potential wins in Charade and Rouen respectively. From pole position in Rouen, Didier had briefly lost the lead at the start to Arnoux before calmly out-braking his rival at the New World chicane a few corners later. Thereafter victory had seemed assured.

'I was perfectly at ease in my head before my puncture,' noted a sanguine Didier when reflecting back on the race at Rouen. 'I had that day a distinct feeling of superiority.'

Modifications made to his Martini together with an engine that was now producing serious power meant that Didier enjoyed a competitive, if not always reliable summer run of form. 'On the straights he was irresistible,' noted Paul Ricard runner-up Marc Sourd, who had finished just 0.3 of a second behind Didier and only 0.6 of a second in front of third-placed Ragnotti! Grandstand finishes were common enough in Formula Renault. Ricard ended in a third victory in seven races. Didier had his mojo back.

Indeed, by the time the series shut up shop in mid-July for a seven-week break, Ragnotti, Arnoux and Pironi were locked in a titanic three-way struggle for the title.

For René and his fiancée Nelly, the holiday turned into a nightmare when fire destroyed their trailer home. Tico Martini came to the rescue with an offer of temporary accommodation. René and Tico becoming ever-closer buddies would not necessarily have been the news Didier was hoping for, not with a championship at stake. Not long after, the Grenoblois couple moved into a caravan in the Magny vicinity. Rivals, friends and neighbours. Formula Renault always was a family affair.

Thanks to a dismal run in the final four races of the season, Didier's title hopes frittered away: a fourth place at Albi and three races in which he picked up a measly four points put paid to any hopes of retaining his mantle as Elf's champion. Bundled off the road by a backmarker while preparing to launch an attack on Snobeck's leading UFP in the season finale in Jarama summarised an entire season: close to success, but ultimately not close enough.

Meanwhile, Arnoux was cruising towards the title. In the rush to move up the motor racing ladder – to F3 or preferably F2 – the little man had manoeuvred himself into pole position. Though they had ostensibly been fighting for the right to call themselves the 1975 champion of Formula Renault Europe, René and Didier had in effect been fighting all season for a much greater prize – promotion to Elf's Formula 2 team. Title slipping away, even by late September Didier was still hoping for a ticket to F2. There was just one problem. With Jabouille, Tambay and Leclère already on board for '76, Elf had a vacancy for just a single driver – the Formula Renault Europe champion, a reality that not even Guiter – benefactor to the young man – could change. Nevertheless, he clung to a frail hope that he could somehow drive F2 in 1976, a prospect that was shattered prior to the start of the 16th round of the championship at Nogaro where, just about to start the race, Didier learnt that Elf had other plans for him. 'Elf then finally convinced me to remain for a season in F Renault, with interesting prospects for 1977 F2 if I win the Challenge.' Patience, dear Didier, patience.

Rumours circulated that the UK-based March F2 team were keen on Didier. For a brief moment, he considered leaving France for England. As well as being a leap into the unknown, such a move would have also meant jeopardising his hard-earned relationship with the petroleum giant, an unthinkable proposition.

Finishing in third place overall in the final standings gave little cause for celebration. Niggling problems with punctures, spark plugs and a frustrating quest to secure high-quality engines had conspired to thwart his ambitions. Worse still, the man who had now become his arch-rival had made a spectacular return from the wilderness: René Arnoux was Formula Renault Europe Champion 1975. Promotion to the Martini-Elf F2 team awaited – a prize that would surely have fallen Didier's way had he scooped the prize.

'Looking back, I realise that bad luck played a big role, and I'm really bitter,' Didier told *Sport-Auto* when reflecting upon his season. The thought of remaining in the lower formula while René moved upwards and onwards was hard to stomach. As matters stood, there really was only one viable option: another season of Formula Renault Europe, a step neither forwards nor backwards.

So where did he now stand in the Elf hierarchy? It was a question that would not go away. Just as his rivals from these golden years – Sourd, Snobeck, Dallest and several other fine drivers – would contrive to miss the cut in the scramble for entrance to the international sphere of motorsport, at the end of 1975, Didier too wondered if his career might have similarly stalled.

There was only one solution: go back to the drawing board. Team Pironi needed a fresh start. In his capacity as chief mechanic, Daniel Champion started work re-imagining the team. Engaging the services of engine specialist Bernard Mange[7] ('Nanar') had been an inspired decision. Engine performance had improved significantly. The addition of aerodynamicist Gérard Duhomet and mechanic Jean-Louis Conré for the forthcoming campaign further strengthened the squad. Didier might have been yearning after Formula 2, but with a highly skilled technical team to back him up, not to mention another generous budget courtesy of Elf, prospects for the coming season did look extremely good. Still only 23 years of age, the young Parisian automatically became a very hot favourite for 1976.

Seven

Perfect harmony

I N many ways, the season ahead would develop into a curiously anti-climactic affair. With all the munificence of Elf and Renault behind him anything less than a conclusive march towards the title would represent a serious disappointment. Not only this, but Didier was acutely aware that 1976 would be his fourth consecutive year as a Formula Renault driver, one season more than ideal.

'It is imperative I win this year,' acknowledged Didier. 'I want very badly for this to be my last season in Formula Renault.' Failure to graduate with honours come season's end would represent a profound, if not lethal setback to his F1 ambitions. Pressure and yet more pressure. The boss gathered his new team around to deliver a pep talk:

'We were not successful last year because we didn't do enough when it was needed, you and me. If we do not take the title this year, Elf for sure will cut us off. There is only one escape route: to deliver a flawless championship. Full steam ahead!'

The subtext was clear enough: 1976 had become a make or break year, a must-win. A fifth season in Formula Renault was as unimaginable as it was impractical.

Poor Richard Dallest, fast, consistent and loyal to his team-mate/manager found himself out in the cold. Écurie Elf had effectively scaled down to a single car team; nothing but nothing was going to stand in the way of their favoured son in 1976.

Inevitably, resentment was never far away. It had been the case at Pilot-Elf and it was still the case in Formula Renault.

'It is true that not everybody likes me. I regret it sincerely, but if it happens, it's my fault,' Didier told *Sport-Auto*'s Francis Reste in a candid interview prior to the start of the new season. Referring to his privileged background, the pilot revealed a hitherto carefully concealed sensitivity.

'Sure, I have had more facilities than others, but what can I do? I chose a democratic driving school, and won. It's not my affluence that convinced the jury.'

The suggestion that money rather than talent explained his rise in the sport clearly hurt. Didier's response was typically abstruse: 'I have never wanted to give proof of demagoguery and disguise my ancestry.' Demagoguery? Not the sort of word to feature too prominently in the vocabulary of your average racing driver. Essentially, Didier was saying there was no point in hiding his wealth – to do so would just add more fuel to the fire. Better to face the cynics and critics full on. It was a battle for credibility he would face throughout his motor racing career.

Niki Lauda had bought a place in F1 before him and Ayrton Senna would do much the same after him. While the Austrian and Brazilian legends had unashamedly used family money to further their ambitions, it was a point of pride in Didier that his own career had not been financed by his own family fortune, rather the support of Elf. Of the many items that can be bought, talent is not one.

On the eve of the new season, optimism flowed through the old stone house. A communal hub to a constant stream of racing folk, the house on the corner was busier than ever. As many as a dozen people would sit down to lunch as the clock struck noon. F1 Tyrrell star Patrick Depailler bid adieu to the residents one day clutching the sketches of the team's bespoke braking system – a Daniel Champion innovation that would be taken up by the Tyrrell Formula 1 team. Team Pironi would hit new heights of professionalism in this most crucial of years. They needed to.

It was not all work though. The gang knew how to have fun. Confrontations on the Circuit 24 Scalextric racetrack took on epic proportions. 'Didier was exceptional, in fact he was unbeatable, I tried everything – changing cars – but nothing worked!' recalled one colleague who foolishly agreed to take up the gauntlet of a friendly race with the remote-controlled cars. When José called by the brothers would go off into the countryside on trials or quad bikes. Upon their return, they would feast on dishes cooked up by Agnes and Daniel Champion's wife. Although Formula 1 had always been the goal, these golden days in the unassuming little town – part of a community of friends and rivals chasing the same dream – were among the happiest days of Didier's life.

He might have been a hard taskmaster, but Didier always balanced his fierce ambition with an impish sense of humour. At the end of the working day, the old house invariably echoed to the sound of laughter. The boss liked nothing more than to play a prank on friends or an unsuspecting guest, a light and frivolous side of Didier known only to the close-knit Magny circle.

Accusations of 'coldness' and 'aloofness' would dog the pilot all the way through his career, at least from a certain section of the press unable to fathom the Parisian's nuances of character. 'The truth is that I am shy,' explained Didier. 'It's that I'm not sure of myself, and I always want to know what people think about me.' Wealth had conferred privilege and with it a tendency to restraint, but it had not blunted the young man's sensitivity – far from it. 'I need to be reassured, and understood; unfortunately this is not always what happens. This lack of security in me is probably due to the way I was raised, and I have perhaps not been confronted with certain realities when I was young enough.' It had indeed been a charmed life, but one according to Didier that might have paradoxically rendered him more vulnerable than he might otherwise have been.

Meanwhile, in the old shed just down the road, Daniel and the team set about furiously modifying the MK18, the latest creation to emerge from the drawing board of Tico Martini. Conré and his fellow mechanics had carte blanche to extract all they could from the MK18. As far as expertise and motivation were concerned, Team Pironi compared more than favourably with any outfit in the business. 'An F1 team competing in Formula Renault,' they said. A team combining the talents of Daniel Champion, 'Nanar' and Duhomet was one to be respected. Credit where it was due,

Didier had created a crack operation of specialists in this somnolent corner of France.

By the time of the first race at Le Mans' Bugatti circuit, the team had already considerably reduced the weight of their MK18. Competitors scratched their collective heads. Martini found himself under siege from customers demanding to know how their rivals had managed to gain such a distinct advantage so early into the season.

'Didier was always introducing all sorts of changes to his car,' recalls Jean-Louis Conré, 'whether it was brake discs, springs, ailerons with adjustable flaps, as well as the mechanical brake distributor picked up by Tyrrell.'

Working on a principle pioneered in aviation, aero efficiency was greatly enhanced with the manufacture and integration of a series of three 'flaps' to the car's rear wing. Duhomet had adapted the concept from the French Caravelle jet airliner. Team Pironi had themselves a car that was literally capable of flying.

Securing a sponsorship deal with the helmet manufacturers GPA further augmented the team's financial health. All told, prospects were looking very good. Could anyone stop the Pironi steamroller?

Old rivals apart, Alain Cudini's return to the fray ensured nothing could be taken for granted. Nonetheless, Didier was cruising to victory in the opening race when he ran out of fuel in sight of the finish, allowing Snobeck through to win by just over a second. Sure enough, Cudini scooped the laurels at round two at Nogaro with a characteristically assured drive, but only after Didier had retired. 1976 was up and running. All he had to do now was win a race!

And oh how he did.

It was a very different-looking Didier who took the flag well ahead of the pack on 2 May at his home race at the Nevers circuit. He may have temporarily lost his long locks, but his potency had remained intact. It was the first in what would turn out to be a run of eight consecutive victories! Shock and awe: Team Pironi had unleashed their power. The competition was rocked on its heels. Monaco, Belgium, Germany – it did not matter where the series went, there could be only one winner.

Aiming for a ninth straight win on 4 July at Ricard, the Écurie Elf finally came unstuck. Forced into the pits from the lead to reconnect a faulty spark plug connection, Didier put on a virtuoso display just for the sheer hell of it, setting and breaking the lap record no fewer than seven times in a drive, which brought him back up to ninth place. While Lauda and Hunt were ripping it up on the Grands Prix circuits during that long, hot summer of '76, Didier was cruising. Autumnal visits to Italy resulted in effortless wins at Imola and Monza.

A team working in harmony, 1976 became a season of unsurpassed dominance. Cudini and Snobeck tried their hardest, but since the season had begun in April the result had never been in doubt. Team Pironi personnel became accustomed to ending races perched on their employer's monocoque, lapping up the spoils of victory.

In the middle of this astonishing season, Didier had his first taste of the Le Mans 24-hour race, Elf's idea. Falling on 12/13 June, sandwiched between races in Pau and Hockenheim (races which Didier won), the Formula Renault Europe championship leader joined a team made up of sports car ace Bob Wollek and Marie Claude Beaumont, both of whom were delighted to learn the identity of their co-driver. Didier was, after all, on a hot streak. After Beaumont broke the clutch, the trio limped home in 19th position. 'I'm pretty happy to have been involved, despite the mechanical problems,' commented Didier, 'but I like to win.'

Getting to the finish line – albeit down the order – was a marginally better result than that achieved by José who had teamed up with Jabouille and Tambay in the Renault-Alpine 442. Le Mans was just another adventure. 'A dilettante' according to a family friend, unlike his half-brother, José never truly developed his motor racing career in any meaningful way, despite being possessed of more than his fair share of talent. It was a major point of departure between the brother-cousins.

Detour over, it was back to the bread and butter of single-seater racing. Pironi and Elf duly collected their second Formula Renault title together. Say what you like about money or favouritism, theirs was undeniably a winning partnership.

It almost ended in grief, however, following another win at Albi in October. Didier had elected to fly down to the nearby Le Sequestre aerodrome, thus bypassing what would have amounted to an arduous five-hour drive from Magny. After collecting his 11th winner's trophy of this incredible season the victor took off the next morning in his single-engined craft, but high winds forced Didier to plot an alternative flight path. Together with Agnes, the pilot set off anew. Just over an hour into the flight, the young couple flew straight into a fierce storm plaguing the Haute-Vienne region. It was a hair-raising moment. The little plane was badly buffeted, Didier drawing upon all his skills to avoid a potentially serious incident. Eventually he was able to make an emergency landing outside the city of Limoges. It had been a narrow escape.

All in all 1976 had been everything Didier had hoped for. He had restored his reputation and was headed for an F2 ride with the Elf-backed Oreca team where he would once again partner with René Arnoux. 'He downright amazed me,' noted Christian Courtel when giving his thoughts on the campaign. 'I followed that year and I have rarely met such a determination in a pilot!'[8]

Even the eye-catching debut of the runaway Formula Renault leader back in Dijon could not dent the sweet taste of a job well done. Such had been the progress of Pilot-Elf's 1975 winner, Alain Prost had been invited to step up into the European series even before he had competed his first year in the sport. The 20-year-old had made quite a splash at Dijon, winning a heat and setting fastest lap on the way. In his autobiography, Prost claims he caught up with Didier in the final lap and was preparing to pass the leader when his car failed him. Whatever the truth, a very potent threat had just joined the Elf stable. Arnoux, Prost, Tambay, all products of France's thriving junior motor racing programme and now, along with Didier, all aiming to assume the mantle of France's undisputed number one racing driver.

On the occasion of Didier's 12th win of the year at the season finale at Imola, Prost was looking to win his 13th race in the 13th and final race of the national championship down in Pau. A mechanical issue robbed Prost of the perfect season, prompting François Guiter to solemnly declare: 'Neither of my two drivers are able to win all the races in their challenge! Where are we going wrong?'

In Prost, Monsieur Guiter had unearthed yet another major talent. Didier had a serious rival for the affections of Elf's sugar daddy. For now, the two drivers moved in different circles, but only the most wilful of individuals could fail to see that these two were on flight paths that must surely one day converge.

Eight

A bigger pond: F2

I T was all change at the end of 1976. After four long years, Didier was finally moving up to Formula 2. Old friend and mentor Tico Martini had thrown the young driver a lifeline for which Didier could hardly express his gratitude.

'My greatest professional satisfaction,' he later told Johnny Rives, 'is the end of 1976 when I knew I was going to F2 with Tico Martini and Hugues de Chaunac. Tico is the person who knows me best and I believe is most able to pass judgement on me. It made me happy to know that Tico was doing everything for me to be on their team.'[9]

Although the Elf-Martini F2 team also had its base in Magny, the newly crowned Formula Renault Europe champion deemed it prudent to move away from France's motorsport 'village'. Didier wished to promote himself as an international driver. The time was ripe therefore to take a step back from this epicentre of French motorsport, to pastures new. Magny had served its purpose. The old team were disbanded. Daniel accepted an offer to join Renault's fledgling F1 team as assistant to Jean-Claude Guénard. It wasn't easy, breaking up this bohemian family after a three-year adventure where loyalty and friendship had seen them through the good as well as occasional bad times.

Overnight, the dynamics of Team Pironi had irrevocably changed. Stepping up on to the next rung of the motor racing ladder meant leaving behind the relative parochialism of what was in effect a cottage motorsport enterprise with Didier as its patron. Rightly, he had sensed the danger of inertia.

The young couple settled in Chantenay-Saint-Imbert, a small town 20 miles south of Magny. A loan secured, Didier and Agnes moved into an old farmhouse set within lush green meadows. After three years of hectic living in that old stone house of multi-occupancy, here was an oasis of calm. Several months of hard work restored the building to its former glory.

On the competition front, 1977 would test the young lion's abilities to the maximum. Counting amongst its ranks the likes of Arnoux, Cheever, Rosberg, de Angelis, Giacomelli and Daly, F2 was a hotbed of motor racing talent. Fields were further enhanced by guest appearances from current F1 drivers Mass, Laffite, Regazzoni and Jones. Ever the mercurial nomad, even José popped up for a one-off appearance in Renault colours at Rouen. And with Chevron and March heavily involved, Martini would not have things all their own way in the chassis department either. On the engine front, BMW, Hart and Ferrari could boast power outputs to rival the 300hp of Renault's own V6. Ultra-competitive, cut-throat even, Formula 2 was the ultimate challenge not only of a driver's speed, but also character, temperament and resolve.

The question uppermost in the mind – at least in the French media – was the question of which of the Martini-Elf drivers would prevail, Arnoux or Pironi? A season of F2 already under his belt, René had an undeniable edge. As was the case with their Formula Renault duel of two years earlier, a greater prize loomed on the horizon. It was hardly a secret that Renault and Elf had been preparing to embark on a campaign to crack F1 itself, 1977 being the year their prototype yellow and black 'teapot' was scheduled to debut on the Grand Prix circuit. While F2 was a useful training ground, Formula 1 was the goal. The Regie's involvement in F2 these past two years had merely been preparatory work prior to launching their future project. Provided they performed as expected, the two young guns currently employed in its F2 team could surely dare to dream of an F1 ride in yellow and black colours. It was a tantalising prospect.

The problem for the newest member of the team was a clause allocating him the status of second driver. After a near miss in

'76, René now had the full support of Martini and de Chaunac to enable him to go one better in 1977. Arnoux had already proven his mettle at this level. From a management point of view, his elevation to senior driver made perfect sense.

Besides, there was still a question mark over Didier's capacity, if not within the Magny community, then certainly within certain factions of the French media as well as members of the wider racing community. 'Last season saw him outclass his rivals,' noted Johnny Rives, 'but no one can say whether this is due to his obvious talents as a driver or as a director.' Could Didier hack it at international level? He might have swept all before him in Formula Renault Europe the previous season, but at what price? Had not Arnoux achieved a similar feat with a much more modest budget? Didier would need to convince a sceptical media that his ascension was fuelled by more than just a generous supply of funds from his friends at Elf.

Rives followed the Elf-Martini team to a wet and windy Silverstone for the opening round of the 14-race season. In his report for *Sport-Auto*, the writer catalogued a raft of technical issues that would plague the Martini/de Chaunac-run team throughout the year. During that wintry March weekend the MK22's teething problems became apparent for all to see, acutely so for a couple of French drivers who never lost their sense of humour despite this unpromising start to their season. As meticulous as he was, Martini was already focusing on a long-cherished dream for 1978: entry to Formula 1.

Arnoux's unexpected victory, as welcome as it was, could not hide some niggling issues for the French outfit. Both cars had qualified well down the field. There was much work to be done. In his first F2 start, Didier had an eventful afternoon. Disputing position with Messrs Rosberg and Patrese at various stages, the debutant was mystified when his car veered off circuit while defending his fifth place: 'Suddenly my car refused to turn. I went straight. The left front wheel did not touch anything. But it was flat.'

Following races at Thruxton and Hockenheim, René headed the title chase with 18 points. Didier, by contrast had yet to open his account. More engine problems had led to retirement in both races – races that had been won by three different drivers driving three different cars. As had been predicted, this 1977 Formula 2 season was wide open – any one of a dozen drivers had genuine claims of winning at any given circuit. 'The toughest European Formula 2 Championship of the past five years,' in the words of *Motorsport*, a specialist monthly UK publication.[10]

Zero points. It was not the start Didier had been hoping for. He never would be able to claw back those 18 points lost to his team-mate. Was it bad luck or just down to inexperience?

The situation with René was not dissimilar to others he would face as his career progressed. Being the second driver in a team could and did lead to disadvantages, often subtle but disadvantages nevertheless. At Silverstone for example, Didier had ceded some 600rpm in power to his team-mate following modifications to his V6 Gordini engine, a distinct handicap on a power circuit such as the British track. Not that there was too much in the way of friction between the rivals. On the contrary, the two men enjoyed good relations despite the undeniable edge inherent when chasing the same prize.

Fourth place on the Nürburgring grid behind Patrese, Mass and Giacomelli resulted in a steady fourth place come race end, one place ahead of his team-mate. Didier's season was up and running. In this freakishly competitive season, every single point would be hard-earned. Even F1 could not claim to be as hotly contested as this category of racing. A fortnight later at Vallelunga in Italy, Didier caught and passed the Ralt-BMW of Eddie Cheever for a superb second-place finish behind runaway winner Giacomelli.

Acclimatising quickly to this new environment, momentum continued apace with a visit to Pau for round six of the championship – one of only a handful of tracks in the 1977 schedule he had experience of driving. The track, which runs through the centre of the picturesque town of the same name in south-west France, past aqueducts, churches and chateaux, had always been good to Didier. His last three visits had all ended on the podium, including victory in '76. As he took his place on the grid on a dark, thundery afternoon, the Martini pilot was quietly confident.

Once Tambay and Cheever had collided at the start Arnoux slotted into the lead pursued by Giacomelli and Laffite, who themselves soon tangled. Now up to P3, Didier had the Chevron-BMW of Patrese in sight. As the skies turned ever darker, the Martini caught and passed the Italian. The young Martini pilot was revelling in the slippery conditions. Next up, Arnoux. Fourteen laps remained to the flag. Didier began to haul the leader in …

The race was heading for a thrilling climax when the dark clouds suddenly and violently burst: a flash thunderstorm, naked, raw, awe-inspiring. The red flags came out, but only after some dithering. As the two blue and yellow Martini-Elfs approached the start-finish line, nose to tail, such was the degradation in conditions and such was his proximity to his team-mate's car in front, Didier failed to notice that the race was being halted. Skating on a treacherously wet race track, unable to slow for the tight virage de la gare (station hairpin) the number two Martini pilot found himself a passenger in his own car. Thud! The car went straight into the straw bales. Unaware that the race had been stopped, Didier tried to extract himself back into the race, but to no avail.

Bitterly disappointed, he had no option but to ditch his mount where it stood. A good job, because seconds later the stricken car was rammed by third-placed Patrese and a succession of other drivers who had similarly lost control of their vehicles as they had crossed the start-finish line.

Approaching the halfway point in the season, Martini-Elf were in a strong position:

1. Arnoux (Martini-Elf)	30 pts
2. Cheever (Ralt-BMW)	19 pts
3. Pironi (Martini-Elf)	18 pts

Those three non-scores at the start of the season had cost Didier dearly. Nevertheless, on recent form there was very little to give between the two Martini drivers. While the European Formula 2 category was highly respected – the presence of so many F1 'guests' proved as much – such was the very nature of its competitiveness, making a name for oneself was nigh on an impossibility. How could a driver hope to stand out?

Didier thought he knew how.

In between the races at Vallelunga and Pau, an opportunity arose to truly stamp his mark on the international scene. An irresistible chance to put himself right in the Formula 1 shop window in the most prestigious race outside of the sport's premier category: the Monaco F3 race.

Nine

Monte Carlo or bust

THE Monaco F3 race long had a reputation of throwing up a potential superstar driver. Jackie Stewart (1964) and Ronnie Peterson (1969) were just two of the illustrious alumni to have won this Grand Prix support race prior to permanently joining the F1 circuit. Future winners would include Elio de Angelis (1978) and Alain Prost (1979). Winning Monaco F3 was the ultimate PR for an aspiring racer.

Twelve months earlier, Didier and Tico had discussed the possibility of a smash 'n' grab raid on the Principality, but riding high during that fabulous Formula Renault Europe season, had never quite got around to implementing their plan. As the 1977 event approached, Martini planned to run Dany Snobeck in the MK21, a car that had been specially prepared with this race in mind. Initial testing at Zolder had gone well enough to suggest the team had a realistic chance of pulling off a spectacular coup.

With Snobeck committed to Formula Renault, and a potential race-winning car on their hands, Didier knew a gift-horse when he saw one. Having sounded out possible sponsorship from the engineering company Bendix, financially the project at least had legs. And there was always the ever-faithful Elf, of course.

'Tico, listen to me. Let me borrow the MK21 for Monaco. Hugh and I will win the Monaco F3 race!'

His employer was unconvinced: 'But you are an F2 driver! Think of the risk to your reputation if you fail to win!'

'It's the only way I have to catch the attention of the F1 teams, the only chance to get a contract for next season!'

Martini had a point. By stepping 'down' to F3, Didier was taking a huge gamble. Should he win the event, then all well and good. However, what if he were to finish down the order? To make a mistake? To get caught up in somebody else's accident? Monaco had a reputation for drama all its own. Take a collection of F3 cars under the influence of 20 gung-ho hotheads and anything could happen. Reputations could be just as easily lost as won on its sinewy streets. Was Didier prepared to take such a risk?

'If you lose, you're fucked!' cautioned Tico, secretly warming to the idea though anxious not to leave his friend under any illusions. If anyone could pull this off, this young guy he had first met as a fresh-faced kid over a decade earlier could do it.

'But if I win, I get into Formula 1. You must help me!'

'Okay. Hugh and I will do all we can. Count on us. But you can't stop us from thinking this scheme is crazy.'

There was barely a chance for Didier to even test the car – just a handful of laps of Nevers – before a small team set out from Magny to Monaco in late May. Former Team Pironi engineer Benito was drafted in to prepare the Toyota engine. Hugues de Chaunac would oversee the raid.

Monte Carlo or bust.

'I don't hide my ambitions,' said Didier upon arrival in the Principality. 'I would do anything to win this race.' He was not the only one. Over 120 applications had been received by the race's organising body, of which just 64 were accepted. Faced with such a large entry the solution would be to run two 'semi-finals' out of which would emerge the 20 drivers who would line up for the final. In their wisdom, the organisers elected to simply hold two qualifying sessions, the fastest 20 times deciding the final grid, be they all from session 'A', 'B' or a combination of both. A few eyebrows raised; what if one session had say, rain or an accident? How could such a disadvantage – a glaring one – possibly be fair? C'est la vie.

On top of all this, for once the Magny raiding party arrived behind the curve. Formula 3 might have been beneath Formula 2 in the pecking order of international motorsport, but it had its own rules and regulations and it certainly had its share of idiosyncrasies. If it had not been for Nelson Piquet, the team would not even have had a suitable gearbox. 'We arrived as amateurs,' joked Didier. He had a point.

For some drivers this race would be a last throw of the dice, a chance to erase what had (or had not) gone before. Like Didier, Gianfranco Brancatelli was stepping down from F2. After an indifferent start to his season, the Italian hoped to re-ignite his career on the streets of Monaco. 'As it's not going so well in Formula 2 right now,' smiled Franco, 'it's worth a try ...' The magic of Monaco. Old rival Alain Cudini was also present, similarly hoping to boost an ailing career. Winner way back in 1968, Jean-Pierre Jaussaud was yet another wild card hoping to pull off his own version of a Monte Carlo heist. All it took was a slice of Riviera luck.

Then there was the present crop of F3 aces, de Angelis, Piquet, Warwick, Johansson and Ghinzani, all hoping to leave their own indelible mark upon the event.

'Didier at that time was the great French hope, so to compare myself with him was a great privilege that enhanced my talent at international level,' recalls Piercarlo Ghinzani, one of several drivers in the field who would make it all the way to Formula 1, but like so many in the sport, a driver who would never enjoy the level of equipment with which to show his true talent.

Certainly, the chance to shine in front of the F1 talent spotters such as Colin Chapman or Ken Tyrrell cannot be underestimated. Come the end of this glitzy weekend, the Monaco F3 winner would be a name on everybody's lips.

Bottom line: whichever driver emerged as the victor would invariably be a class act, a man to watch.

Didier had calculated correctly, but could he pull this off? He was, after all, part of a makeshift team whose car, the MK21, was virtually unknown to him: 'I do not know much about the car, since I only drove her for 20 laps at Nevers...' confessed the pilot. Little wonder Tico had dismissed the plan as 'crazy'. Fearful that the mission would indeed badly misfire, Martini had declined to join the Monaco party, preferring instead to hang about his Magny workshops waiting for news, on tenterhooks.

Damp, miserable conditions abounded during Thursday's first practice session. Along with his small team of mechanics, Didier did what he could to familiarise himself with his mount's quirks. 'There is still a lot of work to do, but I am confident about the race,' he declared after setting the fourth-fastest time of the session.

With a whopping 64 drivers competing for 20 grid slots, Friday's session was set to be a nail-biting day. Split into two groups, this would be a qualifying session like no other. Finding a clear lap on these notoriously tight streets could easily boil down to luck rather than judgement. On a dry circuit, lap times 20 seconds faster than those of the previous day, a titanic battle for pole position began. As is well known, for a shot at victory around these tight and twisty harbour roads, a place on the front row of the starting grid is virtually de rigueur.

Ultimately, European F3 championship leader Piercarlo Ghinzani took pole with a lap of 1'37.93. With his lap of 1'38.26 Didier joined the Italian on the front row, a whisper in front of the Chevron of Elio de Angelis. To illustrate the competitiveness of this race, just 1.5 seconds would separate Ghinzani's pole-winning time from that of the 20th and last-placed qualifier, Geoff Brabham. Motor racing grids do not get any tighter! Indeed, such was the scintillating pace, drivers of the calibre of Piquet, Warwick and Cudini failed to qualify. A collision between two cars at the harbour chicane resulted in a broken arm for one unlucky competitor. Fast and very furious: Monaco F3. By Friday evening, more than 40 disconsolate drivers were packing up, their weekend over before it had begun.

So far so good. However, Didier was still not out of the woods, nor would he be until Sunday afternoon.

At 1pm, adrenaline pumping through their veins, 20 drivers took their places on Monaco's distinctive curved starting grid. Today, one of their number would make a reputation. Tension was sky high. Twice a winner here before, and with just one car ahead, Didier felt serene.

When the red light came on, the Bendix-sponsored car made a textbook getaway, edging into the lead as the field braked for the first right-hander at Sainte Dévote. Ghinzani remembers the start well:

'I had the best time in qualifying, but the organisers had not realised that pole position was on the zebra crossing! I only discovered myself at the start when I skated on the paint stripes and Didier overtook me with ease...' The gods were obviously smiling upon the French driver on this day.

Behind the leading pair came two Swedes, Oloffson and Johansson, the latter who would effectively act as a breaker against a baying pack comprising de Angelis, Gabbiani, Elgh and Schlesser.

In the cockpit of the Martini, it was not all plain sailing. A worried pilot noted that his engine was not responding in the way he expected; the Toyota plant was having trouble reaching its optimum operating temperature. On his second tour, the problem resolved itself. Later it would transpire that a marshall's discarded armband had become lodged in the car's radiator system. Thereafter enough heat was generated to achieve optimal performance. Another piece of luck. Without this unusual aid, it is highly doubtful as to whether the quest of Monte Carlo would have got beyond a few laps.

At the Loews hotel, third-placed Oloffson nudged Ghinzani with the result that the nose cone of his Ralt suffered minor damage, enough to allow the leaders to pull clear of the third-placed man. A lap later the Italian was involved in an almost identical incident as he chased Didier around the Portier corner out on to the seafront which precedes the tunnel section. 'I tried an attack at the entrance of the tunnel that ended with a slight collision between my front and his right rear tyre, causing my nose cone to fly away.' Rounding the corner, Piercarlo had been taken by surprise at the pace of the Martini which had temporarily slowed, perhaps because of a mistake. The second-placed car then 'nudged' the leader. The consequent loss of downforce meant that the Italian's race was effectively over.

Didier was riding his luck, no question. All he had to do now was hold it together for another 24 laps.

Five laps into the race and the Frenchman had pulled almost as many seconds on Ghinzani whose March was now suffering from a distinct lack of aerodynamic efficiency. With Oloffson seemingly unable to capitalise on the Italian's misfortune, and with de Angelis over 20 seconds adrift in fourth place, Didier was looking very strong. The gamble was paying off.

The Grand Prix world looked on as behind the leader a demolition derby unfolded, Johansson singled out for especial criticism. 'At the halfway point,' noted *Auto Hebdo*, 'Pironi had the situation well in hand, and his mastery contrasted with the cowboy style of the guys in F3.' With a clear track in front, the Martini driver was indeed looking a cut above the competition. A heavy collision between Daly (March) and South (March) at Rascasse led to a heated post-race discussion between the two British drivers. Schlesser, meanwhile, was one of several drivers to fall foul of Johansson.

While all this was going on, out front, the implacable Frenchman was in a race all his own. It was a script that the Martini boys had not dared hope would actually happen. Parfait!

Peter Warr was one of several F1 heavyweights positioned at the famous swimming pool section. The ex-Lotus and current Team Wolf manager knew the genuine article when he saw it. Observing this young lion thread his car through the tricky left-right section left F1's weather watchers mightily impressed. Calm assurance radiated from the cockpit. Not only this, but the pilot had conducted himself with maturity the entire weekend. The young man clearly had a touch of class. A driver with flair; a stylist. The name of 'D. Pironi' was on the radar.

Forty years on, Piercarlo still has vivid memories of his duel with the French hussar: 'I recall with great feeling the elation and disappointment of that race and the great esteem I had for Didier. That year I won the European title, but the challenge of Monte Carlo with Didier remained an open account. I remember him with great affection...'

Just under 40 minutes after the race had started, Didier duly took the chequered flag. De Chaunac and the team were ecstatic. Here, under the critical eyes of the Formula 1 fraternity, they had achieved quite a feat: Didier, Tico, Hugues and the rest of the guys – chancers and opportunists – had broken the bank at Monte Carlo. With his improved results at Pau and Vallelunga, in the short space of a few weeks, Didier had contrived to give his career a not unwelcome shot in the arm. The icing on the cake would be to take the crown of European Formula 2 champion.

Ten

Stepping up

FIVE races in as many weeks, midsummer of '77 and Didier's services were much in demand. The Monte Carlo heist was followed a week later with a visit to Pau on the 30th of the month, another stab at Le Mans on 12 June and races at Tuscany's Mugello circuit and back to Rouen on 19 and 26 June respectively. An invitation to race in Canada's Formula Atlantic series in August suggested that Didier was finally forging a reputation as an international driver too.

However, disappointment awaited at the Le Mans 24-hour race. Along with co-drivers Arnoux and Guy Fréquelin, Didier managed to qualify the Alpine-Renault in fifth place, albeit some way off the strongly fancied first-string Renaults, which, after practice, had monopolised the front of the grid. Not that Renault were expecting too much in the way of results from the second-string car whose presence in the race was purely for tactical reasons. In their anxiety to win the race in the face of stiff competition from Porsche, Renault had decided to deploy the services of a 'spoiler' car whose mission it was to simply disrupt the mighty Germans. The blue and white Bendix-sponsored car was therefore handily placed behind the works Renaults of Bell/Jabouille, Laffite/Depailler and Tambay/Jaussaud and in front of a gaggle of works Porsches.

As the leaders entered the fearsome three-and-a-half-mile-long Mulsanne straight on their warm-up lap, car number 16 was, however, already in trouble. Didier was disturbed to note his temperature gauges going haywire. Due to a broken gas pump connector, the car had sprung a fuel leak. For sponsors Bendix, well-known manufacturers of petrol pumps, it was hardly the greatest piece of PR. The back end of the car was soon consumed with flames. Didier continued down the straight until reaching a fire point, whereupon he was already undoing his seatbelts in preparation for an emergency exit before the car had come to a halt. Le Mans 1977 – over before it had begun.

A strong showing at the world's most famous motor race would have undoubtedly done Didier's reputation a power of good. From highs at Monaco to lows at Le Mans, his attention turned back to the F2 championship. With Giacomelli and Cheever proving fast but unreliable, Arnoux's title claims were consolidating by the race. Could he beat the highly rated man from Grenoble? With René holding a solid lead, more to the point, would he be allowed to even try?

Chasing his team-mate hard in the opening laps at Nogaro in mid-July, Didier could smell a chance to overturn the formbook, but an engine failure put paid to his hopes. René went on to win as he liked. Six, if not nine potential points lost; the story of Didier's season.

When the circus arrived in Portugal in early autumn, the title chase had narrowed down to a straight fight between Arnoux and the erratic but fast American-Italian teenager Eddie Cheever. At this stage in the season Didier trailed his team-mate by 20 points, a deficit that was not only down to the Martini team leader's undoubted speed; bad luck had also played a part as had Didier's status as second driver. If the young pilot felt frustrated, he hid his emotions well. Besides, rumours were starting to swirl around the F1 grapevine ...

François Guiter had been in contact with his friends at the Tyrrell Formula 1 team. One year into his contract, Swedish superstar Ronnie Peterson had decided to leave the team to re-join Lotus. A second driver would be required in 1978 to partner Patrick Depailler. Elf had been very good to Ken Tyrrell over the years, and with petrol company cash still accounting for a substantial part of the team's budget, French input carried plenty of weight. Tyrrell had a vacancy. Monsieur Guiter knew just the right candidate. Didier stood on the verge of his dream. All Guiter needed to do was persuade the eponymous team owner to his way of thinking, a task easier said than done.

Cancellations to races in Austria and Belgium led to a seven-week break before the penultimate race in Portugal. Time on their hands, René and Didier tested the MK22 vigorously. The hard work would pay off, spectacularly so.

An opportunity arose in mid-August to race in Canada at the invitation of Fred Opert. A halfway house between F2 and F3, Formula Atlantic was a tough, uncompromising series run using largely Ralt, Chevron and March chassis, all major players in F2. The calibre of driving talent was high. Stars of the series such as Price Cobb, Howdy Holmes and Bill Brack would not have disgraced themselves in F1 and beating the 'foreigners' certainly added spice to the occasion. Attracted by the generous start and prize money purses, European raiding parties had become a common sight by the mid-seventies: Depailler, Jones, Jarier and Laffite were among a host of Formula 1 stars to cross the Atlantic. By attracting F1 drivers – French if possible – to Quebec's Trois-Rivières circuit, entrants like Opert hoped to boost the series' broad appeal as well as its gate money.

For the F1 crowd it was an adventure and a challenge. The Trois-Rivières race usually took place in August when Quebec City would be basking in temperatures of between 20 and 24 degrees. Added to which the F1 guys were always treated like kings. José had twice taken part in the race, finishing fourth in '75, part of an F1 clean sweep, behind Brambilla (1st), Jarier (2nd) and Jaussaud (3rd). He had also taken part in the famous '76 event in which an unknown local boy called Gilles Villeneuve humiliated the soon-to-be-crowned F1 world champion, James Hunt, with Alan Jones also well beaten.

Anxious to catch a flight home that day, Jones had accepted a lift to the airport from José. Big mistake. The Australian had an ever-diminishing window of time to make the flight. José put his foot down …

'Alan shit himself. He was a nervous wreck by the time we got to the airport,' recalls Opert, a husky-voiced New Yorker who was still preparing cars from his garage well into his seventies. 'I saw them off, started up the auto, drove out the airport, put my foot on the brakes and nothing! No brakes! José had worn them completely out on the journey to the airport!'

Wherever José went, Didier was sure to follow. Fred arranged a drive at the St-Félicien circuit where Didier teamed up with fellow European F2 rival Keke Rosberg, an Opert regular. Six weeks remained before the resumption of F2 hostilities. With central France wilting under a customary hot holiday month, a detour to North America could turn out to be a rewarding experience from both a financial and personal perspective. Because if there was one thing the brother-cousins liked, it was adventure. He might have been a tough cookie, but Opert had a soft spot for French drivers.[11] The American team manager had in fact first encountered José's little cousin the previous year in Nogaro during that fabulous Formula Renault campaign.

'José was late to the circuit as he often was in those days,' recalls Fred, 'so we asked Didier to set up the car, which he gladly did. I watched him closely. I instantly knew that he was a special talent. When José eventually turned up, he didn't manage to beat Didier's best time. I knew then this kid was good.'

In an unfamiliar car on an unfamiliar circuit, the young Frenchman's lap of 39.526s proved good enough for sixth place on the starting grid, two places in front of Rosberg. Ahead lay 100 laps of this unusually short track. As expected, Gilles Villeneuve roared off into the distance right from the start. Didier wisely elected to stay out of trouble to collect $3,000 for seventh place following a time penalty. It was at this meeting that he first encountered Villeneuve – by now very much the man to beat in Formula Atlantic. According to Gerald Donaldson's biography, it was Didier who first alerted the Canadian to Ferrari's interest in him, gossip picked up from the European grapevine. Overall it had been an interesting break, one Didier would repeat the following year at Trois-Rivières. Focus now shifted to F2 and the upcoming race at Estoril.

In a rare visit away from his Magny stronghold, Tico Martini joined his boys on the Atlantic coast as summer finally gave way to autumn. Provided he finished ahead of Cheever, Arnoux could wrap up the title this weekend and Tico wanted to be on hand to witness the coronation of a man who seemed to have supplanted Didier in his affections. René had already been engaged for Martini's latest venture, what would prove to be an ill-fated foray into F1 in 1978 with the Martini-Ford, a fact that could not have escaped Didier's notice.

Much fun was had at the hotel just a short hop from the Estoril circuit; golf, swimming, tennis. As an accomplished swimmer and tennis player, Didier enjoyed himself thoroughly between practice sessions, as he always did.

Just as the season was winding down, the Elf driver stepped up his game. Perhaps it was the rumours about the Tyrrell F1 drive, or just an upturn in fortune, but it was a much more polished Didier who turned up in Portugal that weekend. The MK22 seemed to be handling superbly in what were dry, stifling conditions as western Portugal succumbed to an early autumn heatwave. His best lap of 1'33.05 – comfortably quicker than Giacomelli (1'33.46) and Arnoux (1'33.48) – secured Didier his first pole position of the season. Further back in the field a couple of names to conjure with: old Formula Renault foe Marc Sourd (1'35.05) qualified 13th in a rare F2 appearance and current leader of Formula Renault Europe, Alain Prost (1'35.40) had once again catapulted himself into this higher category although on this occasion was well behind Michel Leclère (1'34.67) in the sister Kauhsen-Renault. A driver from the past, another from the future ...

At half-past three the next day, buffeted by one of the region's characteristically fierce winds, Didier led the field of 20 round on to a warm but blustery starting grid. In a season in which so many drivers had won races (Arnoux, Cheever, Mass, Giacomelli, Leoni, Rosberg, Henton), he desperately wanted to chalk up a maiden win.

Six laps into the race the yellow and blue car had a racey Giacomelli for company. Two laps later, the Italian was off into the dirt and on his way back to the pits after miscalculating an attempted pass at one of the hairpins. Didier led from René. Thereafter the gap gradually increased; 3 seconds by lap 10; 20 seconds by lap 40. Mindful of finishing ahead of championship rival Cheever, there were no heroics from Arnoux. Just as well, because Didier had an air about him on this day, a resolve that looked unbreakable. While Rosberg and Cheever breathed down René's neck lap after lap, Didier simply pulled further and further away, imperturbable, serene, in a race all his own.

It was champagne all around at the finish – a Martini-Elf 1-2; a long-awaited race win for their junior driver and the title of European Formula 2 champion for their senior driver. Quite a day (and night) on the Atlantic coast.

A podium in the final race of the season at a cold Donington Park circuit somewhat lacking in atmosphere confirmed Didier in third place overall in the championship. René was champion, but the junior driver was ending the season as at least joint top dog in the Martini stable.

'Pironi approached his first season of F2 with the coolness, resolution and professionalism we know him for,' wrote motorsport journalist Jean-Louis Moncet for *Sport-Auto* when giving his assessment of this unforgettable season of Formula 2 racing, adding perceptively, 'He certainly deserved better than 38 points, but he loyally assumed his role as second driver behind Arnoux when the Martini passed through a bad patch.'

It had not been an easy season, but Didier had demonstrated that he could mix it with the best of them. 'His victory at Estoril shows that he has nothing to prove in F2,' concluded Moncet.

Eleven

Under uncle Ken's wing

RUMOURS that elevation to the F1 grid was a distinct possibility for Didier had been circulating throughout 1977. Certainly, the prospect of another season in F2 held little appeal. The time was ripe to take the last step up the motor racing ladder, one Arnoux had just taken courtesy of the Martini F1 project. In fact, Didier had been cautiously optimistic about his chances of joining the F1 grid ever since Jackie Stewart had taken him aside for a quiet word earlier in the year:

'Don't make any decisions about your future without first consulting me,' cautioned the Scot. 'There is an interesting possibility …' Given that the Scottish legend was still a close confidant of his former employer Ken Tyrrell, Didier dared to hope. Sure enough, a phone call duly arrived from the woodcutter turned racing team owner.

'If you come to England, could you come to see us for a few minutes?' Didier did not hang around. Just one week after the Donington race had rounded off the F2 season, the young Parisian was flying out to London once again, this time en route to the Tyrrell racing headquarters in Ockham, Surrey.

News of Didier's impending promotion to the world's premier motor racing series was met with varying reactions from the French sporting media. The more cynically inclined detected the hand of Guiter at work. Had not Didier finished only third in F2, some way behind Arnoux? Did his season merit promotion?

As impressive as the win in Estoril had been, it still represented the driver's only win of the entire season. Was Guiter using his influence with Tyrrell to promote a favourite driver? Although there was an element of truth in such surmises, Tyrrell and especially Guiter had been keeping an eye on the dashing Parisian since that magical day at Pilot-Elf five years earlier. That recent Monte Carlo demonstration had merely aroused Ken's interest again. Pironi seemed like an ideal fit: young, fast and just as importantly, very sponsor-friendly.

In his biography of Tyrrell, motorsport writer Maurice Hamilton relates how Didier arrived at the 'yard' early one morning to find it closed. According to Hamilton, a hungry French driver then went in search of breakfast. His quest eventually brought him to a typical roadside café where he ate a bacon sandwich.[12]

Back at the old woodyard, which now served as the workshop to the F1 team, Tyrrell promptly offered a two-year contract. 'I accepted the contract without hesitation,' Didier later recalled.

With Jabouille engaged in Renault's fledgling F1 programme and Arnoux fulfilling the same role with Martini, Didier could count himself lucky to have landed a seat with an established stable, a former world championship-winning team at that. Thus, one gloomy November Friday in the heart of the Surrey countryside, the dashing Frenchman readily signed the standard nine-page contract before him. He had made it to F1. The £30,000 salary (approximately £160,000 in 2017 currency), though not unwelcome, felt more like a bonus. A further £70 was on offer for each championship point earned. Tyrrell also promised to pay 'all reasonable accommodation expenses and the cost of economy air travel from London to the nearest convenient airport...' It was hardly a king's ransom, but it *was* a salary. Didier would later say it was the first time in his career that he had earned a proper salary.

Tyrrell in 1978 though was a team in transition. Ronnie Peterson, the team's superstar Swedish driver, had left the team after a single season following a bruising year attempting to tame the team's revolutionary six-wheeled car. There had also been changes in key personnel. Designer of the P34 six-wheeler Derek Gardiner had been replaced by Maurice Philippe, who had taken on the task of effectively designing a conventional car from scratch. Ken's team had seen better days. Certainly, the days of winning multiple Grands Prix and world championships with Jackie Stewart had passed.

Although in many ways Tyrrell was a quintessentially English team, its links with Elf ensured a certain Anglo-Gallic ambience pervaded. In Patrick Depailler, Didier teamed up with a driver he had known since the Lotus Seven days back in '64. One of F1's nice guys, Patrick immediately took his fellow daredevil under his wing, which was just as well given comments made by Didier in an interview with Johnny Rives:

'Patrick had warned me yet I was still surprised by the coldness of relations within the team,' noted a driver perhaps missing the intimacy of the Magny-Cours extended family. 'It's a way of life for the English,' observed a young man who must have been feeling more than a little homesick. Ken oversaw a professional team, but it was a very different environment from those of Martini and de Chaunac.

Didier's Formula 1 career officially began at the Argentine Grand Prix on 15 January. Having never driven so much as a single lap in the Citibank-sponsored 008, this first F1 weekend would prove to be an exceptionally steep learning curve for the rookie. He had briefly driven the six-wheeler at Ricard, but Argentina would represent his first substantial acquaintance with a Tyrrell F1 car.

His objective was simple: to not embarrass himself apropos Patrick.

When both cars ended the first qualifying session propping up the field, the new boy was disappointed but philosophical. The real yardstick was not the Laudas and Andrettis who were engaged in a different race altogether, but rather the comparison between himself and his team leader:

'What comforted me a little is that Patrick was no better placed than me. We were both on the last line after the first day of testing.' Depailler then would prove to be a useful comparison. Paired with Peterson the previous season – many people's idea of the fastest driver of the decade – Patrick had more than held his own. Ergo, if Didier could match his team-mate, he could probably match anyone.

Saturday though was another day altogether. While Patrick improved to tenth, Didier remained anchored to the foot of the grid. Modifications to his team-mate's car were not replicated on his own: 'When I was two seconds off Patrick's times, everyone in the team was satisfied,' reported a perplexed driver. 'It seemed normal, and they did not plan to do anything on the car to fill the gap. Yet I knew that I could be in the same bracket as Patrick.' For the junior partner perception mattered. 'I'm perfectly capable of doing the same time as Patrick with the same car,' insisted an indignant young driver. A spin into the fencing during second practice hardly helped his ranking. Formula 1 was proving an unforgiving mistress.

At 2pm on a warm Buenos Aires summer's day, Didier slotted the 008 into 23rd position on the starting grid. Just one car had qualified slower – the privately entered McLaren of Brett Lunger. Ahead a galaxy of 1970s legends: Lauda, Andretti, Hunt, Scheckter, Reutemann. 'Don't go too fast. Don't get in the way of the others. Don't leave the car…' Prior to the off, Ken Tyrrell had imparted some fatherly instructions to his new driver. Didier started his first Grand Prix with a 'head full of advice'.

The race itself was long and arduous. 'The most difficult race of my life,' according to Didier, who brought his car home in 14th position. Patrick meanwhile finished a splendid third, a whisker behind Lauda's Brabham-Alfa. It had been the proverbial baptism of fire.

Two weeks later the young Tyrrell pilot scored his first ever point in F1 following a gutsy drive to sixth place at the Brazilian Grand Prix. During the weekend, comments allegedly made by Jackie Stewart met with his approval. When asked which drivers would make an ideal Formula 1 team, the Scot allegedly nominated Lauda and Pironi. High praise indeed.

With this eye-catching performance, Didier hoped to dispel certain myths that had grown up around him: 'What made me most happy is to disprove the reputation I tire and cannot stand the heat.' The perception that he struggled to control his weight and that he might not always therefore be in peak physical condition had dogged him throughout his Formula Renault days. True enough, come the end of a race, face reddened and hair drenched in sweat, it did seem as if he required almost abnormal amounts of effort to sustain a level of performance appropriate for the challenges of high-level motorsport.

'That was just him, a quirk,' remembers one friend. 'It didn't mean he was necessarily busting a gut or anything – it was a characteristic.' Nonetheless, the perception persisted that Didier had to work that much harder than his competitors.[13]

In a portrait written in 1980 of the driver, journalist Nigel Roebuck referenced Didier's habitual post-race condition. For a writer used to seeing the face of the young Frenchman 'pumping with sweat' come race end, the contrast with the driver encountered in the hotel lobby or media centre an hour or so later was striking. Washed and showered, Roebuck was amused to discover not the raging bull of half an hour earlier – he of the snorting nostrils and bulbous veins – but a somewhat laconic individual, composed, implacable, inscrutable, one 'watching the razzmatazz around him' with the same 'mocking smile' that had infuriated Imelda on so many occasions.[14]

It was no secret that Didier had a fondness for good food and that he enjoyed a glass of red. While there was almost certainly a genetic disposition towards weight gain, plenty of time spent in the gymnasium, on the ski slopes and on the tennis courts ensured he retained an athletic build. 'Beefy' was the adjective used by Rives when interviewing the 26-year-old. Others would habitually describe his physique as 'muscular'.

'Many people expected that I would stop and faint, or that I would go off road,' Didier further confided in Rives. By getting to the finish in the punishing heat of São Paulo, he had crossed a psychological bridge. 'This reputation comes from the fact that I still sweat when I get out of a car, and observers conclude that I am tired. This judgement is completely stupid, and I was pleased to disprove it.'

The South African Grand Prix, held at Johannesburg's Kyalami circuit, completed the third leg of a gruelling flyaway start to the season. Along with Jarier, Arnoux, Tambay, Jabouille, Depailler and Laffite, in between practice breaks, Didier posed for photographs on the pit wall. Seven Frenchmen were now competing in Formula 1. Elf's investment was paying dividends. After qualifying, just a few tenths separated the Tyrrell-Elf drivers: Didier's time of 1'16.38 compared favourably with the 1'15.97 of Patrick. Another sixth-place finish in the race signalled a further step forward. Progress indeed. Three races into his career had yielded two points' finishes, yet it was hard not to feel underwhelmed. On his way to that second F1 point, the young Elf driver had suffered the ignominy of being lapped by his team leader who, low on fuel, had driven a heroic race, denied victory by Peterson's Lotus only on the final nail-biting lap of the race.

'I was not satisfied at all because I was aware of having missed a very good result. I could have emulated Patrick if my car had been set up as well.' Such complaints are of course not unheard of in F1. The truth, as ever, probably lies somewhere in between. As the team's lead driver, one embarking on his sixth consecutive season with the team, Depailler would almost certainly have enjoyed some benefits that came with that status. On the other hand, he was an extremely fast and durable opponent.

A steady run to fifth place at Monaco was overshadowed by a maiden Grand Prix victory for his team-mate. After many near misses, Depailler finally broke his duck at F1's glamour race. Along with the victor's laurels, Patrick took a surprise lead in the world championship – his total thus far was 23 points, five better than Andretti and Reutemann tied together on 18. While nobody in the F1 paddock would have denied Patrick his moment of glory, Didier must have experienced mixed emotions. Tyrrell led the championship. However, in the 008 did the team really have a championship contender on their hands? Didier was dubious. He was right to be.

Frustration increased at the US Grand Prix at Long Beach. With 45 minutes of practice remaining, a shock awaited the driver when he pulled into the pits for what he thought would be minor adjustments to his transmission: nothing happened. As far as the team were concerned, his practice was over.

'When I asked Ken why, he replied that there was no time. I was dying to repair it myself, but again, that's part of the things not to do. In short, I did not rejoin the circuit, and my time, as I feared, did not do me justice.' Result: 22nd and last on the starting grid.

At Belgium's Zolder circuit, Patrick qualified almost three seconds off Andretti's pole time. Tyrrell were slipping backwards. Indeed, after his sensational start, the championship leader would reach the podium on just one other occasion (Austria) during the entire season. This was the era of ground effect – Colin Chapman's devilishly clever aerodynamic system that glued the car to the tarmac, thus facilitating incredible road-holding which in turn enabled hair-raising speeds, especially in corners. Didier's sixth place come race end was the fourth time he had reached the points in his first six Grands Prix – not too shabby by any standards, but nowhere near good enough for this driven young man.

Life on the Grand Prix circuit was turning out to be very different from the protective hub of the Magny-Cours 'village'. Understandably, a little time would be required to fully acclimatise to this hectic environment. Indeed, many of Didier's comments during his first full year in F1 can be interpreted as a reaction to entering an alien environment. 1978 was, if anything, a year of culture shock.

As the season wore on, results dried up for both Patrick and Didier. The 008 had flattered to deceive. The biggest plus for Didier came on those few occasions he managed to out-qualify his team leader.

Two points earned at a sticky Hockenheim in late July proved to be Didier's last of the season. Dicing with Emerson Fittipaldi did, however, afford the opportunity to learn yet another lesson, this time from a past master. Using his straight-line speed advantage to good effect, the rookie had fended off the Brazilian for several laps. At the Sachs hairpin, however, the double world champion caught the Frenchman napping. Emerson took the place. 'He had never attacked me there before,' reflected Didier, 'so much so that I no longer watched for him in my mirrors at the corner and suddenly I saw him there besides me, on my left. It was a good lesson.' It was a lesson Didier would use himself four years on to execute arguably F1's most controversial overtake ever.

There would be many more lessons in this long, difficult season. True, Ken Tyrrell watched over his protégé with the same avuncularity he did with all his young protégés, but the big, friendly bear could hardly protect his cub from some of the harsher realities of Formula 1 racing.

Although junior drivers are no strangers to accidents, those in F1 tend to be that much bigger than in lower formulae, a reality very much born out at the start of the Dutch Grand Prix. Just moments into the race, the field threaded its way around the tight Tarzan hairpin. Bunched together, the midfield drivers jockeyed for position. Exiting the chicane, Didier was dicing with his old F2 adversary, Riccardo Patrese. The two cars touched. Cutting across the racetrack seemingly locked together, Arrows and Tyrrell smashed into the guardrail, sending up a cloud of smoke and debris, before ricocheting back on to track, right into the path of oncoming drivers who, in order to avoid a potential pile-up, were obliged to take evasive action. Thankfully, both Pironi and Patrese wriggled out of their cockpits. It had been a narrow escape.

In the next race at Monza, Ronnie Peterson was involved in a not dissimilar type of shunt as cars jostled for position. Didier was one of the first drivers on the scene. Though the Swedish ace had serious injuries, his condition was not thought to be life-threatening at that stage. Peterson died during the night. The rookie was learning first-hand that for all its glitz and glamour, F1 had a dark, sometimes brutal side. Did he have the stomach for it?

He might have had his detractors as well as his admirers, but the one thing both factions had to agree on was that as far as bravery and guts were concerned, Didier Pironi had few equals.

Prophecy, divination, call it what you will, at times Didier's life seemed laced with glimpses of things to come. In early September he accepted an invitation for another crack at Formula Atlantic, this time at Trois-Rivières itself. A troublesome qualifying session resulted in the F1 man lining up in 13th spot on the 28-car grid. Saturday brought heavy rain, saturating Quebec and its environs. The race thus started in discouraging conditions. Water seeping into his electrics, the Chevron of Riccardo Patrese gave up the ghost on the parade lap! In the race, Didier was breathing down the neck of the leading duo of Price Cobb and Bill Brack when the black flag appeared on the 21st lap. The race was being stopped. In an eerie foreshadowing of events four years hence, Californian Mike Rocke suffered horrific injuries to his lower legs after losing control of his car on the ultra-fast Boulevard du Carmel. The hapless American could not prevent the vehicle smashing heavily into the guardrail. The March 77B was destroyed on impact. As rescue services gathered, amputation of the right foot had been required. Rocke's career ended there and then in the wreckage of his car on that dismal afternoon. Déjà vu ...

Twelve

Hero of France

ARGUABLY the most famous motor race in the world, the Le Mans 24-hour race is also one of its toughest. Held each June, the race attracts large fields of competitors and vast crowds. It is the ultimate motor racing marathon, 350-plus laps of the 8.5-mile circuit incorporating the awesome 3.7-mile long Mulsanne straight. Racing through the night into the small hours, pilots swoop into team garages where soporific co-drivers rouse themselves from snatched sleep to take their turn behind the wheel. The winners of this gruelling slog are feted, lionised, immortalised. Les 24 Heures du Mans is an event like no other.

As the 1978 running approached, the pressure, which had been mounting on Renault management for several years, threatened to explode. 1978 was going to be their year, a last glorious attack on the world-famous race held on home soil, the board's idea of the perfect finale before a serious attempt to conquer Formula 1. Vast amounts of francs had already been invested in the project, an estimated £20 million, calculated in 2017 exchange rates.

After the fiasco of 1977, failure was not an option. Heads were on the block.

The yellow, matt black and white Alpines had looked impregnable at one stage during that race, running 1-2-3 at the head of the field in all their Gallic pomp. Disaster had then struck. Each of the three cars had, in turn, succumbed to piston failure. Seventeen hours into the race, the Jabouille/Bell combination had been cruising down the Mulsanne straight when Jean-Pierre had noticed a puff of white smoke in his mirrors. Race over. Renault faces turned bright red. Broadcast live around the world, it was nothing short of national humiliation, more so when deadly rivals Porsche took victory. The ruthlessly efficient Germans from Stuttgart had a nasty habit of triumphing on French soil. It was time to fight back, to repel the old enemy.

This year's running would thus become a mission to restore lost pride, to heal wounds that, 12 months on, were still raw. Renault Sport Division manager Gérard Larrousse was told in no uncertain terms that a repeat of 1977 would not be tolerated. Renault had to win at all costs. La Republic expected.

The Regie could at least draw upon a pool of exceptionally gifted drivers: Jabouille, Arnoux, Tambay, Depailler, Jaussaud, Pironi, Jarier, Bell ... the list went on. Larrousse was spoilt for choice. As any soccer manager will testify, winning teams tend to pick themselves, so it was just a case of matching up drivers and allocating them to one of the team's three factory Alpines. After some thought, Larrousse had his team: Jabouille and Tambay would team up in the first-string car, Renault 1; Depailler and Pironi would partner in Renault 2; Bell and Jarier would share Renault 3; and a fourth car would accommodate Jaussaud, Ragnotti and Fréquelin.

Such was the desire to erase 1977 from the collective memory, testing for the 1978 race had begun almost immediately after that calamitous June day. In Ohio's Transport Research Centre, Renault had been alerted to a 7.5-mile track where their A442 could be tested to breaking point. Crucially, the American facility boasted a couple of two-mile-long straights, an ideal environment to replicate the fearsome Hunaudières section of Le Mans, where speeds of 225mph are routinely attained, for almost a full minute – the cause, according to Renault boffins, of the infamous piston failures of '77. The V6 turbo had simply not been able to take the strain. Once bitten. The testing team hit the Columbus circuit with something approaching zeal.

It was in Ohio that Didier was reacquainted with Jean-Pierre Jaussaud, the man he would ultimately partner in the race and whom he had first met when the older man had been observing a

Formula Renault race at Nogaro. That initial meeting had left a lasting impression on the veteran racer:

'Didier had the quickest lap but I felt he should have set his car up better,' recalls Jean-Pierre. 'I noticed he was cornering with only three wheels on the ground … So, I went to meet him to suggest he would do better with four wheels on the ground. He replied it was the way he liked to drive and that there was no reason to change!'

Testing continued apace until halted by snowfall. Renault returned home enlightened, but still with plenty of work to do.

To ensure the fleet were not afflicted with the same problem as per '77, each of the four Alpines would be configured slightly differently. The Regie were not taking any chances. Unveiled two weeks prior to scrutinising, the Renault number 1 of Jabouille and Depailler for example, displayed a raft of modifications. An increase in boost increased its top speed to 360kmh (224mph) – 10kmh more than its compatriots. Jabouille and Tambay rejected the introduction of a plexiglass cockpit 'bubble' to aid aero efficiency, complaining of claustrophobia and a decrease in the field of vision. Having tested the innovation during night runs at d'Istres military airfield north of Marseille in April, Jaussaud was more enthusiastic. Firstly, the hood shielded drivers from the draught. In the same way, it also provided protection from debris such as stones: Didier had found his helmet dented with the imprints of hundreds of tiny stones, kicked up off the military tarmac at the end of the d'Istres session. Not only this, but it resulted in an 8kmh increase in straight-line speed. A hot, cramped cockpit seemed a small price to pay. Whether that would still be the case 24 hours on, nobody could yet tell.

After an accident in which he suffered burns to his legs ruled Tambay out, and Fréquelin injured himself in a road accident, Larrousse needed to shuffle his pack. Then it came to him: Pironi and Jaussaud! Youth and age. The Renault manager decided to take a calculated risk. If maturity could temper the excesses of youth, then maybe, just maybe, this might be a winning combination. Fifteen years senior to his new co-driver, Jaussaud declared himself 'delighted' by developments. That the new partnership came together just in time for first practice did not faze the man from Caen one iota. He had for company a lion, a very hungry one.

Besides, the former French Formula 3 champion had a plan, which he revealed to Martine Camus.[15] The key lay in psychology. The older driver knew that the younger man would wish to prove himself the faster of the pairing; it was only natural. Such inter-team competition was bound to push their car along. It might also jeopardise their race. Jean-Pierre took his team-mate aside:

'If we want to win the trick is to define a range of times and stick to it, regardless of what the others are doing,' counselled J-P, who understood what it took to win this event more than most. If he could channel the young lion's aggression, then they might just reach a level of consistency to launch and sustain a serious challenge. Jaussaud suggested lap times in the 3'40 and 3'45 range, with the younger man aiming to lap at the lower end of the range, while the older driver would content himself him to lap in the higher end. Didier agreed.

In Pironi and Jaussaud, Renault had a wild card, a balance of blinding speed and tactical acumen. Should Depailler and Jabouille falter, in the shape of Jarier/Bell and Jaussaud/Pironi there was plenty of back-up. When the dust settled on this game of musical chairs, José Dolhem replaced Jaussaud in the fourth Alpine, just the type of adventure the older brother-cousin delighted in.

Despite such strength in depth, Larrousse was not taking anything for granted. Porsche also had a strong hand to play. Furthermore, their 935/36s were not only fast, but also durable. When Jacky Ickx broke the lap record during first practice on Wednesday evening, the Regie knew they had a fight on their hands, one the whole world wanted to see. Didier posted a lap of 3'35.7, good enough for fifth on the grid. Playing it safe, Jean-Pierre's practice times were a good few seconds off those of his team-mate.

Aided by their elongated bodywork and extra boost, Jabouille and Depailler had recorded a whopping 228mph on the Mulsanne straight, 15mph faster than the top Porsche. Renault had the speed. The German camp, however, resisted the temptation to go for out and out top end speed. Le Mans was not all about straights – there were corners too. Finding a compromise between top end and cornering speed, the Ickx/Mass/Pescarolo 936 eventually beat Renault to pole position by a whisker under a second. Of the eight top grid spots, the German and French teams shared four apiece, a two-horse race.

On a hot, cloudless June afternoon, the field of 55 cars trooped around the Sarthe circuit on their parade lap cheered on by a crowd of 200,000 ecstatic fans. Nerves already frayed, Renault personnel braced themselves. The smart money suggested that while the French team might enjoy some early showboating, the sturdy German cars would be there to pick up the pieces later. Inside the cockpit of Renault number 2, Didier could already feel the heat, both literally and metaphorically. Warm sunshine spilled into the car, raising the ambient temperature as high as 50°C.

Further down the grid old Formula Renault rivals, Sourd, Matthiot and Debias had teamed up in a specially built Peugeot. Alain Cudini, the man with whom he fought so often in '75, had failed to qualify. Wrong place, wrong time.

Porsche v Renault; Germany v France. As the time approached four o'clock, silence fell across an entire nation as people huddled around radios and television sets. Could the might of Germany be defeated? Let battle commence.

At the lights, Jabouille rocketed into the lead pursued by a trio of Porsches. After a scintillating first lap, Renault number 1 had a lead of 11 seconds! The aim: to break the backs as well as the hearts of the German raiders. The tall, blonde-haired Jabouille had come within an ace of victory in '77 and was out today to right that wrong. Overturning all expectations, it was Ickx's Porsche that encountered trouble first. As early as lap two the Belgian steered his misfiring mount into the pits. Le Mans is a race that is rarely if ever won at the start. The reigning champion was down, but not necessarily out.

After the leading Renault had pitted to remedy vibrations, Jaussaud/Pironi took over at the front, holding the lead for a substantial period, but it could not last. The fastest of the French quartet by some way, Renault 1 had been charging back up the field and was back in contention as dusk fell. Jabouille and Depailler assumed the lead and the race looked all but over.

With the Ickx/Pescarolo Porsche out of contention following a 45-minute stop to change fifth gear, the German team decided on a tactical switch, sending the Belgian to join the Wollek/Barth pairing currently running in fourth place behind the Renaults. If anyone could break the Regie stranglehold, it was Ickx. The undisputed master of Le Mans – already a four-time winner – gritted his teeth. At 11.30pm, the Porsche took the first Renault. A lengthy stop to attend to a brake caliper lost Renault number 2 a fistful of time, dropping Didier and Jean-Pierre behind the swift Belgian and behind Bell/Jarier's sister Renault.

Saturday turned to Sunday. The rhythm of the night: drive, stop, refuel; drive, stop, refuel, swap, eat, drink, sleep; drive, stop, refuel …

His stint completed, Didier would arrive in the garage where Jean-Pierre would be waiting to jump into the cockpit as soon as it was vacated, not a moment to lose. As the car roared back into the race, the young man would try to grab a couple of hours' sleep until his next stint – easier said than done amid the hustle and bustle. As well as sleep, food and drink had to be regulated. 'He didn't eat too much, but he drank lots and lots of water,' recalls Jean-Pierre. 'Whereas each time I stopped to refuel, I went straight to the kitchen to eat as normal. I had ten meals during the race in total.' Some of which, confesses Jean-Pierre, 'were washed down with a glass of red...'

A warm, humid night out on the Sarthe circuit would see fortunes ebb and flow for the German and French teams. In the small hours, Bell's A442 became the race's first permanent casualty. As the night wore on, two of the factory Porsches were also delayed: Pescarolo stopping at 4am with electrical problems, which took half a dozen laps to remedy, while the team's third-string car followed into the garage a few hours later.

In the cockpit of the plexiglass Renault, Didier was already suffering from the heat that had turned the A442 into an oven. Jaussaud remembers well conditions inside the 'bubble'. 'When I got in the car after he stopped, it was like sitting in a bathtub, he sweated so much!' On one changeover the driver could barely move. Painful muscle spasms shot through his entire body, the ever-faithful Agnes on hand to massage the hero's aches. Diagnosing infection possibly due to an open wound or insect bite, doctors prescribed a tetanus jab. It was turning into a painful night for the 26-year-old.

A bright sun rising over the Sarthe region of north-west France, by daybreak Depailler and Jabouille had a comfortable lead over Ickx and Wollek with Didier and Jean-Pierre next up. Barring accidents, Renault number 2 was on for a podium finish as a minimum. Didier was lapping around 3'35 while Jean-Pierre was averaging 3'38, a little quicker than their plan. Steady was the word.

At around 9am the leading Porsche ran into gearbox trouble necessitating another lengthy pit stop. The Regie were now running 1-2. Behind them, a couple more Porsches.

An hour later, when Depailler parked the A443 at the end of the Mulsanne, the groans of despair could be heard all the way from Paris, where Renault had their headquarters at the Quai Pont du Jour next to the Seine. Piston failure ... Pironi and Jaussaud had the lead! The duo now had a very healthy advantage over the Ickx/Wollek Porsche, but six hours still remained to the flag. Anything could happen. A broken gearbox could be replaced but not without a substantial loss of time; a broken piston, on the other hand, would spell disaster. In the Renault garage, Gérard Larrousse's complexion had been healthier. When he became aware of the perilous state of Didier's health – the team's only hope of victory – Larrousse became paler still.

The harsh midday sun had rendered the cockpit of the A442 a Turkish bath. Despite drinking what seemed like gallons of water between stints, Didier was fast becoming dehydrated.

When Jaussaud handed over the car with just four hours remaining, a further headache presented itself. During what would turn out to be his final stint, the veteran had been disconcerted to hear a crunching sound every time he changed gear. 'I found the gearbox cracking, so I asked Larrousse to call Didier to see if he also had gearbox problems,' recalls Jean-Pierre. 'Negative' came the reply. Renault had a dilemma: to allow Jaussaud to drive the final stint, risking the continuation of the gearbox issue, or to stick with Didier in spite of his obvious discomfort. Approaching two o'clock, Didier would soon be in for the final handover. Larrousse got on the radio:

'Didier, do you hear me?' A beat.

'Yes, Gérard, I hear you.' The voice sounded frail. Little wonder. The cockpit was roasting hot. Didier had lost somewhere in the region of eight kilograms, added to which painful cramps shot up and down his legs and arms. The pilot was on the point of exhaustion, a medical condition that on top of severe fatigue, can also entail loss of concentration, nausea and muscular pain. In a few minutes, however, he would coast into the Renault pit for the final time, handing over to Jean-Pierre to complete the final two hours.

'Can you continue? Didier, you must finish the race!'

Didier's heart sank. Two more hours! Impossible! Larrousse's voice came over the intercom once more.

'Do you understand? You must go until the end. Didier, do you understand?'

The words sliced right through him. 'Yes, Gérard. I understand...' Didier's voice trailed off.

Under Le Mans regulations, a driver is permitted to drive a maximum of four hours within any six, not exceeding 14 hours out of the total 24. In the sauna, the young driver steeled himself. He had to hang on. He had to. For Larrousse, for Renault, for France, but more importantly for himself. It would be the hardest two hours of his life. Flicking the turbo boost down, it was time for mind over matter.

At four o'clock, Didier duly took the chequered flag, almost coming to an immediate halt as crowds swamped the car. Only upon opening the bubble did the seriousness of the driver's condition become apparent. Didier had not the strength to extract himself from the cockpit. Amid the euphoria, two police officers helped lift the hero out of the car. When the young man promptly collapsed on to the stinging hot tarmac, panic ensued. Fortunately, medical help was at hand and Didier soon found himself under medical supervision. Through his exertions, the driver had lost just under ten kilos in weight, Jaussaud only three kilos – the average for this gruelling marathon.

'If I had known he was so tired, I would have finished the last turn,' recalls Jaussaud, who had achieved a lifetime's ambition to win Le Mans.

Summoning what little strength he had left, Didier was cleared to join his co-driver on the victory podium. Even spraying the champagne took some effort. It mattered not. With this victory, the Tyrrell driver had announced himself on the world stage. Footage of the celebration reveals a podium awash with emotion; 41-year-old Jaussaud grinning, having just attained a lifetime's ambition; Larrousse, the most relieved man in the whole of France; and the young hero of the hour, exhausted, stripped to the waist, with nothing left to give. Minutes after the ceremony, Didier passed out again. Hospitalisation would follow.

A few days later, Eric Lucas dropped by the castle to find a beaming Didier surveying a new Renault R30 in grey – a gift from a very grateful manufacturer. The pair took the notoriously thirsty car out for a spin around the streets of Boissy, always an adventure with Didier in the driving seat! Indeed, just weeks after that historic day at Le Mans, France's latest sporting superstar would push the limit just that little bit too far. Didier was caught speeding. Rather than imposing the statutory driving ban required under law, magistrates opted for leniency. The hero of France escaped with a fine.

The fairy tale of Le Mans culminated with a suitably glitzy finale. Sat in the cockpit of their victorious A442, accompanied by an entire media corps, a waving and smiling Didier and Jean-Pierre were towed down the Champs Élysées in the ultimate display of French power. The streets of the capital buzzed with national pride. Waiting for the victors at the Renault museum, a raft of dignitaries, among them Valéry Giscard d'Estaing, president of La Republic. Didier's legend was assured.

As for the iconic A442, a supercar with fuel consumption figures to rival those of jumbo jets – 5.5mpg! – like all great race horses, dignified retirement beckoned with an occasional outing for former pilots to reminisce and fans to marvel. For one ex-pilot, the memories of those last, fraught hours driving a car he felt certain would break at any moment came flooding back when he found himself inside the famous 'bubble' once more:

'Years later, with this same 442, I drove it on the Goodwood circuit and found the same gearbox problem!' Nearly 40 years on, Jean-Pierre Jaussaud smiles, an octogenarian still able to recall every twist and turn of that unforgettable day.

With Le Mans at last won, the Regie immediately cancelled their entire sports car programme. All the company's resources could now be deployed in their quest to conquer F1. François Guiter's thoughts turned to '79. Didier would be the ideal driver to join Jabouille in Renault's expanding Formula 1 team. There was just one problem: the apple of Renault-Elf's eye had a two-year contract with Tyrrell.

Thirteen

School of hard knocks

NATURALLY, in the aftermath of *la victoire*, Renault and Elf were very keen to consolidate their relationship with Didier. Thanks to his heroics on that historic day in the Sarthe, the profile and appeal of the young driver had risen considerably. So too had the international profiles of manufacturer and oil company; win-win. Suddenly, he was all over the papers and magazines, and the boyish features became recognisable through France and beyond. After his maiden year with Tyrrell, beset by frustrations on both professional and private levels, François Guiter reckoned the time was ripe to elevate the young driver to the works Renault F1 team, an idea welcomed by Didier. For the 1979 season, the Regie were planning to throw everything they had behind their revolutionary 1.5-litre turbocharged car, one currently making steady progress in the right direction up the F1 grid.

After initially agreeing to 'sell' his driver's contract, Ken Tyrrell reconsidered. Although results had not been forthcoming, the wise old owl sensed that in the young Frenchman, he had a talent on his hands. The second Renault seat eventually went to that man Arnoux. After a bruising introductory season to F1, and with his career hanging in the balance, it was a lifeline that when offered, brought tears to little René's eyes. Didier was gutted.

Over at Tyrrell the promise of a ground-effect car in the mould of the all-conquering Lotus 79 helped to cheer his spirits a little, even if the wisdom of copying a car that had now clearly been superseded seemed questionable. For better or worse, Didier was set for a second year with uncle Ken. In its current guise, the team from Ockham were a shadow of their former selves however, and their young Frenchman knew it. Renault meanwhile were a team on the move. Bitter pill as it had been to swallow, Didier shook off the disappointment to focus his efforts on the season ahead, one in which in terms of results he knew had to surpass those of his rookie year.

Now living in an elegant first-floor apartment in Neuilly, Didier and Agnes faced a new life that would only intensify under increased media exposure. France's new hero was a man in demand. Always attractive to women, entry to the Grand Prix circuit only seemed to compound that allure further. One member of the Argentinian paddock club could not hide her admiration: 'Didier was an amazing guy, simply amazing.' The lady in question, still vivacious in her late 50s, declined to elaborate further. As part of the glamorous jet-set world that is Formula 1, temptation lay everywhere, not least on aeroplanes ... With the delicate Agnes now acting almost as a secretary-cum-PA to her man, perhaps inevitably, relations between the couple cooled. Twelve years after they had first met, the sheen was fading on what had begun as an adolescent holiday romance. Didier was embarking on what one friend would describe as his 'playboy' years. Rich, famous, handsome and in demand, the world was his oyster.

Back on the racetrack, 1979 looked wide open. Indeed, it would prove to be an unusually competitive season in F1 terms with Ligier, Ferrari and Williams all enjoying various periods of dominance during the year. As for Tyrrell, the team pressed ahead with the Maurice Philippe-designed 009, a dead ringer for the all-conquering Lotus 79. The addition of the quick but inconsistent Jean-Pierre Jarier to the team helped impart the secrets of ground effect he had picked up in a short stint with Lotus at the back end of '78. Sleek and prepared to Tyrrell's usual high standards, the car certainly looked the part. Moreover, it might well have developed into a consistent front-runner had not the team lost its main financial backer, Citibank, at the end of '78. Going into the new season, Ken's team found themselves bereft of major sponsorship.

When the team rolled up in Argentina for the opening race of the season, stripped of sponsorship insignia, the new car looked strangely naked when viewed next to its competitors. Compromise, watchword for a season. The team from Surrey were headed into a season in which budgetary concerns could only restrict potential.

The season started, however, on a promising note. On a hot Buenos Aires afternoon, an 80,000 crowd watched Jarier cling grimly to Depailler's leading Ligier in the early stages of the race. Didier's race had ended within yards of the start when he was caught up in somebody else's accident. After a single kamikaze lap in second place, it soon became apparent that Tyrrell number 4 was holding up a raft of faster cars, a cork in a bottle. Once Watson and Laffite had squeezed past, the floodgates opened. J-P was going backwards, fast. Once again, the team had flattered to deceive.

Of more concern to Didier were the frequent accidents he began to experience, some technical, others brought about by a young driver forcing too hard, desperate to compensate for his machine's deficiencies. During practice at South Africa, the young pilot had, in the words of *Motorsport*, a 'monumental' accident while travelling at 150mph. The impact destroyed the front end of the car. Didier escaped with minor bruising and a 'good migraine'. It would not be the first nor the last time the Tyrrell man would emerge from a potentially serious incident with nothing more worrying than superficial injuries.

Despite such scares, Didier remained upbeat. 'The car is on the pace and both cars are evolving the same way,' he told *Auto Hebdo* early in the season, fears that he would play second fiddle behind Jarier seemingly allayed. 'The 009 has great potential, and planned changes which will be effective after Monaco will make it quite competitive and will help to secure a sponsor.' The 009 had, it seemed, potential, but without funds to develop the car, realising that potential would prove to be virtually impossible.

Having qualified a career best of P7 in Brazil, Didier steered his car to a superb fourth place behind the rampant Ligiers. When the Lotus of third-placed man Carlos Reutemann was adjudged to have had a push start, he found himself standing on his first F1 podium, gulping water while one of the Coca-Cola promotional girls attached herself to his waist from whence she seemed reluctant to let go. Later, the Argentinian was reinstated to third. Notwithstanding, fourth place seemed to suggest that the team were headed in the right direction. And anyway, Didier had had his first taste of champagne à la F1. He liked it, too. Stood there with Depailler and Laffite, one of three French musketeers glugging champagne on a sultry Rio afternoon, he had looked at home, as if standing on the F1 podium was his natural habitat.

Three races into the season, however, the midnight-blue cars were still searching for sponsorship. Talks with drinks company Martini had not progressed. Lack of funds meant lack of testing. Ken was running his team on a shoestring. The team would thus fight the majority of their battles in midfield, fighting against perennial also-rans such as Arrows and Fittipaldi, nowhere near what Didier had envisaged.

By the time the teams arrived in Monaco for round seven however, Didier had taken his first legitimate podium after a third-place finish in Zolder. On their day, Tyrrell had a squeak of a chance of finishing in the top three, even if victory was out of the question. The 009 might have been an improvement on the 008, but any improvements were offset by the advances made by their rivals.

Fresh from his third place in Belgium, and with a fine pedigree around the famous streets of the Principality including that famous F3 win in '77, Didier arrived in a hopeful mood. Monaco was a playground, one in which this sophisticated young man felt entirely at home.

On Friday's 'rest' day, the pilot invited some of the Tyrrell crew for a ride on his powerboat moored in the harbour. These powerful 'Formula 1s of the sea' had always held a fascination. There was something in the brute power of these craft and their unpredictable handling characteristics that appealed to the risk-taker in Didier. Taming one of these monsters was a challenge to be relished. Didier led a small group of Tyrrell mechanics along with Jarier down to the harbour where his Lamborghini-powered 'cigarette' awaited. Tyrrell mechanic Steve Leyshon takes up the story:

'And what a boat! I was used to skiing behind Fletcher Arrow or Shakespeare speedboats, not a 20-odd foot cigarette with Lamborghini engines! We left the harbour in the appropriate manner – slowly, then when we hit the open water it was a different matter. The water was generally very calm – mill pond if you like. So, in order to create some excitement, Didier carried out some very large turns at speed – we didn't go slow after we left the safety of the harbour. Having created a "non" calm environment he proceeded to cut across the waves he generated. This enabled him to demonstrate (a) his boat control – which was as you would expect considerable – and (b) the lack of suspension on his toy!! Didier allowed all of us to have a turn at driving. That to us meant he was either very generous or brave – the jury's still out on that one!'

The one abiding memory shared by associates and colleagues alike of Didier is indeed his generosity of spirit. The young Frenchman liked nothing more than entertaining friends on land, sea or air, whether in boat, plane or car. It was not just white-knuckle rides in the bay of St Tropez; Didier always took care of the mechanics. Forty years after it was presented, one ex-Tyrrell man still has the bottle of aftershave the young driver gave him in recognition for his hard work: 'Best of all, after all these years it still smells nice too!'

The party eventually made it back to the harbour: 'Jarier brought the boat home with Didier sitting right at the front of the boat with his legs either side hanging over the edge! And Jarier wasn't in the habit of driving anything slowly!' Shaken and not a little stirred, Steve Leyshon and the Tyrrell crew went straight back to the race transporter to prepare the cars for Friday's practice. 'It does not get any better than that, a weekend to remember!'

When Didier qualified in seventh place, the weekend started to look even brighter. The Tyrrell driver was less than a second away from Jody Scheckter's pole-winning Ferrari. If he could make a good start in Sunday's race, anything was possible, perhaps even victory.

The Tyrrell pilot certainly had the bit between his teeth this May weekend. While the Ferraris of Villeneuve and Scheckter ran away at the head of the field, Didier found himself handily placed behind the previously dominant Ligiers, who were undeniably being held up by Lauda's obstinate Brabham-Alfa in third position. Anxious to chase after the Ferraris, and suffering from the kind of frustration unique to Monte Carlo, Didier would encounter both the Gitanes-sponsored cars within a few laps, Laffite obliged to pit while Depailler dropped right out of contention following separate brushes with the Tyrrell. 'Didier behaved very badly,' growled Jacques later. 'He's a very silly boy.' Frustration increasing by the lap, Didier had nudged both Ligier cars with the result that the race of both blue and white cars had been compromised. Patience is a virtue in life and, very often in motorsport, especially at Monte Carlo. Unperturbed, the Tyrrell driver pressed on. Besides, the 009 was working well on the street circuit, handling the bumps, slow corners and short straights better than at any race in the season so far. Didier sensed a result.

The manner in which the Tyrrell proceeded to attach itself to Lauda's Brabham suggested he might be right. For several laps, Didier menaced the great Austrian. Ahead lay only the two Ferraris, but the gap was increasing. Somehow he had to clear Lauda; then and only then could the chase of the Italian cars begin.

Such were his thoughts on lap 22 as the Brabham and Tyrrell came hurtling through Casino Square together and down the bumpy Mirabeau section towards the right-hander. Preparing for the corner, Niki edged to the left. A gap! The Tyrrell shot down the inside. Bang! The blue car was launched into the air, smashing into the guardrail with some force before finally coming to rest. The force of the impact threw the poor steward stationed at the corner some distance backwards. Didier wriggled out of the cockpit and slumped down behind the barrier. When F1 cars fly, the landing is very rarely of the smooth variety.

'I saw an opening to pass and Niki was much slower than me. He had slowed dramatically,' reported a shaken driver. 'When I arrived in the middle of his Brabham, however, it was so tight I could no longer avoid hitting him.' The young driver had decided to 'send one up the inside', a move that always requires the full co-operation of the guy in front.

Lauda saw things differently: 'I was travelling quietly in third position, not forcing it, setting the ideal line for the corner when I saw, almost side by side, on my inside Pironi. I could not do anything and the Frenchman crashed into me. At that moment I no longer understood anything.'

A 'racing incident' then, one in which the young Tyrrell driver took the lion's share of the blame. Ready to mix it up with the big guns, certainly there was an urgency about Didier that afternoon. F1 wisdom is gained, as in any professional sport, not without some hiccups along the way. Scheckter eventually took the win. Considering Clay Regazzoni's surprise second place for Williams, the runner-up spot had been there for the taking. A lesson learnt.

Shortly after this eventful weekend Didier's old Tyrrell mucker and daredevil par excellence, Patrick Depailler, smashed his legs in a hang-gliding accident in the Massif Central. Patrick was lucky to survive the fall. Given that his Ligier contract specifically forbade participation in dangerous sports, current boss Guy Ligier was not best pleased. Although Jacky Ickx was drafted into the team, a vacancy had just arisen in a front-running team, a French one too …

Although he had settled in well at Tyrrell after the initial culture shock, Didier was not immune to interest from other teams and plenty of attention was being paid to the young French ace.

On a personal level, Didier and Ken were getting along fine: 'Relations between Ken and I are a little like those of a father and son,' Didier told *Auto Hebdo*. 'When I arrived in the team, they dictated to me and did not ask my opinion. I was pretty disappointed. But I now think Ken intended this course of action and he was right.' Eighteen months on, Didier trusted Tyrrell completely. When his employer vetoed a possible Le Mans return with Porsche, Didier accepted the decision without too much fuss. Ken had heard all about Le Mans and did not want a repeat of '78. He needed a fully fit driver, one whose focus was entirely on F1. Moreover, with Elf no longer sponsoring the team, there would be no outside pressure to release the driver.

The year wore on. Disconcertingly, early pacesetters Ligier slipped gradually back into the field as Ferrari and Williams came to the fore. As for Tyrrell, the team remained in mid-pack. Despite the arrival of some welcome funds from Italian engineering company Candy, the 009 would continue to suffer from a chronic lack of investment. The second half of Didier's season would be one of unfulfilled promise punctuated by a catalogue of worrying incidents.

One of the most serious occurred at Dijon during practice for the French Grand Prix. Going into Courbe de Pouas, the sweeping final corner that leads on to the home straight, heading for a potential place on the front two rows, the Tyrrell flew off the circuit into the catch fencing. The front end of the car was mashed, prompting *Motorsport* to declare that only by a 'miracle' had the driver 'escaped totally unscathed'. The impact of the crash split the Tyrrell chassis in half! Such accidents spooked the driver no end. Rear suspension failure in the race compounded his insecurities even further. After an 'off' Ken Tyrrell would always be the first person to apologise to the driver, but it was all wearing a little thin. Didier was now *expecting* to have accidents.

Misgivings aside, when Ken offered a new contract for 1980 on improved terms in the shape of an enhanced performance bonus, Didier readily accepted. By the time the teams had assembled in Montreal in late September for the penultimate race of the season, agreement had all but been reached – at least verbally. Certainly, Ken Tyrrell was anxious to secure Didier's services for the forthcoming season. As the months had passed, the woodcutter had warmed to the young Parisian, impressed by not only his speed, but moreover the driver's calm, methodical approach to racing. After an accident, Didier simply brushed himself down and started all over again. No drama, no hysterics and absolutely no accusations. Ken appreciated that.

Nevertheless, from inside his room at Montreal's Regency Hyatt hotel, Didier was considering his options. Tyrrell was not the only team manager eyeing the Frenchman. Colin Chapman, Bernie Ecclestone and Guy Ligier were rumoured to be monitoring developments. Not that the rumours unduly disturbed Ken Tyrrell, who had shaken hands on the agreement with his driver and thus considered the matter closed. So when Ken received a letter over breakfast on the Thursday before the race, the team owner was taken aback. In the letter, Didier expressed his resolve to seek his future elsewhere. As far as he was concerned, the apprenticeship was over.

It was time to win races, to challenge for championships, optimistic if not plain fantasy with his current team. As ever, Agnes it was who acted as messenger, going back and forwards between rooms, surreptitiously slipping a series of notes under the door of Ken's hotel room.

Qualifying a season-best sixth on the grid, Didier would steer his car into a solid fifth place come race end behind a couple of Williamses and Ferraris, a highly commendable performance given the superiority of those cars. Ken Tyrrell's anxiety was understandable: in Pironi, he had a young charger, a driver capable of extracting the maximum from his limited equipment. After the race, the two men sat down to discuss the situation. Ken outlined his ambitious plans for the 010, the team's challenger for the 1980 season. Didier listened. Suitably impressed, the two men shook hands. Back in his hotel room, the driver reflected on the promises made: could the team really make the gigantic step from midfield to front-runners? Ken seemed to think so. Didier was not so sure. Late on Sunday evening, Agnes was once again heading for Ken's room, where she softly pushed a final note under the boss's door, one that had been composed a few days earlier but had been kept back. After careful consideration, Didier had decided not to resign after all.

Early on Monday morning before he set off to Montreal airport, Didier received a plaintive, even doleful reply from his employer: 'It was a shock to receive your letter stating that you did not wish to drive for me in 1980,' wrote Ken, reminding his driver that agreement had been reached with 'a handshake'. Hailing from a school that considered a gentleman's word to be his bond, to Ken, handshakes were much more than symbolic gestures as he made clear further on in his letter: 'I trust there is some misunderstanding that can be cleared up, but I must warn you that I consider our agreement to be legally binding ...'

It was not the first time in F1 history nor would it be the last whereupon a talent had been incubated by a small fish only to be lured away by a bigger species. At the dawn of a new decade, the F1 pecking order was changing. Newer teams such as Ligier, Renault and Williams were usurping the old order of Tyrrell, McLaren and Lotus. Upon returning from Canada, Didier set up a meeting with Guy Ligier.

Third position in the season finale at Watkins Glen provided further evidence of the young charge's progress. Speculation mounted that Didier was about to become part of an 'Equipe Nationale' with Guy Ligier's talented but frustratingly inconsistent team based at Vichy.

When Didier therefore signed for Ligier on 26 November in Paris, F1's worst-kept secret was finally out. The relatively modest 100,000-franc retainer suggested that the desire for a competitive machine far outweighed any pecuniary interests. The pilot wanted not merely to compete, but to win. In Guy Ligier's team of swashbucklers, he had his wish. The late '70s/early '80s would see the French team enjoying the most competitive period of their history, regularly challenging for race victories. OK, after a bright start to the 1979 season the team had lost its way somewhat, but general wisdom suggested that if Les Bleues could overcome some organisational issues, then Guy's boys had the potential to become genuine world championship contenders. There was just the usual issue of hierarchies to sort out.

Before his accident, Depailler had refused to extend his contract, citing what he perceived to be Ligier's preferential treatment towards team-mate Jacques Laffite as his reason. Patrick had no desire to play second fiddle and so had already decided to seek pastures new. Having had similar experiences himself – most notably with Arnoux and ironically Patrick – Didier sought assurances from Ligier and his chief designer Gérard Ducarouge. Parity assured, Didier agreed to sign. Pironi and Ligier; it seemed a perfect match.

Christmas celebrations that year centred around a family gathering chez Didier and Agnes. The family descended on Chantenay. Guy Ligier and Jacques Laffite joined the family to toast the future. The next day Didier set out with his mother and aunt en route to Paris. It was late and a thick winter fog hung over this part of central France. Passing the Magny-Cours circuit in all its dark tranquillity, skirting the town of Nevers, the party joined the national road that would lead them all the way up to the southern outskirts of Paris. A two-and-a-half-hour journey lay ahead. Nothing stirred.

It all happened in a split second: the impact and the windscreen shattering into a thousand pieces, then the fear, the shock, the disbelief. There had been no time to react.

From out of the gloomy darkness, a figure had stepped out on to the highway into Didier's path, a ghostly spectre unseen, unheard, unknown. The figure had been tossed into the air like a skittle. Miraculously, the party escaped serious injury although Imelda suffered a perforated eye, fractured wrist and broken tooth, pain enough. Profoundly shocked, Didier ran to the victim's aid. It was too late. The unfortunate man had died on impact.

Deeply distressed, the party groped and stumbled its way back along the highway through the dank night air. Eventually, the bright, familiar logo of Elf pierced the gloom. Upon reaching the petrol station, Didier cleaned his mother's bloody face and called Agnes who arrived minutes later. Imelda was taken to the nearest hospital at Nevers where doctors treated her wounds. Later that night an ambulance transferred her to the emergency department of the Hôtel Dieu, Paris where she underwent surgery to preserve her sight. The victim it transpired was a homeless vagrant who, under the influence of alcohol, had stepped out into the road oblivious to the danger.

1979 had ended on a ghastly note. Wherever he went, whatever he did, danger and drama were never far away. If there are such things as jinxes and curses, could such an affliction have been shadowing a young man who, up until this point, had lived such a charmed existence?

Fourteen
Royal hussar

OIL and water, the sometimes tentative and at times fractious relationship between Didier and a team owner in Guy Ligier whose operating temperature was either volcanic or iceberg cool – with little in between – would come to define an entire season. Small, squat and pugnacious, ex-international rugby player Ligier had a well-earned reputation for outbursts quite unsurpassed in the F1 pit lane. Fiery tantrums were the norm chez Ligier. How then would Le Patron get along with a driver renowned for uber cool detachment? A clash of temperaments. Could these opposites attract?

As in '79, Ligier hit the ground running at the start of 1980. Following extensive wind tunnel testing at Saint-Cyr – a luxury that had been restricted at Tyrrell – the JS11/15 had benefitted from improved road-holding and aerodynamics. Resplendent in the iconic livery of the Gitanes cigarette brand, if the blue and white machine replete with red trim went as well as it looked, 1980 could be a season to remember. Optimism abounded at Vichy.

The team thus arrived in Buenos Aires for the opening race of the season quietly confident. Yet as with so many races in 1980, the Argentine Grand Prix promised much, but would ultimately deliver little. Nonetheless, on Saturday evening the mood in the garage was upbeat. On his debut for the team, Didier had qualified in third, one place behind team leader Laffite. Only the Williams of Alan Jones was faster. So, was the Ligier a better car than the

Tyrrell? 'Better brakes, better steering, better handling, better traction...' Oui!

The blue and white cavaliers made a good start to the race, and for a brief moment, Didier was looking to relieve his team-mate of second place. Just as he was harrying Jacques, the Ford engine started to misbehave. His race was effectively over before a single lap had been run. Sadly, it would not be an isolated incident, rather a portent of things to come. Laffite meanwhile hung in there fighting for positon with Piquet's Brabham and the second Williams car of Reutemann. Clearly, the JS11/15 had bags of speed. However, did it have stamina? The million-dollar question. Laffite's race would also end in retirement. Jones took the win with something to spare.

It was not until the Brazilian Grand Prix two weeks later that Didier had the opportunity to show what he could really do in a front-line car. The Ligier driver's 'flair' and 'sheer car control' during practice left *Motorsport*'s Alan Henry breathless: 'To watch the blue Ligier bobbing over the bumps at top speed and its confident driver hurling it through the turn with unshakeable confidence was truly exhilarating.'[16] His reward? A place on the front row – his first in F1. In between practice days, the driver enjoyed soaking up the sunshine on Rio's spectacular Copacabana beach in company with Agnes. Swimming, surfing, relaxing, this was the good life. There was also time to indulge in a spot of illicit hang-gliding along with old friend Depailler, out of sight of Ligier and Alfa Romeo personnel.

All the evidence pointed to a first Grand Prix victory here in Brazil. To see the number 25 Ligier then struggling to keep up with pole man Jabouille, Laffite's sister car and Andretti's Lotus suggested all was not well. Sure enough, after a handful of laps plagued by understeer, the Ligier was in the pits for adjustments to its skirts. Laffite's race ended just a few laps later. Predictably, before even a quarter of the race had been run, Ligier had thrown away a potentially winning hand.

Way down the order, Didier re-entered the race with a point to prove; flat out to the end. The Gitanes car started to fly.

Ten thousand kilometres away in Modena, Italy, as was his habit, Enzo Ferrari watched the race on the small black and white portable television set in his office. The blue and white car was on fire. A motor racing connoisseur who knew a fine vintage when he saw one, Ferrari savoured the spectacle. There was something about this pilot, his style, his panache with just a hint of arrogance, which reminded the old man of champions past. Young Pironi eventually hauled himself up to fourth place. *Il Commendatore* was impressed. Turning to his assistants, the great man is famously rumoured to have declared: 'I want Pironi.' And what the great man wanted, he usually got. Contact between Ferrari and Didier was established soon after. Just two races into the season and Didier it seemed was already planning a future that did not involve his current employers.

Before the South African Grand Prix, there was time for a three-week holiday hopping around various Caribbean islands with Agnes and a group of friends. Didier enjoyed the holiday tremendously. In his heart, though, he knew the relationship with his childhood sweetheart had run its course. Stood on the verge of a novel and exciting phase of life, new horizons were presenting themselves.

Around the same time as negotiations began with the legendary Italians, the team from Vichy started to show its potential. A double podium behind Arnoux's uncatchable Renault in Kyalami signalled the start of a particularly competitive phase for Guy's cars. After a shaky start to 1980, the JS11/15 was proving itself the equal of the Renaults, Brabhams and Williamses. Notwithstanding, just two days after the South African race, Didier signed a pre-contract agreement for 1981 with Ferrari.

All the signs suggested that a maiden Grand Prix victory was close. At round five in Zolder it all came together. Sandwiched between Jones's and Reutemann's highly fancied Williamses, Didier and Jacques lined up in second and third place respectively on the Belgian grid: Williams v Ligier, British efficiency versus French flair. A race that had looked set to be a four-way battle for supremacy ended, however, after 100 yards when Ligier number 25 calmly out-braked Jones's Saudia Leyland car at the first right-hander. It was the first time the young Parisian had led a Grand Prix. Could he hold it together? More to the point, would his machine hold out? Little by little, the Ligier increased its advantage.

After 20 laps, the lead stood at around seven seconds. By the end of the race, it had increased to almost 50. Total domination. On his slowing lap, Didier removed his helmet and balaclava, a gesture that would become a Pironi trademark. Boy, was it hot inside that cockpit! 'Bravo Didier!' Ligier mechanics held a sign up to greet their man.

'Pironi has not only achieved a great feat, his victory has restored confidence in our team and serenity in a sensitive period,' enthused a jubilant Guy Ligier. 'Our results have not corresponded either to our expectations or our ambitions.'

On the winning driver, the team owner was lavish in his praise: 'I realised that he had the technical and psychological potential of a winner. It would have just been enough to provide the necessary material, i.e. a competitive car. His victory in Zolder was impeccable in both how he obtained it and in his behaviour. Pironi now belongs to the great legend of F1 and I don't think it will stop at this.'

All smiles at Team Ligier, though not according to Imelda. It had long been the pilot's habit to call home after a race, whereupon mother and son would discuss on and off track developments. Although she disliked motor racing and the dangers it entailed, the matriarch insisted her beloved son keep her up to date with all issues pertaining to his career. Thus, in her memoir Imelda speaks of Ligier's 'lukewarm reception' towards Didier's victory. It appears that Guy would have much preferred his great friend and number one driver Laffite to be stealing the limelight, not the young man hired to support him. This attitude, she notes, 'disappointed' Didier. Whatever, the team held a celebration dinner that evening. The hero of the hour thanked all the right people and shook many hands. Meanwhile, the more extrovert Laffite spent the night cracking jokes:

'Hey Didier, you do realise after I won my first Grand Prix, I didn't win another for two years!' grinned Jacques. Didier merely smiled. What a preposterous thought. Weren't the team on a roll? Entering the European stage of the season, the JS11/15 was arguably the fastest machine on the Grand Prix circuit. The thought of the categorical winner of the Belgian Grand Prix waiting another two years to taste victory seemed absurd ...

Indeed, a first F1 pole positon in the next race at Monaco looked set to be converted into a certain victory until a light rain shower tripped the leader up after 55 laps. Approaching the right-hander which follows Casino Square, Didier had simply lost control of the car and skidded off into the barriers. Human error. 'Making mistakes at Monaco can be very costly,' Didier had told Jackie Stewart in an interview earlier that day. The young man kicked himself. The race had been his for the taking. Despite this lapse, he had undeniably announced himself as a star performer. Including Zolder and up to the point of his Monte Carlo retirement, Didier had led the last 127 laps in Grand Prix racing. 'Didier Pironi,' wrote *Autocar*'s Grand Prix correspondent Peter Windsor, 'has established himself as the fastest man in Formula One.'[17]

Was Mr Windsor getting ahead of himself, caught up in the moment? Not if you'd seen the Ligier screaming around the Monte Carlo harbour at 10am on a wet Thursday morning when the pilot had ended the session almost 1.5 seconds faster than the entire field!

On the face of it, then, summer 1980 should have been a time of serenity, of enjoying his ascension to the top rank of his chosen profession. After all, the young cavalier had just won his first Grand Prix with the promise of more to come; with the JS11/15 going so well, a shot at the world championship seemed a realistic goal. There was also that Ferrari pre-contract agreement filed away in his briefcase. On top of which F1's hottest talent had just established a lucrative St Tropez-based business selling and renting Lamborghini-powered luxury boats in partnership with the Abbate brothers. And yet the months ahead would prove to be some of the most tumultuous in his 28 years.

In the early 1980s, Formula 1 would witness a brutal power struggle for control of the sport between Jean-Marie Balestre's FISA[18] and Bernie Ecclestone's FOCA.[19] This duel of egos inevitably spilled over on to the track. By 1980, tensions that had been simmering between the two organisations for a few years finally boiled over. In a series of tit-for-tat moves, FOCA advised its drivers to flout the FISA requirement for all drivers to attend the 45-minute pre-race briefing at the Belgian and Monaco races. As members of FOCA, Ligier's drivers did not attend the briefings, a show of defiance that resulted in a fine, which Didier, Jacques, Piquet, Jones and others were advised not to pay. FISA responded by threatening to withdraw drivers' licences. Subsequently, threats and counter threats were made on both sides. The whole affair started to become rather petty. Things took a turn for the worse when the FISA teams – Ferrari, Renault and Alfa Romeo – retaliated by boycotting the Spanish Grand Prix on 1 June. As a result, the race would subsequently be downgraded to non-championship status.

Politics aside, following a front-row lockout in Madrid, the French team once more conspired to throw away a race they really should have won. First, Laffite tangled with Reutemann. Later, coasting to victory, Didier was aghast to notice his front right wheel wobbling violently. Much to his astonishment, the wheel simply fell off! Fingers pointed at Ligier. Had the team failed to secure the wheel nuts properly? Outlandish, a beginner's mistake – some observers thought exactly that.

That evening and the following day, Didier spent some time with his race engineer Lionel Hublet searching for clues. How could a wheel just drop off? The problem seemed to be ground effect: in the JS11/15 had the team perhaps perfected the dark art a little too well? Such was the level of downforce generated by the Ducarouge-inspired design, the pressure exerted appeared to be causing instability vis-à-vis the car's Gotti wheel rims, which had cracked under the pressure, leading to the punctures. It was a technical dilemma that would ultimately be the straw that would break the Gitanes's back.

Meanwhile F1's civil war rumbled on. With the threat of a suspended licence, Didier's plans to drive for BMW at Le Mans were placed in jeopardy. Without a FISA-approved licence, there would be no race. Thus, the day before practice started on 13 June, along with some other rebels, Didier paid the $2,000 fine. Guy Ligier hit the roof. Having forbade his drivers to comply with FISA's demand, in Le Patron's mind the gesture equated to nothing short of mutiny. To the team owner, paying up was a move that could only strengthen Balestre's grip on the sport, a man Ligier considered to be a danger to his own interests and those of his team. In some ways, it need not have mattered. With the BMW

M1 never a serious contender, Didier's Le Mans swansong proved a low-key affair.

Back in F1, the up and down atmosphere within Ligier would come to a head over the next two races scheduled for France and England. As ever, these were races Ligier were strongly fancied to win, but as ever with the French team, it never quite happened.

On home ground in France, pressure mounted on the two national teams, yellow and blue. While Renault looked composed, there was little in the way of harmony in the Ligier camp. Stung by what he regarded as Didier's disloyalty over the fines, Guy Ligier was threatening his number two with suspension from the race. 'He was really mad,' recalls Jacques Laffite, 'completely resolved not to allow Didier to race.' Significantly, although the team leader had also paid his fine on the same day, Jacques escaped the worst excesses of his boss's wrath. Writing for the legendary *Grand Prix International* magazine, Eric Bhat summarised the situation in typically colourful fashion, when he described a Ligier garage with team boss and driver 'glaring at one another like a couple of fighting cocks'.[20]

Guy's bark, however, proved to be worse than his bite. Both blue and white cars lined up at the start, Laffite on pole, Didier slotting behind in third. As Jacques scampered away in the lead, Didier diced with his old rival Arnoux for second place. Whichever way, a home win looked assured. Judging by the size of Laffite's lead as they flashed across the line at the end of lap one, there might have been more than some truth in the suspicion that the team leader's engines were, on occasion, that bit more powerful than those of his junior partner. One or two observers certainly believed this to be the case. Still, the blue and white cars were clearly the fastest out there on a sultry afternoon in southern France.

Yet 90 minutes later it was Alan Jones waving a Union Jack flag from the cockpit of his triumphant Williams – hardly the most diplomatic gesture ever seen in F1.

Put simply, Ligier had imploded once more, almost literally. Having passed the leader, Jones was getting away. The faster of the two Ligiers, Didier needed to overtake his team leader, which given his inferior rank within the team pecking order, presented something of a conundrum. Oh, what the hell... Flying down the endless Mistral straight, the number 25 car pulled out of the slipstream of car number 26. Going into the ludicrously fast Signes right-hander, the junior driver duly dived down the inside of his senior partner. Jacques, however, turned into the corner as usual ...

Only a last-second correction by the second-placed car averted disaster. The two cars came within inches of touching.

Didier managed to squeeze through, but with time running out it was too late to challenge Jones; a defeat on home soil. Guy Ligier was not best pleased. 'You fucked up Jacques' race!' stormed a raging bull of a team owner. The good ship Ligier was starting to creak.

'If Pironi had contained Jones better, maybe things would have been different and Laffite would have had an easier run,' snapped Ligier. More creaking. Worried by tyre wear, Didier had been unable to resist the Australian on this sizzling French afternoon, not that Guy cared. Le Patron needed a scapegoat.

Things finally came to a head at Brands Hatch for the British Grand Prix two weeks later. An entire weekend if not an entire season summed up in just two words: wheel rims. If the motor racing world had not known about wheel rims before this race, after the chequered flag had fallen (on Jones's Williams), they knew all about them, and some more.

From an easy pole position, Didier drove a sensational first lap around the Kent track. Could anyone live with him today? Short answer: no. The JS11/15 was handling superbly. Didier was driving with customary panache, a motor racing d'Artagnan, imperious, dashing and supremely confident. Pironi-Ligier were the class of the field. When asked who would win the race on race morning, 'Didi Pironi,' had replied Jackie Stewart without a second's hesitation. What could possibly go wrong ... ?

Wheel rims.

First Didier then Jacques, both Ligier drivers had the sinking feeling that comes with deflating tyres. Leading with something akin to serenity, Didier was forced into the pits after 18 laps. An agonisingly long pit stop, which James Hunt described as a 'cock-up', ended his hopes, while the Brands Hatch catch fencing ended those of Jacques, who spun off while fighting a desperate battle to control his own puncture. A sanguine fellow at the best of times, the fury on Jacques' usually happy face was clear for all to see. Ligier had thrown it all away, again. Back in the race, Didier proceeded to break the lap record for fun. From last to fifth place, a Brands masterclass. When the blue car pulled off the circuit late in the race, this time its left rear tyre shredded, Ligier could be forgiven for thinking the gods were against them on this particular day. Three punctures in a single race! What had started as a mission to avenge defeat on home ground by Williams had ended in all-too-familiar chaos.

Arriving back at the Ligier pit, Didier found himself assailed by a French media that seemed to be laying the blame for this disastrous day firmly at the door of the drivers, not the cars. Quietly, Didier articulated what he knew, which was not that much: the car had felt superb; he was leading easily, when suddenly the puncture had occurred. No, he had not driven over the kerbs, had not made a mistake of any description whatsoever on either occasion. The accusatory tone irked, more so as he started to suspect the real reason for the calamity.

What happened next convinced Didier his future lay not with the blue of Ligier, but with the red of Ferrari. As usual, the disappointed young man phoned Boissy after the race.

'Hi mum.'

'Hey, not such a lucky boy today.'

'Well, you know that's racing mum.'

It was what Imelda told her son next that confirmed his many misgivings about the team and his future with it.

'You know, Ligier just declared on the radio that if Jacques and you had not banged over the kerbs, you would not have had your punctures.'

'What! Are you certain?'

'Yes, yes. We heard the interview just now.'

Furious at the way the race had been lost, the pugnacious team boss had simply decided to blame his drivers rather than any shortcomings with their equipment. 'The machines,' said Guy only just managing to contain that famous temper, 'are made to go on the track, not in the meadows!' Didier was outraged. How could Ligier say such a thing, and on national radio too? When both drivers suspected – correctly – that the reason for the catastrophe lay with an incorrect choice of tyre rim, at best the boss's declaration seemed presumptuous, at worst downright malicious.

It was at this moment he decided to quit Ligier. Coincidentally, he had agreed to inform Ferrari of his intentions viz-à-viz 1981 this very weekend. A no-brainer.

Yet the weekend had all started so well. Le Patron's 50th birthday had been celebrated with cake adorned with tricolour candles, champagne and good cheer. As Didier, Jacques and Guy laughed and joked, agreement or no agreement, Ferrari had seemed a distant prospect. Besides, 1980 was turning into a nightmare for the Italian team. A glance down the Brands Hatch grid proved as much: Villeneuve and Scheckter stuck in 19th and 23rd places respectively. 'I do not see why I should change a team that is fighting for pole position and the win with another fighting just to qualify,' remarked Didier when rumours of a Ferrari switch for '81 started to circulate around the Brands Hatch paddock. He was, however, bluffing.

In addition, with Ligier announcing a lucrative new deal with Talbot for 1981, who but the most optimistic of gamblers would have chosen Ferrari over Ligier at this moment in time?

Yet just 48 hours later Didier had made up his mind to do just that.

The moment Jody Scheckter announced his retirement from the sport, the media went into overdrive. Who would take his place at Ferrari? As ever, there was no shortage of candidates, especially among the new wave of Italian racers: Patrese, Giacomelli, Baldi … ? All the while, the man of Friulian heritage, a fluent Italian speaker, kept his counsel.

Any hopes of either Ligier man competing for the world title had similarly deflated with their flat tyres. After his win at Brands, Alan Jones led the race with 37 points, six ahead of Nelson Piquet. Didier's total of 23 points put him fourth. The tough Aussie was starting to edge away. In contrast to their French rivals, Frank Williams's team did not make basic errors. Those 18 points lost from what would have been certain wins in Monaco and Britain had cost the young Frenchman dear. 1980 was slipping away, fast.

Laurence (right) with Didier and Jose, the long lost brothers that would be lost to her all too soon
© Laurence Villaume-Dolhem

The golden child: Rio 1982
© Bernard Asset

Didier (left) and Rene Arnoux (right) chillin' at Rio 1982.
© Bernard Bakalian

Young man in a big hurry. Didier's Tyrrell launches over Lauda's Brabham-Alfa during the 1979 Monaco Grand Prix
© Eric Lemuet

With Manfred Schurti at the 1980 Hockenheim Procar race scene of a particularly tenacious Pironi performance
© Jurgen Tap

Royal hussar. The Ligier JS11/15 though fast, often flattered to deceive as it did here in the 1980 Austrian Grand Prix
© Emmanuelle Zurini

Cheever (15) takes the lead at Rouen 1977 F2, as Didier slots into second. Meanwhile teammate Arnoux (4) collides with Tambay.
© S le Bozec

Familial accord. Throughout his life Didier could always rely on the support and counsel of his father (centre) and brother (right)
© Laurence Villaume-Dolhem

Riviera Days – Having fun in St. Tropez cerca 1980
© St Tropez Magazine

They seek him here, they seek him there ... Michelle Thieme offers some moral support prior to the off
© Emmanuel Zurini

Early days in Formula Renault. Didier (14) tails Bochet (18) at La Châtre, May 1973
© Christian Courtel

Time-out at Albi, September, 1973
© Christian Courtel

A beaming 'baby' Pironi (left) takes his first ever podium behind Couderc (centre) at Nivelles, September 23, 1973. Mathiot (right) finished third
© Christian Courtel

Didier and Douchka
© Laurence Villaume-
Dolhem

Best behaviour: Louis
(third from right) with
his daredevil sons,
Jose (fourth from
right) and Didier (fifth
from right)
© Laurence Villaume-
Dolhem

"He had a soft voice,
looked shy, but had
the inflexible will to
reach his objectives."
Serenely calm prior to
the start of the 1972
Pilot-Elf competition
© Jeff Lehalle

40 Rue de Valenton, The 'Castle' at Boissy
© David Sedgwick

War hero, athlete and businessman: Louis Dolhem, a name to be reckoned with in post-war Paris
© Laurence Villaume-Dolhem

Ephemeral summer – Didier and his 126C2 emerged as the combination to beat during the 1982 season
© *Emmanuel Zurini*

Always time to listen to big brother, Jose, even as world champion elect
© *Laurence Villaume-Dolhem*

An exhausted Didier faces the 1982 post-Imola media as Laurence (far left) looks on
© *Laurence Villaume-Dolhem*

In recognition for the work he did restoring his legs, Didier sent Professor Letournel this personalised photograph at the end of his stay at Porte de la choisy. The inscription reads:
"No word can express the admiration and the respect which I bear you but you will find in my look all the hope and the trust which I have in you."
© Francine Letournel

Monaco Grand Prix 1987 with protege and fellow powerboat enthusiast Phillipe Streiff
© Phillipe Streiff

'Always on the razor's edge' powerboating with Tullio Abbate, Lake Como 1979
© Emmanuel Zurini

Fifteen

The French lieutenant's Ferrari

FURTHER turmoil arrived that summer when Didier decided to end his 14-year relationship with Agnes. Although there had been 'blazing rows' during the Tyrrell years, to most outsiders the couple had seemed happy enough. However, Didier was moving in different circles. Anxious not to hurt the woman who had shared all the highs and lows of the past decade, Didier broke the news as gently as possible. Understandably, Agnes was inconsolable. Over the years, this waiflike young woman had become part of the Pironi-Dolhem family, and especially close to Imelda who comforted the young woman as best she could through some very difficult days.

A bachelor boy – one sitting at the very summit of the world's most glamorous sport – if Didier enjoyed his new freedom in the months that followed the break-up, he could hardly be blamed. F1's 'pretty boy' had the looks and appeal of a pop star. During that summer, amongst others, he had a brief dalliance with Michelle Thieme, the daughter of Lotus sponsor David Thieme of Essex fame. Shortly after, he would be seen around town in company with a stunningly attractive young woman of flawless complexion and natural elegance, whom he had met the previous year through mutual friends in St Tropez. It had been love at first sight. Didier and Catherine Bleynie became an inseparable item. 'The apartment at Neuilly already bears marks of her presence,' notes Imelda in her memoir. Young, blonde and seemingly perfectly suited to one another, the Formula 1 paddock lit up the very moment the golden couple arrived.

On the racetrack, the relentless professionalism of the Williams team allied to the grit and determination of Alan Jones was proving an irresistible combination. The Aussie marched towards a first F1 world crown. Didier's season would become, in his own words, one of 'missed opportunities'. Frustratingly, with a little more in the way of organisation, the Frenchman knew he could have easily been a genuine world championship contender in 1980. Fate dictated otherwise.

Thoughts of world championships were banished completely, however, on the first day of August. At noon that day Didier answered a call from a journalist who questioned him about his great buddy Patrick Depailler – a not untypical scenario and thus Didier was happy to speak about his fondness for Patrick, his reactions to the hang-gliding crash of the previous year and his thoughts on his friend's return to F1 with Alfa. 'Your friend has been killed in a test at Hockenheim,' blurted the journalist and with that bombshell put the receiver down. Didier was stunned. Such was the shock, he turned to tranquillisers. Patrick was a true friend, one who had gladly helped the young man navigate his way through the often-choppy F1 waters of Tyrrell. Heartbroken, Didier immediately liaised with the unfortunate driver's wife. Having made arrangements for repatriation of the body, he then flew to Clermont-Ferrand to pick up the grieving widow en route for the sombre onward journey to Hockenheim.

Although it would become fashionable in some circles to label Didier as 'cold' and 'unemotional', his actions in the aftermath of the Depailler tragedy proved he was anything but.

So just who was Didier Pironi? Racer, playboy, philosopher, even by 1980 the Pironi legend was already growing apace. *Grand Prix International* had posed such a question in its Belgian GP edition: *Who is Didier Pironi, a demon or an angel?* The magazine was not alone in its musings. Others too had noticed incongruities aplenty. On the one hand there was the softly spoken, impeccably mannered Parisian, a young man of education and sophistication, a polyglot who studied astronomy and in his spare time cultivated his beloved orchids. On the other, there was the individual who once inside the cockpit of his car, would become uncompromising, confrontational, almost warlike in bearing. Jekyll and Hyde. A total transformation.

'Didier Pironi is a man of contrast, paradoxes even,' wrote Johnny Rives for *Sport-Auto* in June that year. The writer marvelled at how a man with 'weightlifter deltoids' could at the same time display such a 'boyish smile'; how an adult with such a 'serious' nature could also delight in 'childish pranks'; how a driver who demonstrated such 'strength' on a dry track could so effortlessly switch and become 'subtle and elegant' on a wet track. Pironi: a mystery, an enigma.

Never more so was the enigmatic nature of his character on show than at Hockenheim in late summer.

Procar was the intriguing title given to an unprecedented motor racing challenge that bloomed for a couple of glorious years between 1979 and 1980. In this series, held at European circuits, top sports car and Formula 1 drivers would compete in identical 3.5-litre BMW M1 saloon cars, in what amounted to a Grand Prix entrée. A generous prize fund ensured the attention of the F1 boys. The format dictated that the top five qualifiers from Friday's practice would automatically line up in Sunday's Procar race. These shortish sprints were always eagerly contested. As in F1, points were awarded and a 'Procar champion' declared at season's end. Although billed as a bit of fun, races were anything but. The wheel-to-wheel racing that invariably characterised the series made it hugely popular among fans and drivers alike.

As one of the fastest Friday qualifiers at the German Grand Prix weekend, Didier had earned himself a place in Saturday's Hockenheim support race. Then the fun began.

Reflecting on this weird and wonderful format some years later, Alan Henry would call the 1980 Hockenheim Procar race, in which Didier was to play such a central role, his most 'vivid' memory of the entire series. With good reason.

After qualifying, Didier had his M1 up at the sharp end of the grid. A lone Frenchman surrounded by a glut of local heroes –

Schurti, Stuck, Danner and Heyer amongst others, it seemed as if he was up against the whole of Germany on this day. It was the Swiss driver Marc Surer though who took the fight to Didier initially. But the Ligier man was in no mood for compromise. Whenever the Swiss showed intent, he found the door firmly slammed in his face. Forced to brake harder than he liked on more than one occasion, Surer slipped back to be replaced by a trio of German sports-car drivers each determined to put the surly Frenchman in his place. Cheered on by a lively crowd, Stuck, Heyer and Schurti shadowed the leading M1, but Didier grimly repelled their attacks, causing Stuck to take an excursion in the Hockenheim mud. Agitated, the crowd showed their displeasure. So too did Stuck.

At the end of the race, steam pouring out of his ears, the former Brabham driver sought out his French nemesis. Didier had scrambled home a second in front of Schurti with a recovering Stuck in third. 'Muscular' was the term most commonly used to describe his performance and even that might arguably have been tinged with understatement. True enough, he had certainly taken no prisoners out there. Stuck was incensed. The German caught up with a nonchalant Frenchman.

Back to Henry and his most 'vivid' memory:

'Stuck uncoiled his six-foot frame from the confined cockpit of his M1 to unleash a furiously vocal critique of Pironi's driving straight to the Frenchman's face,' recalled the writer. '"Hanschen" was visibly quivering with rage, but Pironi just faced him down with that impassive stare which he'd made his hallmark.' Henry was one of several F1 journalists to witness the icy control of the victor, the more impressive given the highly provocative manner of Stuck's address: 'Didier, quite frankly, couldn't have cared less.'[21] Here was that same imperturbable boy who had not even flinched under his mother's thrashings all those years ago. They did not come any cooler than Pironi.

More drama followed on Sunday in the Grand Prix proper. Not for the first time, early doors Jacques' car looked demonstrably the quicker of the two Ligiers. Were the team-mates driving equitable cars? It did not look that way. As the leaders pressed ahead, Didier appeared to be holding his team-mate up. After just a handful of laps, Laffite slid past into fourth place, waving an angry fist out of his cockpit as he completed the manoeuvre. Though he would ultimately take his first and only win of the year, happy Jacques he most certainly was not:

'Pironi kept me behind illegally for more than a lap, even though he was slower, and it made me lose contact with those who were ahead. He is an immature boy.'

Nevertheless, Guy Ligier promptly offered contracts to both men for 1981. To ensure Didier's signature, Le Patron offered a substantially improved financial package. Didier hesitated. In his mind, he had already committed himself to Ferrari. Still, he was intrigued to see how far Guy would go to retain his services. Not far enough. When the boss announced on that same Sunday evening that the team would be focusing all their efforts (and resources) on Jacques for the remainder of the season, misgivings he had since the beginning of the season crystallised.

The last third of 1980 saw Ligier lurch from one crisis to another. With their Gallic flair and buccaneering spirit epitomised by the iconic gypsy motif of their Gitanes sponsors, Guy's squad had always been a vibrant addition to the F1 paddock. However, in F1, it is pragmatism, not romanticism, that wins prizes. From their positions at the head of the field, the blues started to slip backwards à la '79. A season of two halves.

Will Pironi join Ferrari? There was only one question in the motor racing press as summer turned to autumn. Some newspapers such as Italy's *La Stampa* sincerely hoped not: Pironi and Villeneuve in the same team, the paper cautioned, would be like 'two roosters in a hen house...'

But Didier knew better. The Ferrari pre-agreement, signed as long ago as March, had provided him with both security and options. The deteriorating situation at Ligier merely confirmed that decision. Thus, his transfer to Ferrari was officially announced on Monday, 15 September, the day after the Italian Grand Prix, news that disappointed the hopes of any number of young drivers, most notably those of McLaren's Alain Prost. Enzo Ferrari made the announcement in front of a packed media room. Why had he plumped for the French driver?

'I am a sensitive person,' replied the great man from behind his trademark dark glasses, 'and I trust my emotions. Pironi has impressed me and many people have told me he's a smart guy.' Some journalists seemed unconvinced. 'You tell me I have a fixation on Pironi, I answer you that I am simply objective.'

The grand old man paused.

'I have to take you into a little confidence. There is also a sentimental reason. Didier is a native of Friuli and I have Friuli in my heart ...' For a brief moment, Ferrari's voice wavered. 'Just a few years ago, a team from this region have worked with marble slabs to reconstruct the grave of my son Dino, which vile people have devastated. I will never forget their altruism and generosity.'

When quizzed over the potential difficulties of housing two superstar drivers in his stable, the 82-year-old could not have known just how prophetic his words would turn out to be: 'Ferrari does not need a second pilot, but only men who can go fast. If they are combative, and their antagonism is damaging for the team, then we will intervene.'

The atmosphere was light. With the signing of the French hussar, the old man believed he had the best two drivers in the world.

'No, they have not found anything in my head,' joked Villeneuve when attention turned to the drivers. Ferrari's current superstar driver had just returned from a hospital visit for a head scan after a testing shunt in Imola. Everybody laughed. 'As for Pironi, I think Ferrari has made a wrong choice...' The Canadian did not elaborate any further.

When it came to his turn, Didier, 'elegant and smiling' in the words of La Stampa, delighted and surprised the assembled media by answering their questions in fluent Italian. Who even knew he could do that? Always full of surprises, Pironi: 'I am naturally happy to have arrived in Maranello, because I know I'm in the best team. Even if Ferrari at this time are not so strong, I am certain that they will return to the top.' The hacks hung upon his every word. It seemed the new driver had made a very favourable impression upon the journalists. 'It was an investment,' he explained when discussing the tricky issue of contracts and money. 'I did not have a rich engagement, but if I win races the money will come in abundance.'

On hearing the news, Guy Ligier had an epic meltdown. Despite the many difficulties of this rollercoaster season, he desperately wanted Didier on board for '81. Ligier tried one final pitch. Too little, too late. Monsieur Le Patron had lost his dashing French lieutenant.

'I wanted to be on an equal footing with Jacques Laffite. That means an equal car, the same money, and more than anything, the same psychological backing.' Didier was clear about his reasons for leaving the French stable and reacted with uncharacteristic irritation to accusations that he had broken an agreement with his employer: 'I never verbally agreed to drive for Guy. I simply said I would drive for him if certain conditions were met. They weren't, so I left.'[22]

The 1980 season was fizzling out. At the penultimate race of the year in Montreal there was nothing Didier could do about Piquet and Jones, who pulled effortlessly away from the Ligier, enacting a thrilling duel for the world championship. Even Giacomelli's Alfa loomed large in his mirrors. Somehow, Ligier had lost their magic formula. Later, when Jones let the French car through to the lead, he did so in the knowledge that Didier was carrying a time penalty. Its clutch threatening to melt, car number 25 had moved forward a fraction of a second before the green light had signalled the start of the race, hence the penalty. Although Didier crossed the line in first place, a 60-second penalty dropped him to third overall. A bitter disappointment.

His only comment: 'The least I can say, for a fault so common, the penalty was severe and hardly consistent.' There, the matter dropped. Being demonstrative never was his style.

Although he was relieved to be leaving L'equipe Francais, Didier genuinely regretted the way his Ligier career had ended. Ultimately, his status as second driver had compromised his season. On that basis alone he had to move on: 'Jacques has too much power, everything revolves around him.' Depailler had uttered just such criticisms a little over 12 months earlier.

At the final race of the year at Watkins Glen, his mechanics attached the Ferrari prancing horse emblem to his steering wheel. Lionel and the crew were sad he was leaving. What ought to have been the start of a beautiful partnership had become rather ugly, tetchy. Fifth place in the final world championship standings was an underachievement and the driver knew it. Didier's tally of 32 points represented neither his own potential nor that of the JS11/15. Six retirements, including those fateful races at Brands and Monaco when victory had been assured, had conspired to undermine his season.

His final run in a Ligier occurred in novel circumstances. Just Jaeckin, the flamboyant director of the infamous *Emmanuelle* films, had been commissioned to direct an episode of the sports-themed television drama series *Salut Champion*. Episode 12 would be set in the intoxicating world of Formula 1. Thus, the show's producers arranged to film their motor racing sequences with the Ligier team.

In the episode, dedicated to the memory of Patrick Depailler, to a press fanfare, the fictional F1 team of Brabant announce the re-entry to F1 of ace driver Joel Pasquier, whose glittering career had been cut short by ... a serious boating accident! A career interrupted by serious injury, a return to Grand Prix racing following a period of convalescence, the struggle to re-establish himself in the top echelons of the sport he loved, accidents at sea ... Had the scriptwriter been gazing into a crystal ball when he had penned this script? Omens and portents – never far from the surface of a life far from ordinary.

Once upon a time at Paul Ricard, a strange vision had sought Didier out predicting glory but also death by fire for the young driver. Now a television scriptwriter had conjured up a plot of pure fiction that would foreshadow future events with disturbing accuracy. Coincidence? Perhaps. Perhaps not.

Little wonder the press and the Formula 1 community in general had always wondered about the French ace. Whispers surrounding his background had always circulated on the F1 grapevine and the gossip pages. So, just who was Didier Pironi? It was a question nobody seemed able to answer, journalists and competitors alike.

1980 ended with trips to Italy and Australia. On 15 October, ten days after the US Grand Prix, he journeyed to Maranello for a symbolic test drive of the disappointing T5 at Ferrari's Fiorano test track. Naturally, the Italian media turned up in large numbers. New additions to the scarlet team are, and always have been, front-page news in Italy. With his Italian surname, fluent language skills not to mention his Friulian heritage, Didier found himself the object of some curiosity. Had the Scuderia finally found an 'Italian' champion to drive their scarlet cars?

Didier completed 65 laps in the T5. His best lap time of 1'09.72 proved to be just under a second off the track record. He might have looked odd, still clad in his blue Ligier overalls, but he felt very much at home in the scarlet enclave. Enzo Ferrari declared himself more than satisfied with proceedings. *Il Commendatore* then went on to pay his latest recruit the ultimate compliment when comparing him to the legendary Italian racer Count Felice Trossi, aka 'Didi'. A gentleman racer of great talent and charisma, like Didier, Trossi was a speed freak, racing cars, boats and aeroplanes – anything with an engine. Tragically, the aristocrat's life was cut short by illness. After decades searching, in the Franco-Italian Enzo Ferrari seemed to believe he had found a latter-day Trossi, a swashbuckler who just like his late friend, exuded class and finesse. In Signor Ferrari's eyes, Didier would always simply be 'Didi'.

Based on what they described as the Frenchman's 'round face, blonde bob haircut, blue eyes and muscular frame', the Italian media conjured up their own name for the new man, 'Cicciobello', the name of a toy doll popular with children. Whether Didier was flattered or not by the comparison is not known. He might have been French by birth, but as of winter 1980, Italy had reclaimed the Parisian as one of her own.

Didier rounded off an eventful year by accepting an offer to appear at the Australian Grand Prix in November. Although billed as a 'Grand Prix', the race was in reality a Formula 5000 race with the addition of Alan Jones's world title-winning Williams FW07 and Bruno Giacomelli's Alfa Romeo 179. The brainchild of Australian entrepreneur Bob Jane, the three F1 stars had been invited to boost the gate, a given since Melbourne-born Jones had only just been crowned F1 champion of the world. Up against the F1 trio, a pack of tough Aussie professionals led by Alfredo Costanzo. Didier teamed up with John Bowe, an up-and-coming driver who was honoured to partner a Grand Prix superstar.

'He was a very cool cat with a gorgeous girlfriend who my mates all lusted after,' recalls Bowe. 'I was young and quite inexperienced but I really liked him and he had a great sense of humour which we loved.'

Enjoying a substantial performance advantage, it was no surprise that the F1s of Jones and Giacomelli ran riot at the front of the field. Best of the rest, Didier finished a distant third, leading home a gaggle of local drivers. It was a blisteringly hot day in south-east Australia. Stood on the victory podium the three F1 men gulped copious amounts of water as Jackie Stewart conducted interviews. During the race, the triple world champion turned pundit recalled how, once upon a time, as a judge at Pilot-Elf, he had cast his vote for a certain 'Didi' Pironi, 'in my opinion,' the Scot added, 'one of the best drivers in the world, I expect him to be world champion within the next two or three years. Tremendous talent the young man has, very nice young boy, he almost looks like a teenager ...' Ever since he had laid eyes on the young French kid at Ricard that auspicious October day eight years earlier, the Scottish legend had monitored Didier's progress with something akin to parental concern. Now, he delighted in watching his 'son' blossom. Similarly, when asked which drivers he admired most, Didier invariably nominated Stewart. In particular, he admired how the Scot had chosen to quit while still at the top of his profession. Didier never did intend hanging around F1 longer than necessary.

It was not just JYS who was blown away. The new Ferrari driver left quite an impression on Bowe: 'As all talented drivers show, he had a very smooth style, and was very quick. He asked me lots of questions which flattered me, but the bottom line to me was that he was an ace driver and an ace bloke.' Respect was mutual: 'Didier was very encouraging of coming over to race in Europe the following year. Unfortunately it was way too big a step for a boy from Tasmania, but my memories of Didier are full of pleasure.'

After three years in Formula 1, Didier had graduated to the most famous racing team in the world, one steeped in folklore. It somehow seemed appropriate. There was just one snag: a pint-sized Canadian who with his bravery and daring had already won the hearts and minds of an entire nation. His name, Gilles Villeneuve.

Sixteen

Riviera days

O N a sultry afternoon in late summer 1980, an Italian television crew headed for the French Riviera. Their mission: an interview with Didier Pironi. Ferrari rumours had been mounting for some time, the ensuing speculation at least partly accounting for this pilgrimage. Did the programme makers hope to obtain a scoop perhaps? If so, they would be disappointed. Weeks later, the French lieutenant would indeed be announced as a Ferrari driver.

Leaving the chic resort of St Tropez behind, the crew ascended the tight and twisty roads that led them to La Garde-Freinet, a medieval village nestled in the hillside overlooking the spectacular Gulf of St Tropez. The Pironi-Dolhem villa was one of several similar properties that peppered the landscape, the retreat of people like themselves, well-to-do Parisians who would think nothing of jetting down to the Riviera for a weekend break to escape the hustle and bustle of the French capital. Ever since Brigitte Bardot first strutted her stuff in the movie *And God Created Woman*, the port had become a magnet to the international jet set. Its quayside crammed with superyachts, St Tropez had a reputation for hedonism. Venture just a few kilometres inland, however, into the hillside villages, and the vibrant, at times brash ambience of the port could not have been farther away.

During his teenage years, Didier had spent much time in this area, holidaying at the same rented property year on year.

139

Subsequently, the family had constructed their own villa complete with swimming pool. Tucked away in a secluded spot deep in the hillside, the property boasted breathtaking views of the surrounding countryside. Paradise, or near as dammit. Seclusion and tranquillity certainly, a place where the Pironi-Dolhems could unwind far, far from the madding crowd. Characterised by a climate in which endless sunny days would morph into even balmier evenings, this was an environment cherished by the whole family. A piece of heaven.

His celebrity rapidly growing, Didier would become an instantly recognisable figure in and around St Tropez and its environs. Appearances at one of the resort's swish bars or restaurants would inevitably draw a crowd of onlookers, female fans proving particularly adept at grabbing (and keeping) his attention. At other times, he might be found tearing along the twisting roads that connect villages such as Grimaud and Cogolin on his Honda CBX superbike, sans helmet, naturally. Capable of hitting speeds of 135mph and with fearsome acceleration, the Japanese-built machine had a notorious reputation. Indeed, the bike had already claimed the life of one of Didier's circle.[23] Riding this supercharged monster without a helmet was asking for trouble – not that it deterred either Didier or José. On the contrary, the brother-cousins seemed to revel in the brute power of a machine for which the moniker 'death-trap' could have been specifically coined. Long hot days, comprising adrenaline-fuelled adventures in car, bike, boat or plane followed by frivolity and adulation down in the bars and restaurants of St Tropez. At 28 years of age, the golden child stood at the peak of his considerable powers.

At the height of that dreamy summer of 1980 on a languid Mediterranean afternoon, the Italian film crew arrived in the Côte d'Azur to be afforded a rare glimpse into the milieu of this otherwise fiercely private family.

Airing on Italia 1, *Grand Prix* was a half-hour television programme devoted to all things motorsport, with a bent towards F1. Produced by ex-Ferrari driver Andrea de Adamich, the show often went behind the scenes, gaining unrivalled access to motorsport personalities. Somehow, the producers had sought and gained permission to join the Pironi-Dolhems at their splendid hillside retreat. Footage of the programme survives to this day: Imelda is present, so too aunt Ilva. Louis Dolhem appears briefly, observing proceedings not altogether incuriously from a balcony.

As for Didier, he answers the interviewer's questions in that calm, polite way of his. The voice is soft, gentle, composed. Revealingly, as he speaks, Imelda sits at hand scrutinising his every word. It is the usual chatter: racing, winning, ambition, as well as some questions pertaining to Ferrari. Though he had all but joined the Italian squad, you would not have guessed it by the young man's demeanour, which never changes despite the interviewer's subtle probing. The crew then follow Didier out to the patio. Beside him, the swimming pool shimmers. It is a balmy, almost indolent afternoon in the south of France. Later, the crew accompany him to his Port Cogolin office where the business of boat sales and rentals is conducted. To top off the day, some lucky members of the production crew are taken for a spin in his powerboat. As a snapshot into a particular moment in time, the film offers a fascinating insight into the life of a sporting hero for whom the terms enigmatic, unfathomable and taciturn might have been invented. A day with Didier, pure whimsy, fantasy.

As elusive as a butterfly, catching up with Didier Pironi was never an easy task at the best of times. It was not just journalists. Friends would often find themselves in the dark, unsure as to his whereabouts or indeed his schedule. Didier had a habit of keeping people guessing. Whether it was the castle at Boissy, the villa at St Tropez, or the apartment at Neuilly, depending on commitments or the mood, pinning him down was no easy task. The *Grand Prix* film crew had done themselves proud.

When he was not taming the streets of Monte Carlo or flying over the bumps of Jacerapaguá, he might be found on the shores of Lake Como where business partner Tullio Abbate crafted some of the most beautiful boats ever to set sail. When he was not talking boats with Abbate, he might be found pounding around the Ferrari test track near Modena. As 1980 ended, he was also spending ever more time at Catherine Bleynie's Geneva home where his glamorous new girlfriend ran a high-end boutique for the Givenchy fashion brand. Geneva, Paris, Milan, St Tropez,

Modena – Didier never stayed in one place too long. So, what was it like to live with such a man, to be engaged to such a man?

In 1981, Catherine Bleynie shared her thoughts with Italy's *Autosprint* magazine. *Who is Didier Pironi? What type of man is he? What is he like?* Like many before and after her, the French ace seemed to intrigue the journalist who conducted the interview.

'He is a very picky person, a perfectionist,' replied Catherine when asked about Didier's character. 'He loves that everything is done perfectly and detests approximation. He wants to have the most beautiful house, the nicest car.' Bleynie then delineated two very different Didiers: 'He is a kind and considerate guy by nature; he hides torment, any jealousy, and even anxiety very well. When he is happy he is smiling but when angry he does not speak and everything closes within himself.'

As a new year dawned, Didier's thoughts turned to the forthcoming F1 season, his fourth in the sport. Development of Ferrari's 126C – the car the team hoped would turn their fortunes around after a disastrous 1980 campaign – had started in earnest even before the last leaves of autumn had fallen. Regular trips to Fiorano were interspersed with tests at Paul Ricard and Imola. Ferrari was desperate to avoid a repeat of 1980. Thus, the team were pinning their hopes on a new turbocharged engine. Although work had started the year before, Ferrari were already behind Renault whose turbocharged car had first appeared at the British Grand Prix in 1977. There was much work to be done. It was during these long, hard days that Didier became properly acquainted with his new team, its personnel and way of working.

In January, he spoke frankly to *Sport-Auto* revealing a hitherto unknown anxiety regarding his Ferrari move:

'I was not really convinced of having made a good choice,' he told Johnny Rives, 'until I visited the Ferrari factory and met the people. It was a relief. Prior to this, I had never been that fascinated by the Ferrari myth, less than most drivers and other professionals. My first visit to Maranello has however completely changed my opinion. Today, Ferrari represents to me something quite apart.'[24]

The question uppermost in many people's minds revolved around his new partnership with Gilles Villeneuve. After three years at Ferrari, with his blend of speed and courage that sometimes bordered on the abnormal, the French Canadian had carved out a niche all his own. Italy adored Villeneuve. Moreover, the little Quebecois was generally agreed at this time to be the fastest if not necessarily the most complete driver of his generation. Could Didier hope to compete against Gilles in what amounted to the Canadian's own team? There was also the question of backgrounds. While Gilles' idea of haute cuisine began and ended with burger, fries and Coca-Cola, Didier's tastes were of an entirely different nature. The Canadian was a family man married to his childhood sweetheart, a doting father to two young children; the Parisian, meanwhile, was the archetypal motor racing playboy.

Many in the French and Italian media had predicted friction between the two men, but contrary to expectations the two 'peacocks' hit it off from the start. 'We share a sense of competition,' noted Didier. 'We are both of us dominated by an uncontrollable desire for speed and acrobatics. I love fast boats and I have introduced Gilles to this world. His main hobby is to frolic in the sky in his helicopter.' The opposites had attracted. 'We're both,' concluded Didier, 'as crazy as one another.'[25]

They might have been poles apart in terms of their backgrounds, habits and tastes, but a shared love of white-knuckle riding – risk-taking – bonded the two men together. Keen competition on the test track at Fiorano followed the daredevils off track. Upon his arrival at Maranello, as was company tradition, Didier had been presented with a Ferrari 308 GTS, a sleek supercar with a top speed of 150mph.[26] More toys for Didier and Gilles to play with. It was in these iconic supercars that the Ferrari pilots indulged in some hair-raising stunts, walking a precarious line in terms of not only legality but morality too. Decades have passed, but there are still those who recall their antics. Amongst their favourite pursuits was a game of chicken. The rules of this 'game' were simple: keep the foot planted on the 308's accelerator for longest without lifting, the winner being he who drove the car flat out for the longest unbroken period of time.

A 600-kilometre run, starting at Paul Ricard and ending at the Fiorano test track, taking in the delights of the French and Italian Rivieras, Cannes, Nice, Sanremo, the journey would normally be expected to take about six hours; Pironi-Villeneuve in a Ferrari 308? Less than half that time.

News of these Riviera white-knuckle rides even made it into the pages of the Italian media. In early spring, the media reported that the Carabinieri had been involved in a high-speed car chase in which they pursued a Ferrari being driven at astonishing speed. Rumours soon spread regarding the identity of the two male occupants. At least one of the occupants in the 308 was rather adept at shaking off police pursuits, having earned his spurs on the streets of Boissy some years previous. On the rare occasions when such chases ended in the Carabinieri's favour, sanctions invariably ended in nothing more onerous than autographs and photographs.

Both Didier and José craved speed, but did the brother-cousins also crave danger even more? What else could explain their audacious plan to take part in the London to New York Transatlantic air race, a reprise of the famous race held in 1969 sponsored by the *Daily Mail* newspaper? With this aim in mind, the boys had taken ownership of a Second World War B26 bomber. Stripping the plane of its artillery and other weight-inducing accoutrements to reduce some of the craft's 10,500 kilos, Didier and José were preparing themselves for a serious crack at the race should Ferrari management give their blessing. 'Between too many private practice sessions and political problems, Formula 1 tires me. I am beginning to know saturation.' Didier's rationale for devoting his energy to this project is revealing. Work continued on the plane through spring 1981. 'I think I will find F1 more fun upon my return from New York,' prophesied the driver, revealing a hitherto unknown antipathy towards his chosen profession. On the subject of danger, he was unmoved: 'I think Turin–Modena is much more dangerous in a Ferrari than Paris–New York by plane.' Once Ferrari management intimated their objections, however, the project stalled indefinitely.

Meanwhile, testing continued apace at the Fiorano track. The new turbocharged 126C was progressing steadily. Pre-season and Didier took the new car around the circuit in a time of 1'09.61, a whisker away from the lap record for a turbo. Ferrari had the power – of that there could be no doubt. The Mauro Forghieri-designed chassis was a different matter altogether, an Achilles heel that would compromise the car's potential the entire year.

Ten-year-old Moreno Weffort had a rare glimpse into both these worlds, Riviera and Ferrari that year. Thanks to the exalted status of his French uncle, the schoolboy was immensely popular among his fellow Villesse school friends. 'My pals were always asking me when Didier would come to Villesse,' recalls Moreno, who would follow his uncle Pepi into the building profession as an adult. 'They even formed a Didier fan club! I was a very popular boy in the village!'

'One day my dad and I went to the big house in Paris,' recalls Moreno. A visit to Paris! To the home of his superstar uncle, Ferrari F1 driver! The Italian connection duly arrived at the castle. Moreno walked around in awe. Then he spotted that familiar blue and white design, his uncle's favourite colours. 'Above the mantelpiece I saw Didier's helmet. I couldn't resist ... so I asked if I could try on this famous helmet.' Carefully, Imelda removed the helmet from its position and handed the precious item to the excited youngster. 'I can't explain how I felt at that moment. I was in the Ferrari!' Little Moreno's vacation continued when from Paris, he flew with his parents, Imelda and Ilva down to St Tropez to be greeted by his illustrious uncle. 'I have these scenes before me, like a movie,' says Moreno.

'One day we went to the grocery store and Didier was driving us back from town. At some point in the road he braked suddenly. There was a kitten. Didier got out of the car, gently picked up the little cat and took him back to the villa.' Moreno and his parents went on to spend an idyllic few days at the villa enjoying its seclusion and not least the divine waters of its swimming pool. 'A dream!' repeats Moreno. When Didier offered to drive his Italian relatives home, the holiday just got even better.

'Arriving in Maranello we came to a queue at some traffic lights. I was in the back seat with my mother,' continues Moreno. 'Didier turned around to me: "Watch carefully!" Suddenly, he accelerated hard, pulling out of the line of cars at incredible speed. Somehow, we managed to avoid all the cars coming in the opposite direction! I have never been so scared before or after! Didier laughed. "That's how the adrenaline feels at the start of a race," he told me with a smile.' Young Moreno had just done a dummy Grand Prix start with one of the world's fastest drivers! From here the party headed to Fiorano where Didier insisted on taking his young cousin for a spin around the test track in the BMW hire-car he had used to chauffeur the family to Italy. 'I did not realise what I was actually experiencing at that time,' recalls the older Moreno. What the young boy's friends had to say about this fantasy adventure can be imagined.

Seventeen
In Villeneuve's shadow

O N the eve of the 1981 Formula 1 season there was reason to be optimistic. Ferrari had arguably the strongest driver line-up in the whole field – perhaps the squad's strongest ever – added to which the V6 engine was producing power readings at least the equal, if not better than those of the turbocharging kings Renault.

When racing began, however, the 126C's teething problems became all too apparent. After his fabulous 1980 performance, Brazil proved to be a race to forget for Didier and his new team. Plagued by poor handling, both cars went off the road in practice. Didier went off road again on Saturday, forcing him to use the down-on-power spare car. The Ferraris lined up in 7th and 17th places on the grid, Didier a second off the pace of his team-mate. His race would end in a collision with Prost. Unstable, unpredictable, the 126C t-boned the Renault as it came up to put a lap on the Ferrari. 1981 in a nutshell: power to spare, but bolted to a chassis sometimes described as 'evil'.

Didier never would manage to tame this awful machine. With a background in racing snowmobiles – machines that require bending to the will – Gilles would fare much better in his attempts to tame the unwieldy Ferrari.

'That 126C really was a truly rubbish car,' recalls Ferrari assistant team manager Dario Calzavara. 'Only Gilles could have succeeded with that car. It was terrible. Didier was a different type of driver, used to more finesse while Gilles would simply drive through a problem.' Calzavara, who joined the Scuderia in January 1981, has fond memories of the daredevil pairing. 'Although they had different temperaments, they got on very well together, at least initially. I might be alone in this opinion, but for me, Didier and Gilles were evenly matched in terms of ability as well. Didier was a very quick guy. He just happened to have all of the bad luck in the team during 1981.'

Fortunes briefly improved at San Marino, a home race for Ferrari. Taking advantage of increased turbo boost, Villeneuve took a clear pole position, but not without cost. As Ferrari number 27 streaked over the line, the V6 engine was already smoking, unable almost to cope with its own power. 'I hate to think how much that lap cost,' drily remarked Alan Jones. Didier meanwhile qualified sixth. Ferrari were cautiously optimistic.

On a bleak afternoon in Emilia-Romagna, Didier made a lightning start to the race, slotting into second place behind Villeneuve. Ferrari were running 1-2! An entire nation held its breath. For the first dozen or so laps, the two red cars edged away from the field, Gilles sliding his 126C into the corners in his own inimitable style. Less spectacular, Didier duly followed, chipping away into his team-mate's lead by a few tenths each lap. Indeed, when the leading Ferrari dived into the pits for slicks on lap 15, the number 28 Ferrari had closed to within a couple of seconds of the French Canadian ace. Didier now led his first race in red. However, there was a problem: Brabham, Arrows and Williams. As the race settled down, rival cars started to handle much better than the Ferrari. Didier clung on for 30 laps. Ultimately, bereft of grip, he was powerless to stop first Piquet, then Patrese, Reutemann and Rebaque getting past. Reaction to his fifth-place finish in the Italian media was, however, positive. The turbocharged 126C had shown potential.

Back-to-back wins by Villeneuve in Monaco and Spain seemed to suggest that Ferrari were indeed back in play, but looks can be deceptive. Ferrari had in fact stolen both wins. Monte Carlo had been inherited after Jones and Piquet had clashed. While Gilles was earning the praise of the paddock for his heroics – and rightly so – Didier was forced to take a back seat. Fighting against the 126C, he had crashed three times in practice at Monte Carlo. While Gilles had grabbed a place on the front row – a crucial factor in his subsequent victory – Didier had been unable to set a representative time, lining up way back in 17th place on the grid, as good as the kiss of death at Monaco. Under the circumstances, a fourth-place finish round the streets of the Principality was a decent result.

At the Spanish race, Gilles had used the fearsome power of the turbo engine to keep a queue of cars behind him for virtually the whole race. Never had track position counted for so much. Didier, meanwhile, had suffered no fewer than three turbo failures. A desultory weekend culminated in a lowly 15th-place finish, some four laps behind the winner. Tough times for the young Parisian.

If Didier envied his team-mate his success, he never showed it. Besides, Villeneuve was a motor racing phenomenon. Competing against the great French Canadian was clearly going to test his abilities, a challenge he professed to relish: 'We will each make our own races,' Didier had said prior to joining the team. 'Racing with a fast driver like Gilles will be a further incentive for me to go faster.'

During the Monaco weekend, Didier had agreed to take part in an experiment conducted by Henri Mondor University Hospital. Doctors found some wild, though not unexpected variations in the driver's heartbeat: a resting rate of 60–70 beats per minute rocketed to over 200 during certain parts of the race, namely at the start and while completing overtaking manoeuvres. The researchers also noted some interesting spikes and falls in between: peaks occurred when the driver changed into gloves and helmet and at the green light signalling the start of the race. Cocooned in the Ferrari cockpit prior to the off, sealed off from the pandemonium around him, Didier's heart-rate returned to normal, until that is the engine fired up whereupon another peak was recorded. On catching sight of an attractive girl hanging around the pits, yet another spike was recorded!

If Didier wished himself back at Ligier during these troubling times, he could hardly have been blamed. Laffite's pole and runner-up spot at the Spanish race marked the start of a rich vein of form for his old friends at Vichy. Wins at Austria and Canada would bring Jacques right back into world championship contention. In contrast, Didier's maiden Ferrari season would yield not a single podium.

'Is it possible,' asked Didier as much to himself as to anyone else, 'that I am not able to drive like I used to?' It was not easy, listening to the plaudits that came the way of his team-mate following these sensational Monaco and Spanish wins. For the first time in his career, the French driver was on the back foot, up against a man imbued with an abundance of natural talent. 'It is probably a period of bad luck that I will try to overcome and you will see that I will succeed sooner or later to climb the top step of the podium.'

Didier endured mixed emotions at the French Grand Prix. Fifth place in the race, albeit a lap down on Prost's victorious Renault, followed an incident on Saturday night when thieves broke into his 308, ripping out the car's radio necessitating a costly repair bill.

A welcome diversion from this less than satisfactory season occurred in the run-up to July's British Grand Prix. Some years previous, it transpired, Louis Dolhem had fathered a third child. This incomparable man had subsequently contrived to live two separate lives. As his two sons had been growing up, the gallant's wanderlust had led him further away from the castle into the arms of Daniele, an attractive younger woman with whom he would conduct a relationship lasting many years. Theirs was a love story however that would not end happily. When Daniele had given birth to a daughter in 1964, Louis had been torn in half. The businessman loved Daniele and doted upon the young girl they would christen Laurence, but from whose presence he would ultimately be banished. That summer, Didier was astonished to discover the existence of his half-sister and was naturally curious to meet this 'new' member of the family. Following Friday practice on the eve of the British Grand Prix, he thus dialled a telephone number, which connected him to a house in Brighton, a seaside town situated on the south coast of England. The call was answered by Laurence, an attractive student staying in the UK with the aim of improving her language skills. Brother and sister spoke into the small hours of the morning.

'We understood one another immediately,' recalls Laurence. 'It was just so easy talking to him. We only stopped when we realised how late it was!' Growing up she had followed her brother's sporting achievements from a distance. No more. Before parting that night, Didier arranged for his sister to come to Silverstone the next day as a guest of Ferrari. It was a nervous but excited French student who set out from Brighton that summer morning. Didier's personal assistant met her in London, and thence chaperoned her back to the Northamptonshire circuit.

'Just as I feared,' said Didier, breaking into a wide smile upon the entrance of his sister into the Ferrari trailer. In a scene straight out of Shakespeare, long-lost brother and sister stared at one another. The family resemblance was striking. The young girl and racing driver shared many of the same physical characteristics of the Dolhem clan. Ice broken, it was laughter all the way. Laurence spent a fascinating day at her famous brother's side that July weekend. At her brother's invitation she joined him for an extended stay at his Geneva home. There was a lot of catching up to do.

On the racetrack, Silverstone proved to be the first race weekend that Didier could claim to have had the upper hand over his highly regarded team-mate in 1981. A power circuit, the Ferrari V6 really came into its own on the Northamptonshire track's long, fast straights, but not enough to trouble the Renaults of Prost and Arnoux, which wrapped up the front row of the grid. With Laurence looking on, Didier's fourth place on the grid saw him handily placed. When the race got underway, however, both Ferraris were soon going backwards, unable to hold back the Brabhams, Williamses and even the McLarens. Brute speed it seemed was not enough in itself to conquer the British track. It was the story of a season: the fast-starting Ferrari a sitting duck as the better-balanced cars of Piquet, Jones, Reutemann and co, hit their stride. Didier's race ended before halfway with a smoking turbo. Another blank.

Undeniably, Ferrari had a very powerful car on their hands. The problem was handling; the 126C handled like a shopping trolley. Thanks to their turbo power, lightning starts often propelled Didier and Gilles to the front of the field, but as the races wore on, the red cars would invariably fall into the clutches of the less powerful, but better-balanced British cars.

Ferrari's season hit a plateau at Zeltweg, venue for the Austrian Grand Prix. Didier and Gilles were way off the pace. Mauro

Forghieri, chief designer and the architect responsible for Niki Lauda's huge success just a few years earlier, was philosophical: 'We have chosen a difficult road, that of the turbo, and now we are paying the consequences as always when you enter in unknown fields. I am convinced, however, we will have better times already by the end of the season.'

After pulling a muscle in his back frolicking in the powerboat, Didier spent an uncomfortable couple of hours in Austria en route to a ninth-place finish. As ever, the Frenchman spent most of his race fending off quicker cars. And as ever with Didier, there was no quarter given on track: 'Someone accused me of defending with too much aggression, but I am a Ferrari driver and I cannot give in without a fight.' In agony throughout the 53-lap race, Didier refused to give up his place easily, be it first or tenth place. Driving on pure adrenaline in the early laps, he clung to third place with tenacity, holding back a train of cars comprising eventual winner Laffite as well as Piquet, Jones and Reutemann. 'He is a born winner,' Catherine Bleynie had told her Italian interviewer earlier in the year. 'He just will not accept defeat.' The lady knew her man.

Later in the race, Ferrari number 28 even came under attack from Nigel Mansell's Lotus, Watson's McLaren and others. 'Every time we see a Ferrari,' remarked James Hunt in his role as television pundit, 'there's a huge queue behind it.'

When the acclaimed aerodynamicist Dr Harvey Postlethwaite joined the team in late summer, the overriding feeling at Ferrari was one of enormous relief. Didier had played his part in the Englishman's appointment, urging Enzo Ferrari to allow a 'foreigner' to enter the inner sanctum. Too late to affect the current car, Postlethwaite's appointment augured well for 1982.

As much as the team from Maranello might have wished it, 1981 was not yet over. The Italian Grand Prix followed a race to forget in Holland. If Ferrari were going to pull out something special, what better place than here on the Autodromo Nazionale Monza, spiritual home of Italian motor racing?

In qualifying, a huge shunt left Didier unhurt and seemingly unmoved: 'I entered the second Lesmo curve in fourth gear, travelling between 220 and 240 kilometres per hour,' recalled the driver. 'Suddenly the car veered off on a tangent and ended up against a guardrail.' This characteristically cool description did not tell half the tale. The impact crushed the left side of the car. His 126C a write-off, only by a miracle had Didier escaped serious injury. Human or mechanical error? The jury was out.

Two seconds short of Arnoux's qualifying pace, the Ferraris lined up eighth and ninth on the grid. Despite making a customary rocket start into second place at the end of the first lap, on current form, it would be only a matter of time before Didier started to go backwards. A mobile chicane, Reutemann, Laffite and Arnoux quickly stacked up behind the number 28 car. Only the awesome power of the V6 kept the Frenchman ahead; 1981 in a nutshell. Renault, Ligier, Williams, Brabham – the team from Maranello would never quite get on terms with F1's leaders in 1981. At times, the red cars struggled to keep pace with Lotus, Alfa Romeo and McLaren. Indeed, Didier's fifth place at the flag arguably flattered the team's true performance. The rather sobering fact was that his 126C had finished over 90 seconds down on the winning turbocharged Renault.

1982 could not come quickly enough. When quizzed about the team's very visible woes, Didier's resolve never once wavered. Ferrari, he insisted, were on the right track. 'I am super happy with my personal situation,' he told *Auto Hebdo* halfway through the year. 'Technically, I have no concerns for the team. She will be world champion very soon.' He also praised the team's V6 turbo, labelling it 'the best engine in F1'.

Just days after the Italian Grand Prix, Ferrari called a press conference. Piqued by what it called 'recurring' and 'unsubstantiated' rumours which had suggested Didier was on the move to Williams, his place in the team to be taken by Elio de Angelis, the team officially confirmed Pironi and Villeneuve as its drivers for 1982.

It had been a difficult year. Though he had somehow managed to get the unwieldy 126C into the lead at Belgium and San Marino, Villeneuve's sensational Monte Carlo and Jarama wins had put those efforts somewhat in the shade. After establishing himself as one of the world's fastest drivers with Ligier in 1980, this first year with Ferrari – though not without promise – had been a disappointment. Imola, Zolder, Silverstone, Hockenheim and

Monza provided enough evidence to suggest that if things went his way, Didier could indeed compete with the incomparable Canadian. The key word was *if*. Significantly, the Parisian had endured the lion's share of Ferrari's misfortune, especially with the turbo engine, which demonstrated such worrying fragility in Didier's hands that the driver had sought the advice of the team's technicians in the hope of adapting his style. Verdict: plain bad luck.

However, Didier's detractors had ammunition. With a haul of 25 points compared to the nine of his team-mate, Gilles had won the internal Ferrari battle, at least statistically. Even so, the long-term future of the team's senior driver had not been entirely concluded. Villeneuve was growing frustrated. Although he had re-signed for the Scuderia in May, Ron Dennis and Frank Williams had not given up hope of one day securing the services of arguably the sport's biggest superstar. Would Gilles be driving a Ferrari beyond 1982? There had even been talk of an F1 venture of his own – Team Villeneuve.

Didier, on the other hand, had no such concerns as regards his own future: 'I will not drive for a team other than Ferrari, world champion or not,' he declared. 'If I survive F1, I will probably finish within three years, like [James] Hunt.'[27] He also revealed his admiration for Enzo Ferrari, whom he referred to as a 'grand gentleman', a man in whose presence he confessed to sometimes finding himself 'lost for words'. In Ferrari, he had found his spiritual and material home. Working with Forghieri had been a revelation too. As for Gilles, predictions of friction between the two 'peacocks' had been wide of the mark. The white-knuckle Nice–Modena rides continued throughout the year and would do so into the new year.

Yes, 1981 had been difficult, but Didier felt very much at home in the Italian squad. With Harvey Postlethwaite now on board and the fearsome V6 turbo arguably the most powerful power plant in the sport, 1982, he instinctively felt, would see the team take its rightful place at the top of the F1 summit.

If he could win the 1982 world title, might he not quit in the manner of Stewart or Hunt, while at the very peak of his powers? It seemed more than likely.

Eighteen
President Pironi

ENZO Ferrari leaned forwards on his desk: 'Madam, do not think I want to take your son away from you, I do not.' Imelda Pironi smiled. It would take quite a lot to take Didier away from her. 'I wanted to assure you of this. My own son Dino was taken away from me by disease. Fate, you see. It can strike any time!' Ferrari raised his hands upwards towards the heavens. Imelda felt a pang of sorrow for the old man.

Il Commendatore had been anxious to meet the mother of his French driver. Steeped in the traditions and folklores of the country of his birth, Enzo Ferrari knew a thing or two about Italian mothers, knew also the strength of bonds that could exist between a Friulian matriarch and her only son. In his own way, Ferrari was reassuring what he assumed to be an apprehensive mother. Therefore, when Imelda had arrived at Maranello as a guest of her son, she had been ushered into Ferrari's inner sanctum for a private audience, a privilege reserved for very few. As the meeting ended, the old man gallantly escorted his guest out of the office.

'Goodbye madam! Your son is a great driver. He has all the qualities required to become a world champion.' Ferrari took Imelda's hand. 'And Ferrari is going to give him the means, I promise you!' 1982 – a year that promised so very much, a year in which Didier might have expected to cement his reputation as a world class sportsman, one in which he was also looking forward to marrying the woman of his dreams and living happily ever after.

1982. Oh, ill-fated year! Decades later it still seems unreal, the ambience, the climate, the sheer scale of intrigue. Not in his wildest imagination could the French lieutenant have foreseen just how fast events would overtake him in this, a year in which anything had seemed possible. Swept along by an unseen power, at times Didier appeared helpless, an unwitting star actor caught up in a film noir entitled simply, *1982*.

Tumult, upheaval, tragedy, words barely begin to adequately describe this remarkable 12-month period. 1982 would leave its mark indelibly printed upon both the driver's body and soul. A tangled mess, Didier's life would never be the same again.

Yet on a crisp morning in early January, optimism had been there for all to see when Ferrari unveiled their new car. Didier and Gilles knew instinctively that 1982 would be Ferrari's year, their year.

Energised by its British designer and its powerful engine, Ferrari had been a hive of activity throughout the winter of 1981/82. Determined to regain their place at Formula 1's top table, its personnel worked round the clock in order to perfect the 126C2. The team had just two days off over the holiday period – Christmas and New Year's Day. It was all hands on deck as a team of 170 technicians went about constructing the new machine. Didier too had never been busier.

Effectively, the team had gone back to the drawing board. 'It's a completely new car,' announced Mauro Forghieri at the machine's launch on Wednesday, 6 January, 'not just the chassis, and the aerodynamics, but the entire mechanics as well.' Dr Postlethwaite had indeed created a brand new car. Drawing upon his aerospace experience, the British designer had introduced a sandwich structure for the car's bodywork – aluminium panels reinforced with carbon fibre and Kevlar. The 126C2 thus represented a significant improvement over the car that had caused so many problems in 1981, not least of which was a 40kg saving in weight. Thanks to this new technology, Ferrari had a lighter car with the added bonus of greater rigidity. The omens looked good.

Initial testing at Fiorano had indeed convinced the team that they had a potential winner on their hands. Both drivers had already lapped under the circuit record with the promise of more to come. A few days after its launch, with a lap of 1'07.10, Villeneuve shattered the existing record for the test circuit by almost one and a half seconds! The Canadian completed 60 laps, never once missing a beat. The 126C2 was not only quick, it was reliable too. 'We believe we are on the right track,' said Forghieri with masterly understatement. Although officially enjoying equal status with his superstar team-mate, Didier had spent a large proportion of his time testing the hybrid car, an updated version of last season's model. Gilles meanwhile had been focused solely on the new car, the 126C2, a subtle but crucial distinction regarding Ferrari hierarchy.

On the eve of the new season, Ferrari looked worthy favourites. The 126C2 was fast, reliable and strong. Along with fellow turbo teams, Brabham-BMW and Renault, the Italians would surely have too much power for those outfits still using normally aspirated engines, Lotus, McLaren and Williams among others. Only time would tell.

If January's Kyalami testing times meant anything, Ferrari's confidence was well placed. Didier finished the tests just a few tenths shy of Piquet's best, the Brabham and Ferrari men comfortably ahead of a field that included both Williamses (Reutemann and Rosberg) and both Renaults (Prost and Arnoux).[28]

F1 cars were getting ever faster.[29] There was, however, a fly in the ointment. In the race to extract ever-greater performance, the cars were becoming lighter, while thanks to ground-effect technology, speeds – particularly while cornering – were reaching dangerously high levels. Light cars and high speeds – a potentially lethal cocktail. Didier was not the only driver in the field gravely concerned about the way the sport was headed: 'The speed of these ground-effect cars increases the chances of a serious accident,' observed Didier in a pre-season interview, adding prophetically, 'In the instance of an accident, it would be all too easy for a car to become airborne at which point it would become an aeroplane. Under such circumstances, the pilot would become a passenger, helpless. If there is a serious accident, then the FIA[30] must take the blame.'

As ever, Formula 1 was pushing the barriers. Even as he spoke, Didier could never have known just how prescient his words would prove to be. At least he was now in a position that enabled him to express his reservations formally, to those who mattered.

Since the previous year's Canadian race, Didier had represented his fellow drivers on the Grand Prix Drivers' Association (GPDA), a sort of F1 drivers' trade union. When the association had required an articulate spokesman, his fellow drivers had immediately turned to their calm, unflappable French colleague. Intelligent and cool in equal measure, the French driver was the ideal candidate to represent drivers' interests, be that in relation to the sport's administrators, circuit owners or team bosses. Didier took the position seriously. Always a vociferous critic of the era's ground-effect cars, he began what amounted to a personal crusade, the goal of which was to make Formula 1 safer, and not before time.

Meanwhile, Didier and Gilles continued their own unique form of macho bonding. Despite the Carabinieri's best efforts, the legendary runs to and from Fiorano showed little sign of abating. On one such occasion, the daredevils agreed to meet up in Milan. Arriving from Geneva in his 308, Didier duly collected his Canadian team-mate. Full speed ahead! Hitting top speeds of nearly 150mph as they roared along the A1 autostrada, the Ferrari soon caught the attention of the Italian motorcycle police who, unable to keep pace, radioed their colleagues further down the line.

'Expected! Two fugitives in a red Ferrari!' Upon reaching the toll at Modena, police armed with machine guns greeted the drivers. In a gesture of surrender, Didier and Gilles raised their arms.

'Is it really you?' The police could not quite believe their eyes. 'It is! It is you! What are you guys doing?' An excited gaggle of police officers surrounded the car.

The Ferrari colleagues happily autographed the scraps of paper thrust into the car. Following a phone call to Enzo Ferrari, half an hour later the officers finally released the pair of firebrands. The old man had simply contacted the Ministry of the Interior. Friends in high places. Chastised, the two friends drove on to Maranello where they fully expected to be read the riot act upon their arrival. Au contraire. When the drivers sheepishly presented themselves in the office of their employer, an animated Ferrari sprung up from his chair.

'Bravo boys! What an advertisement for Ferrari!' Didier and Gilles exchanged bemused smiles. 'Go ask the accountant for a bonus! Bravo!' Enzo Ferrari was nothing if not a capricious employer.

As far as Villeneuve and Pironi were concerned, Mr Ferrari took an almost parental interest in his two drivers, an old headmaster looking out for the interest of these, his errant pupils.

A man of contrasts, paradoxes even, as well as this carefree, adolescent side of his nature, Didier had a deadly serious side too. The boy-racer, who could drive at speeds in excess of 150mph on public roads for the sheer thrill of it, was the same one who fretted over the ever-increasing risk of ever-faster F1 cars. Perhaps it should not have come as a surprise then when in January 1982, the scourge of the Carabinieri assumed the GPDA presidency and with it ever more responsibility in matters of safety. Ironically, it was a position that in just a few weeks' time would thrust this shy, private man into a pivotal role in one of the sport's most infamous episodes, a drama that was broadcast and reported on around the world: the South African Grand Prix drivers' strike.

It all started when Didier received a telephone call from Niki Lauda while on a skiing holiday at Megève in the French Alps. Returning to the F1 fray after a two-year sabbatical, upon receiving his super-licence contract – the document that grants drivers permission to compete in international motorsport events – the Austrian legend had smelt a rat. The double world champion was disconcerted to note certain amendments to the licence, granted by FISA, the sport's governing body. Didier and Niki spoke at length. It was a conversation that would set in motion a chain of unprecedented events.

Two clauses in particular aroused concern. The first involved a potentially profound change in relations between team and driver, employer and employee. Under FISA's proposals, drivers would effectively become the property of their team, commodities to be traded between manufacturers in much the same way as footballers are transferred between teams. Such a move would not only undermine driver autonomy, but also erode any negotiating power they had when it came to matters contractual. Another clause forbade drivers criticising FISA and its irascible president, the autocratic and ever pugnacious Jean-Marie Balestre. Sign the new contract or do not race. FISA's message had been stark enough.

1982 had started with dissent in the air. In the run-up to the South African Grand Prix – scheduled for 23 January – Didier and Niki discussed countermeasures. Many of the drivers had, however, already signed the new contract, and now bitterly regretted having done so. Just days before the race, Didier attended a raft of meetings where, according to an impressed Lauda, he showed himself to be 'diplomatic but firm', arguing the drivers' cause 'completely unemotionally'. FISA though remained intractable. Soon enough the dispute escalated. On the advice of the French and Austrian ringleaders, the drivers simply refused to drive their cars. The stakes were getting ever higher. Team bosses were not impressed. A standoff. The South African Grand Prix came within an ace of being cancelled.

Come 9am Friday – start of official practice – the Kyalami circuit stood eerily silent, a hire coach having spirited the drivers away to Johannesburg's Sunnyside Park Hotel, some 20 miles from the circuit. Thirty-one of the world's top drivers would famously barricade themselves in the hotel ballroom for 24 hours eating, sleeping and joking together, lest team managers should attempt to break their resolve. Solidarity, F1 style.

In many ways, Didier was in his element during this surreal showdown. Flown back and forth by helicopter between his hotel and the Kyalami circuit, he seemed to revel in his role as chief arbitrator. Certainly, his calm, analytical approach came to the fore. From holding press conferences to negotiating with FISA and the Kyalami organisers, the Frenchman articulated the drivers' position clearly and precisely.

A few years previous when guesting in Japanese F2 he had already shown a definite affinity in matters legal as Beppe Gabbiani recalls: 'We were both racing in Japan and I had a big accident involving another driver. The stewards decided I caused the accident and I had to go to conference to explain myself. Didier heard about this and offered to come with me. It lasted two hours! I remember him acting like my lawyer. He helped me enormously that day.'

Back in Kyalami when Balestre resorted to underhand tactics, in Didier he found his equal. 'He [Pironi] accepted the terms of the super-licence in December,' argued the FISA president, firmly on the back foot and coming under increasing pressure from all sides. True enough, Didier had attended a meeting of the Formula 1 commission in Paris on 16 December where the terms of the new super-licence had been discussed. 'I had five minutes to read the documents, written in English,' complained Didier, 'and I specifically expressed reservations about certain clauses.' To no avail. His presence at the meeting largely ceremonial, he was powerless to affect proceedings. Besides, the views of the GPDA cut little if any ice with the governing body's autocratic president. The suspicion remained: Balestre had hoped to sucker the drivers into accepting the new contracts. Had Lauda not been so wily, he might have succeeded too.

A battle of wills unfolded. FISA threatened fines, suspensions and retraction of licences. Similarly, the teams, a significant proportion of them represented by Bernie Ecclestone's FOCA (Formula One Constructors' Association), threatened to bring in reserve drivers. Backed by Lauda, Didier remained resolute. With the threat of cancellation of the South African GP very real, and with the prospect of long and protracted legal battles to follow, a truce was eventually agreed, or so it seemed. Telephoning Lauda back at the hotel, Didier relayed the message the Austrian had been hoping to hear: the drivers' demands had been met. The race was on.

Turbo country – when the South African Grand Prix finally started, thanks to the high altitude, the turbocharged cars ran away at the front of the field. As the super-fast Renaults of Arnoux and Prost made the break, Didier looked more than comfortable in fourth place sat on his team-mate's tail. Although Gilles often ended up the faster of the two Ferrari drivers in qualifying, racing it seemed was a different matter altogether. The Frenchman's pace was more than equal to that of his esteemed colleague. After Gilles' early retirement, Didier clung on to the leaders, just. Renault had produced an awesomely fast car. Even the vastly improved 126C2 struggled to keep the yellow and white cars in sight. Tyre wear would, however, blight what had looked like a promising run for the new car's debut. Following a long pit stop, Didier fought his way back to second place only for a further stop to end his hopes.

During this sensational comeback drive, the Ferrari had blown past Watson's McLaren and Rosberg's Williams, cars that had so often left the red car standing in 1981. Not any more. Renault apart, Ferrari had clearly been the best of the rest in the southern African veldt.

No sooner had the race finished than FISA launched what amounted to an attack on not only Didier's integrity but also his competency. Post-race, the sport's governing body wasted no time imposing fines and suspensions on drivers who had only agreed to race provided the terms of the super-licence were revised. As far as Didier knew that is precisely what FISA had agreed to do. The administration begged to differ. No, retorted the sport's governing body, no such concession had been made. Had Didier misread the signals? On the other hand, had he been the victim of a classic double cross?

Having obtained a verbal guarantee from Balestre and Ecclestone that the contentious clauses in the super-licence would be dropped, Didier had assumed the battle had been won. On that basis, the drivers had decided to race. FISA's lawyer, Max Mosley, disagreed: 'There is no agreement, secret or otherwise, except to have a meeting to discuss the drivers' demands,' declared Mosley. The battle might have been won, but clearly not the war. Just days after the race, along with Villeneuve, Prost, Laffite, Giacomelli and Patrese, for his part in the strike, FISA slapped a $10,000 fine on Didier. The remaining drivers were each fined $5,000. The governing body then gave the drivers 48 hours to pay or face suspension.

Didier vowed to fight on. 'We are determined to get justice. Our aim is not to overturn the FISA, but to arrive at a solution of our problems, both as regards the profession and safety.' Time to marshal the troops. Using the services of a firm of international lawyers specialising in sport, the drivers convened at offices on 44 Champs-Élysées, central Paris. Among other things discussed was the possible formation of a new group to supplant the somewhat impotent GPDA. Hence, the PRDA (Professional Racing Drivers' Association) came into being with Pironi and Lauda as president and vice-president respectively. Where the previous organisation had been largely perfunctory, this new incarnation promised to have teeth. Didier threw himself into his new role. The question of circuit safety was just one aspect of his role that occupied much of his time, especially the provision of and access to on-circuit medical facilities, another foreshadowing of events yet to unfold.

Uncertainty, however, still hung in the air. Balestre it seemed was not prepared to compromise: 'We have to use an iron fist,' said FISA's president. 'If the drivers refuse to submit to the decisions, the situation will become untenable.'

When the sponsors of the Argentinian Grand Prix withdrew their support, leading to the cancellation of the 7 March-scheduled event, the dispute threatened to spiral out of hand. Formula 1 could not go on this way. Ultimately, common sense prevailed. The teams decided to pay the fines, a gesture that allowed the drivers to save face while also saving the blushes of the governing body; a goalless draw. From start to end, it had been an unsavoury affair. Nevertheless, for the dignified and calm way he represented their interests, Didier won the lasting respect of his fellow drivers.

Nineteen
Calm before the storm

TESTING of the 126C2 continued. In early March, the team rolled up at Le Castellet in the south of France. With a little more work, Ferrari sensed they had the capacity to overhaul the dominant Renaults. Entering the ultra-fast Signes corner at an estimated speed of 180mph, Didier's heart jumped into his mouth when the car showed no sign of wanting to turn into the right-hand corner. Instead, the Ferrari went straight on. Smashing through three barriers, the car eventually came to a halt. Incredibly, Didier extracted himself from the cockpit, hobbling away from the wreckage with nothing more serious than a badly bruised pair of knees. The Postlethwaite-designed monocoque had proved its worth. The 126C2 had already shown itself to be a fast car. In the light of this incident, it had also proved its mettle in terms of its structural integrity. As for the cause of the crash: a jammed throttle.

Happenings off the track were just as eventful as those on it. While Didier flew to Brazil for testing ahead of the upcoming Grand Prix, Catherine busied herself preparing for the couple's wedding scheduled to take place on 14 April. Spring 1982, it was all happening: strikes, miraculous escapes, Grands Prix, marriage plans …

At this juncture the picture becomes somewhat cloudy. Keeping track of Didier during this period – any period – was no easy task. From his favourite Italian haunts of Lake Como, Modena and Milan, to Paris, Nice and St Tropez in France, Geneva in Switzerland, and not forgetting Grands Prix races in South Africa, Brazil and beyond, criss-crossing countries and continents was all part of the Didier experience. Journalists at the time described him with any number of adjectives: distant, aloof, enigmatic, secretive, mysterious. There was more than an element of truth in such charges. Attempting to unscramble his personal affairs around this time leads inevitably to speculation and conjecture. Never more so is this apparent than when charting his relationship with the beautiful Catherine.

It fell to Imelda to accompany her future daughter-in-law on all the usual pre-wedding errands that spring. With the bridegroom busily engaged some 5,000 miles away testing in Rio, it was left solely to the women to arrange the ceremony, banns, catering and the thousand and one other details weddings entail. 'What a faculty for organisation has this little, young girl,' notes Imelda in her diary, adding somewhat archly, 'she clung to her wedding! For in no time at all she had everything settled.' Catherine it seems was determined to have her wedding, and sooner rather than later.

Imelda was not the only one to notice Catherine's sheer resolve. In order to arrange the civil ceremony, the two women met with the mayor of Neuilly, a certain Nicolas Sarkozy, who, bemused to note the absence of the would-be bridegroom, is alleged to have quipped: 'You know Mademoiselle, in order to marry, in principle there must be two!' The mayor's joke must have gone down well, for according to Imelda, Catherine burst into her 'crazy and irrepressible laugh'.

Was Didier just too busy to get involved in the wedding plans? Could he even have been a mite reluctant to tie the knot? If so, he would not have been the first bachelor to vacillate at the prospect of impending marital union. Yet those who encountered the golden couple could not doubt the extent of their devotion. 'They radiate so much joy in one another's company,' notes Imelda.

Wedding arrangements concluded, Catherine, Imelda and Ilva flew to Brazil to attend the Grand Prix. In the fortnight after the race, in the period leading up to the United States race in early April, the group planned to take a vacation, which would coincide with Didier's 30th birthday on 26 March. Holidaying with mothers and aunts might strike some as rather quaint, but family mattered, always had. Though he had spent his youth in cosmopolitan Paris, Didier had been raised, lest we forget, in a household of pure Friulian values where modesty and loyalty prevailed. It is also a culture where the bond between mother and son is especially strong. Besides, was he not riding the crest of a wave? An F1 driver – a *Ferrari* driver? It was only natural therefore to share his good fortune with the people who mattered most to him – his family. He and Catherine might have been living together in the white house with its long sloping garden sweeping all the way down to the edge of Lake Geneva, but somehow Didier contrived to spend more time away from the Swiss city than he did in it. When asked by *L'Automobile* magazine to describe his ideal woman in an interview in 1980, he had responded with, 'A girl who respects my freedom.' In Catherine, he had met that woman, seemingly.

On the evening before the Grand Prix, the party gladly accepted a dinner invitation from Ferrari's sporting director, Marco Piccinini. Up in the young couple's hotel room, mother and aunt enjoyed a pre-dinner whiskey and soda. While Catherine occupied the bathroom, Didier chatted away to the ladies. The sisters had certainly come a long way from their humble roots in Friuli. Sprawled out on the bed, Didier was, however, becoming ever more impatient. Time was getting on. What on earth was Catherine doing in there? Eventually, she came out of the bathroom dressed all in white, 'a fairy-tale princess', according to Imelda. Didier was not impressed.

'You'd better spend more time in the kitchen and less in the bathroom!' he snapped in reference to his fiancée's supposed indifference to matters culinary. Cracks, hairline, but cracks all the same. Asked which human trait he disliked most in the same 1980 *L'Automobile* interview, he had replied with just a single word: pretension.

A tearful Catherine returned forthwith to the bathroom. Didier, his mother and aunt meanwhile went off to keep their appointment with Marco. Just as they had given up hope of the young woman's company, having changed her apparel from white to black, Catherine took her place at the table. Dinner proceeded leisurely enough. Although the gentlemen avoided talking shop for much of the evening, Didier eventually raised the topic of safety. The Paul Ricard accident had been his second such shunt. Twice he had walked away from huge crashes, what chance a third time?

'Marco, you must do something! You saw what happened at Paul Ricard. You know when the car takes off like that, there is nothing more we can do. I have survived thanks to a miracle!'

'Didier, hold on. Wait a minute!' As Ferrari's right-hand man and good friend to the French driver, the man known affectionately as Monsignor found himself in a potentially awkward position.

'No, Marco! Wait for what? Somebody to die?'

'Didier! You exaggerate.' Ever the diplomat, Marco steered the conversation into less controversial waters. Didier remained unconvinced.

With Gilles lining up second on the grid, Ferrari was cautiously optimistic of a good showing, perhaps even victory come race day. After a fraught qualifying session, Didier had only managed the eighth fastest time. Still, prospects for the race looked good. However, on a humid Brazilian afternoon, not for the first time, Ferrari's hopes evaporated. It was difficult not to reach the conclusion that it was 1981 all over again: plenty of promise, but little in the way of end product. Until spinning off under pressure from Piquet's Brabham and Rosberg's Williams, Villeneuve had led from the start. Didier, meanwhile, had a race to forget. The hitherto dominant Renaults did not show. 1982 in a nutshell: unpredictable, topsy-turvy.

Race over, the French party headed up to the Caribbean. Sailing from island to island, Didier, Catherine, Imelda and Ilva observed with wonder the incredible diversity of the region's warm, turquoise waters. Embarking at Fort-de-France on the magical French enclave of Martinique, the party dined on freshly caught lobster at the restaurant of a friend. From here, they sailed to a remote, private island as guests of John Caldwell. Days spent enjoying the golden beaches and crystalline waters, evenings spent dining on succulent delicacies hewn from the sea as the sun dipped under the horizon, retiring thereafter to the peace, tranquillity and not to mention sheer novelty of straw huts. Paradise.

Sailing northwards, the party next arrived at the exclusive island of Mustique where they stayed at the famous Cotton House complex. While preparing to board a flight for a short hop over to St Vincent one day, the pilot – an old friend – made a surprise offer to the quiet, unassuming Frenchman:

'You want to do the piloting?'

'Sure,' replied Didier, unable to resist such an opportunity.

Not surprisingly, the other dozen or so passengers looked on in trepidation. They need not have worried. To a resounding round of applause, the temporary pilot executed a textbook landing upon arrival at their destination. This dreamlike interlude ended where it had started, back on Martinique. From the island capital, it was a three-and-a-half-hour flight to Miami, followed by a five-hour connecting flight to Long Beach, California, venue for the United States Grand Prix.

April of 1982 was certainly shaping up to be a busy month. A little over one week after the US race on the fourth of the month, Didier and Catherine would return to France to marry. Oddly, just a few days after the couple were scheduled to say their vows, when the happy couple might naturally have expected to be enjoying their honeymoon, Didier had in fact agreed to race in an event at the Montlhéry circuit. No matter, the Caribbean trip had been an unforgettable experience, a honeymoon in advance.

Long Beach saw Ferrari off the pace, despite or perhaps because of their infamous double rear wings, a ploy calculated to draw attention to the vagaries of the F1 rulebook. Officials later disqualified Villeneuve from third position, the wing having been adjudged to contravene F1's strict regulations. The previously anonymous Marlboro-sponsored Alfa Romeos and McLarens proved the cars to beat on the Californian streets. Returnee Niki Lauda won in grand style. Renault, Brabham, Williams and Ferrari had never looked better than candidates for minor placings. With any one of a dozen drivers having legitimate claims as race winners depending on circuit and conditions, predicting a winner in 1982 was proving to be an almost impossible task. Formula 1 has never been so competitive. It all added up to a most compelling world championship.

After three Grands Prix, Ferrari had amassed just a single point. In the wake of disqualifications to Piquet and Rosberg, winner and runner-up in the Brazilian race and whose cars had subsequently been declared illegal, Didier had been upgraded from eighth to sixth place, accounting for that solitary point. All very underwhelming. When would Ferrari's season begin? The team needed finishes, points-scoring finishes, podiums, race wins. It was not happening, yet.

Before the team could muster in preparation for the San Marino Grand Prix later that April, Didier had another pressing matter to attend to on the 14th of the month: his marriage. For a venue, Catherine had chosen the small town of Eugénie-les-Bains, a long way from Paris, but base to celebrity chef Michel Guérard whom she had engaged to provide the catering. France's gastronomic guru concocted a banquet fit for a king: lobster, truffles, caviar, pigeon wing, pomerol jelly, foie gras; mille-feuille and croque-en-bouche for dessert; 1973 Krug champagne or Château Beauregard 1970 to drink. No expense had been spared. Did such extravagance meet with Didier's approval?

The honour of best man fell to Marco Piccinini, a move that surprised some onlookers who had assumed this important role would have fallen to José to perform. Soon enough the whispers started. Was this decision, as some observers insisted, a political move – a cynical one at that? Alternatively, was it simply one of those occasions when a difficult choice had to be made? Critics thought the former. According to this line of reasoning, Didier had purposely overlooked his brother-cousin in order to curry favour with his Ferrari boss, a move ultimately calculated to undermine Villeneuve's position within the Scuderia. The fact that the French Canadian and his wife Joann did not attend the ceremony added further fuel to the conspiracy theorists' fires. Pironi, they concluded, had snubbed Gilles on purpose. The Frenchman was a snake, they said, plotting the overthrow of his own team-mate.

'Bullshit,' says photographer and raconteur Allan de la Plante, Gilles' friend and confidant throughout his racing career. 'I saw the wedding invitation with my own eyes.' A no-nonsense Canadian himself, the photographer had known the Villeneuves for many years. 'Truth is Gilles and Joann were going through a rough period at the time,' explains de la Plante. 'Going to a wedding together, the happy couple, was the last thing they wanted. Gilles had a woman friend in Montreal ... Let's just say things were very rocky between them. Besides, Gilles detested formal affairs, suits, ties and all that crap. Not his scene at all.'

Added to which, since his arrival at Ferrari Didier had become good friends with Piccinini. Intelligent, discreet and humble, the two men had much in common. During the drivers' strike, Marco had supported his driver fully, even though its aims at times ran counter to those of the team. Mutual trust, call it.

On a warm, sunny afternoon in the unassuming church of Saint Eugénie, Didier and Catherine exchanged vows. The golden couple dazzled the assembled guests, he in his pearl grey morning suit and she in her splendid bridal dress. No doubt, Madame Bleynie made for an extraordinarily beautiful bride. 'She is, it's true, irresistible.' remarked Imelda, 'Very sweet, always smiling, sleek, and radiant with beauty.' In his regular column for *Auto Hebdo,* Didier spoke of his 'pleasure' upon marrying 'an exquisite woman'. Indeed, pictures of the day present a young couple who appear to be deeply in love.[31] After the ceremony, the couple exited the church hand-in-hand to discover a guard of honour made up of a dozen chefs who lined the path that led across the road to Guérard's restaurant. The newlyweds then posed for pictures in the restaurant grounds as Imelda, Ilva, Louis and José looked proudly on. Meanwhile, Didier's nieces and nephews played happily together. Perfect weather, perfect food: a perfect day. And yet … something lingering in the fresh spring air, distant clouds, imperceptible, thundery.

'Strangely enough,' recalls the bridegroom's mother, 'the wedding pictures, and God knows there were many, Didier never showed them to me. I do not have any!' Strange is indeed the word. As Imelda correctly notes, plenty of photographs were indeed taken – none of which found their way into the family album …

The day after the wedding, Didier flew to Bologna for Imola pre-race testing. Ferrari arrived in the midst of persistent rumblings that the team might withdraw from F1 in protest over what it felt were the attempts of some of their competitors to cheat the sporting regulations. With the 126C2 finally hitting its stride, withdrawal would have come at a most inappropriate time. Villeneuve (1'32.11) and Pironi (1'32.22) both dipped under Prost's lap record set the previous week. Ferrari were coming to the boil.

Before joining the family in St Tropez where they had congregated post-nuptials, Didier first had a date at the Linas-Montlhéry circuit to drive a Ferrari P4 in an exhibition race. Catherine remained in Paris. As honeymoons go, unconventional is a word that springs immediately to mind. Curiouser and curiouser.

Didier enjoyed himself immensely at Montlhéry. Sprinting ahead of a field of privately owned Porsches, Ferraris and Lolas, he professed to have rediscovered his love for competitive driving. In order to preserve the mechanical integrity of his car, a vehicle owned by the collector David Piper, Didier pulled out of the race at the halfway point. 'In F1, we no longer have any fun at all. The suspensions are so hard the car is shaken to the point sometimes where the driver misses the pedal or gear change during manoeuvres. This causes stupid mistakes. Moreover, because of ground effect the limit is less perceptible, as it depends on the contact of the skirts with the ground, which varies with the inequalities of it.'

After this all-too-brief thrill, it was back to business, back to F1. Ferrari were desperate for a good result on home soil at the San Marino Grand Prix, round four of the championship. With dissent once more in the air, however, a chain of events was just beginning that would ensure that the 1982 running would become one of the most controversial races not just of the season, but in the whole of Grand Prix history.

Twenty
Much ado about nothing: Imola '82

EVERYBODY it seems has an opinion on the 1982 San Marino Grand Prix. Much has been written about events that April afternoon and the part Didier played therein. As with other contentious issues, a standard version of events from that extraordinary weekend has emerged, a version largely the creation of a certain media faction with avowed biases and prejudices, of which more later.

Just what was it about that year? *That* weekend? *That* race? Even as the team transporters were arriving in the Imola paddock, controversy once more stalked the air. Formula 1 was bristling. In response to the Piquet and Rosberg disqualifications, Bernie Ecclestone's FOCA resolved to boycott the race; retaliation pure and simple. In common with their fellow Cosworth-powered teams, come the end of the Brazilian Grand Prix Brabham and Williams had topped up their cars with various 'coolants' and 'lubricants' in order to meet the minimum weight of 580kg stipulated in the sporting regulations, a perfectly legal if not morally correct interpretation of FISA's somewhat opaque rulebook. Desperate to gain parity with the much more powerful turbo-powered teams, it was a ploy designed to level the F1 playing field. 'Cheats!' cried Ferrari and Renault.

Subsequently, Piquet and Rosberg's disqualifications were upheld.[32]

Hence, the FISA–FOCA war, dormant for a couple of years, had just re-ignited. The Williams transporter duly turned around and headed back for England. McLaren, waiting at the Mont Blanc Tunnel, followed suit. Brabham did not even leave the UK. By Thursday morning only Renault, Alfa Romeo, Tyrrell, Toleman and Osella remained at the Dino Ferrari circuit, ten cars all told, that would soon become 12 upon Ferrari's arrival from their Modena base. As it stood, the San Marino Grand Prix would not go ahead – it could not. Under the terms of the sport's Concorde agreement a minimum of 14 cars were required in order to run a Grand Prix.

'I have my helmet around here somewhere,' joked Renault's Gérard Larrousse as the teams anxiously awaited the arrival of the ATS team, who as members of FOCA were expected to also boycott the event. When the Anglo-German squad eventually rolled up in a half-empty paddock, monsieur Larrousse could put his helmet back in mothballs. We had a Grand Prix, just.

With Brabham, McLaren and Williams absent, the race would clearly boil down to a Renault v Ferrari battle. First and foremost a power circuit, even if they had turned up, it is doubtful whether the English teams would have troubled their turbocharged colleagues to any great extent on the Imola circuit. That was not the point. At stake was the sport's reputation. Following hard on the heels of the South African strike, needless to say the worldwide perception of Formula 1 had never been so precarious.

Events leading up to the race are not entirely clear, but it seems that the Renault and Ferrari drivers met to formulate a mutually beneficial race strategy. Although the precise location of the meeting is subject to some dispute – some reports suggest a restaurant in Imola, others the Ferrari motorhome – the upshot of the encounter is not disputed.[33] Aware that fuel consumption could play a potentially crucial role on the day, the drivers agreed not to race for position until after the halfway point had been reached, after which the spoils would be up for grabs. It was an eminently sensible agreement. After all, with the FOCA teams not in play, one thing was certain: either Renault or Ferrari would win. If, however, the red and yellow turbocharged quartet went hammer and tongs from the green light, the chances of fuel consumption issues could only increase. Turbo engines – fragile at the best of times – could become compromised and the possibility of non-finishes increase. Furthermore, despite its infancy, Imola had earned itself a reputation as F1's thirstiest circuit. Prost, Arnoux, Villeneuve and Pironi all agreed: after half distance, the gloves would come off.

Muddying the picture further is a comment some years later by Ferrari's chief mechanic Paolo Scaramelli.[34] In the event of both Renaults retiring, according to Scaramelli, it had been agreed that whichever Ferrari happened to be leading at that time would run unchallenged to the end. Oddly, for a claim with such profound implications for what followed, it is one that has never been repeated, not even by Gilles, who would surely have been the first to recall such a clear-cut instruction.

Forty thousand fans turning up for Saturday's practice quelled any fears that a depleted field might negatively affect the event's appeal, and how. Renault and Ferrari battled it out for the fastest times. As expected, the turbo-powered cars were considerably faster than their non-turbo powered rivals headed by Alboreto (Tyrrell) and De Cesaris and Giacomelli (Alfa Romeo).

Didier's practice days ended in frustration and disappointment. Approaching Acque Minerali towards the end of Friday's session, about to set his fastest time, the 126C2 suddenly went off into the barriers. It was a big shunt, his third such incident in this troublesome year. 'I felt a collapse of my right rear suspension,' recounted Didier. 'I tried to correct my trajectory but there was nothing I could do.' Technicians attributed the crash to a right rear tyre, which had burst without warning. No option but to use the spare car. Sometimes disparagingly referred to as the 'mule', as the name implies spare cars often lacked the finesse and attention lavished on the team's race cars. The 'mule' did the dirty work. Any chances of challenging the Renaults or his team-mate for pole had effectively ended. Indeed, out of the entire 14-car field, Didier was the only driver unable to improve his time during Saturday's qualifying session. In the team garage Ferrari's mechanics worked frantically to renovate the car that Didier had crashed the previous day, but time was against them. Didier was stuck with the 'mule'. It was doubly disappointing for the Frenchman. Only a few days ago he had set a new lap record for the Imola circuit.

Although often overlooked, this unfortunate turn of events for the driver of Ferrari number 28 is in fact a crucially important element when it comes to interpreting the controversy that would soon follow. With minutes to go before the end of the session, Ferrari declared Didier's car ready. Too late. The Frenchman was 1.3 seconds slower than his team-mate.

Thus the grid was settled. Two yellow and white cars (Arnoux and Prost) at the front, with the two scarlet cars sitting right behind:

Arnoux	1'29.765
Prost	1'30.249
Villeneuve	1'30.717
Pironi	1'32.020

Based purely on qualifying form, Renault had this in the bag. Of more significance perhaps were the times from the 30-minute warm-up session on Sunday morning which told an altogether different story:

Pironi	1'35.036
Villeneuve	1'35.136
Arnoux	1'35.313
Prost	1'37.734

In race trim, Ferrari it appeared had a slight edge over their French rivals. Practice woes behind him, and back in his own car, Didier had been finally able to show his true speed. Nearly three seconds off the pace, Alain Prost's time suggested all was not well with his Renault – more evidence that warm-up rather than qualifying times were more representative of actual pace.

On a sunny but windy day an estimated 100,000 spectators made their way to the Dino Ferrari circuit. The absence of the FOCA teams had seemingly not dampened the public's appetite for the event. As the start time approached, four turbo and ten normally aspirated cars took up their places on an uncharacteristically empty starting grid. Formula 1 was about to witness arguably one of its most contentious ever races.

At the lights, the turbo foursome all made good starts. Thus, into the first corner, Arnoux led from Prost, Villeneuve and Pironi. Renault's joy was, however, short-lived. Confirming his warm-up problems, Prost was unhappy though hardly surprised to find his engine misbehaving even before a single lap had been completed. First Gilles and then Didier slipped past the sickly French car. Four became three. Blisteringly quick in a straight line, by the end of the first lap Arnoux had already pulled out several lengths over the scarlet cars. Catching the little Frenchman was clearly not going to be easy. Were the remaining three drivers mindful of the pact they had made just days ago? Take it easy until half distance, no heroics, then the real race would begin? Perhaps. One thing was certain: René was not hanging around.

Later, Gilles would claim that had he wanted to, he could easily have left his French team-mate behind in a cloud of dust at Imola. 'I could have given him [Pironi] a couple of laps,' Gilles would tell the media after the event, going on to cite the 1.3-second gap he established in qualifying as evidence. However, as already noted, the 1.3-second gap had materialised due to a set of extraordinary circumstances which in no way reflected Didier's true race pace. Nonetheless, for a partisan media, the 1.3-second gap struck a chord. It was all the evidence needed to confirm that Gilles had been the faster of the two Ferrari drivers, and by some margin. Ergo, the faster driver should win the race.

Yet as Villeneuve honed in on the leading Renault, Didier was sticking right with him, the gap never more than three seconds between the two men. Far from dropping the number 28 car, Didier seemed able to maintain a similar pace to that of the sister Ferrari. Just as the warm-up times had indicated, in race trim there was little if anything between the scarlet cars. Even so, the supposed disparity in speed between the Ferrari mavericks has become part of Imola mythology, a soundbite repeated ad infinitum and one upon which many opinions have been based, erroneously so.

As a spectacle, the race was warming up nicely. To the delight of the packed grandstands now witnessing a thrilling three-way duel for the lead, Villeneuve was soon sizing up the very swift-in-a-straight-line Renault, confirmation once more of the veracity of the warm-up times. While the red cars seemed to have better speed in the corners, such was the power generated by the French car's awesome V6 engine, the Renault pulled away on the straights. On lap 22, Didier signalled his own intent when slipping by his team-mate into second place only for Gilles to retake the place a few laps later. At this stage, it looked as if the red cars were taking turns to have a crack at the yellow and black car out front. The peace pact, such as it had been, appeared to have ended. The gloves had definitely come off.

Gaining a run at the Renault as the leading trio approached Tosa, Gilles slipstreamed into the lead a few hundred yards later. Lap 30, half distance, a red-yellow-red turbo-charged train flashed across the start-finish line nudging 190mph. A few corners later, René powered past Gilles to retake the lead as Didier audaciously attempted to leapfrog both cars. With the Renault the meat in a Ferrari sandwich, the leading trio entered the hairpin three abreast.

For a brief moment, it looked as if Didier's gambit had come off, but a couple of corners later Ferrari number 28 was back in third place! F1 had not seen anything like this for quite some time. As the Ferraris squabbled over second place, Arnoux managed to pull out a few car lengths over his scarlet tormentors. Even at this stage of the race, it seemed clear that Villeneuve and Pironi were battling for position – and battling hard, all of which makes subsequent claims even harder to justify. Indeed, such was the intensity of their struggle they soon cruised up again behind the Renault's gearbox.

Over the course of the next few laps the Ferraris swapped places on two more occasions, each time catapulting out of the other's slipstream on the straight leading to the Tosa hairpin – the shape of things to come.

Rounding the Tamburello corner having just started its 45th lap, flames licking out from its back end, the Renault cried enough. After a sterling drive, Arnoux was out. Ferrari had outstayed their French rivals. Alboreto's Tyrrell over 40 seconds down in third place, the scarlet cars had a comfortable lead over their nearest pursuer. Game over? Not quite. With 15 laps to go, the fun was about to really begin.

Prior to the Renault's exit, the leading trio had been lapping in the 1'35 bracket. Arnoux gone, and ever mindful of fuel consumption, Villeneuve dropped this pace by a couple of seconds to somewhere in the 1'37 region. As far as the Canadian was concerned, the race was over. The duel between himself and his French team-mate was therefore also over. From Gilles' point of view, it must have made perfect sense: drop the revs, save fuel, coast to an easy victory. Rightly or wrongly, Gilles had decided that the San Marino Grand Prix was his for the taking. Not so fast. At any moment now the Ferrari pit would issue instructions, wouldn't they? Yes, eventually …

Making a small error of judgement at Rivazza, the Canadian acrobat went off the road for just a brief moment, no more than a couple of seconds, but enough to hand the initiative to his French comrade. 'Pironi did not follow the instructions, he passed me. And in a dangerous place,' said Villeneuve later. 'Dangerous?' asked *Auto Hebdo* in reply. 'Not quite. Let's say Didier took advantage of a slight fault of his team-mate …' In this craziest of races, accusations and explanations were coming thick and fast, not all of them entirely accurate. Whatever, the boot was on the other foot; Didier now led Gilles.

When exactly had the first pit board been hung out? On lap 45 – the same lap as Arnoux's demise, when Gilles led, or, as seems more likely, at the end of the following lap when Didier led? When the cars screeched over the line to compete lap 46 the board duly read:[35]

1 Didi	+0.3	SLOW
2 Gilles	- 0.3	

Since assuming the lead, Didier had once more started to lap in the 1'35 bracket, an unnecessary risk in the eyes of the management, given the unassailable lead of their two cars. Hence the 'slow' instruction.

What exactly though did 'slow' mean? Did this message mean that the two cars were to hold position from this point onwards, to refrain from overtaking for the duration of the race? After all, in terms of battling Renault, the race was over. No point taking unnecessary risks. According to sporting director Piccinini, the signal simply warned the drivers not to take 'excessive' risks. Gilles, however, interpreted the signal differently. In his view, 'slow' approximated to 'no more overtaking'. If so, in accordance with Gilles' own interpretation Didier's position as leader should have been unopposed until the end of the Grand Prix. Yet when the Canadian swooped back into the lead on lap 49, the meaning of 'slow' seemed to mean anything but hold station. Gilles' mistake on lap 46 had changed the dynamic. A few laps later Didier responded in kind. At this point, neither man seemed to be interpreting the 'slow' signal as shorthand to hold position. Just the opposite in fact. The crowd whooped and cheered. The San Marino Grand Prix was turning into a classic.

Explaining Ferrari's pit-board symbols to readers of his *Auto Hebdo* column, Didier was unequivocal in his understanding of the Ferrari system.[36] 'Slow', he repeated, meant just that: drop the pace, don't take risks, thus: 'The day you see "P2 Didi. OK" that is an instruction to hold second place and to respect it absolutely. At Imola, the panels indicated "P1" and "P2" to each of us according to our positions on the previous lap.' At no time during the race had Ferrari displayed the 'OK' sign. As far as Didier was concerned therefore, he and his team-mate were in a race, and what a race!

As for fuel, preserving it had been the last thing on Gilles' mind as he had stalked his team-mate between laps 46–49. Slow signs or not, he had only one thing on his mind: to take Pironi and the lead.

Seven laps to the flag and the scarlet cars circulated in formation. It was anyone's game. Having driven within the limit of fuel projections, Didier was relishing a fight to the flag. 1981 had been a pig of a year. Here was an opportunity to start 1982 on a completely different note. May the best man win! It was, however, a sentiment not shared by the man in the cockpit of the number 27 Ferrari. For Gilles, if not Ferrari management, the crowd or Pironi, the race was over. According to the Quebecois, the duel between Ferrari 27 and 28 had all been part of a spectacle, an orchestrated way to entertain the 100,000-plus spectators jammed into every Imola nook and cranny. Post-race, the largely pro-Villeneuve media seized upon this assertion. Gilles, they said, had been the faster of the two Ferraristas by some way and had jousted with Pironi for 50 laps purely for the crowd's benefit. He could, they said, easily have left his French team-mate behind at any moment had he wished. Had he not been 1.3 seconds faster in qualifying?

If this was indeed a charade, it was a good one. If Villeneuve really did believe himself to be taking part in some sort of 'show' he was in a minority. Up in the BBC commentary box James Hunt was in no doubt: 'There's certainly no team tactics here,' observed the 1976 world champion. 'They're both going for it hammer and tongs.' The manner in which the two drivers had been passing and repassing each other since the start of the race seemed to support Hunt's contention.

However, Gilles apparently still believed he and Didier were putting on a synchronised show. If this was the case, then the two cars would need to engineer a swap for position, and soon. Laps 53 through to 58 found the Ferraris locked together, Didier just yards in front of his team-mate. With two laps remaining to the flag, Gilles tried his luck at Tosa only to be firmly rebuffed. If this was indeed play-acting, it was play-acting of the very highest order. To Hunt and 100,000 spectators, it looked real enough. 'Pironi is defending his position with all he's got,' noted the ex-McLaren driver.

Were the Ferraris racing? Each time he took over the lead, Didier increased the pace, in the absence of team orders, a perfectly legitimate course of action. Indeed, in his biography of the Canadian ace, Gerald Donaldson is also clear that the scarlet cars were not showboating. On the contrary, Didier and Gilles were involved in a titanic battle for supremacy:

'On lap 58 he [Villeneuve] moved alongside Pironi at Tosa and was again cut off in no uncertain terms and the crowd began to sense that the Ferrari manoeuvres were not being made light-heartedly.'[37]

Arriving at Tosa for the 59th time, Ferrari number 27 pulled out of the leader's slipstream and seized the lead. Game. Set. Match. To Gilles, it was a concession, albeit a rather late one. Didier had decided to finally end the 'show' and accept team orders. But what team orders? As Harvey Postlethwaite later confirmed, there never had been any team orders. From Didier's perspective, the race was still very much on. Neither was fuel a problem. Professionals that they both were, he was expecting a thrilling final couple of laps. Nonetheless, Gilles relaxed. Despite the glaring lack of team orders, in his own mind the 'show' was now definitely over. Although Donaldson's biography portrays a sporting hero, it also presents a picture of an individual who could occasionally veer towards intransigence, a man who was absolute in his convictions. Gilles had won the San Marino Grand Prix. Case closed. He could now lead this glorious Ferrari procession home to the acclaim of the grandstands and an entire nation. It would prove to be a fatal act of presumption.

'Pironi is going to have to be well placed as they come on to the long straight,' mused James Hunt, just as certain the race was *not* over. 'He's got to start within four lengths of Villeneuve when they come on to the main straight,' he cautioned. 'If he can do that, he'll get him at the end of it.' The two Ferraris duly approached the pit straight to begin their final lap. 'Can he close up? Can he get himself into position?'

Hunt's question was answered moments later as Ferrari number 28 squeezed past the leader as both cars braked into Tosa. Gilles had left a small gap. While there is no doubt that he believed the race to be over, and thus did not expect his team-mate to attack, it was a supposition entirely of the Canadian's own making. Gilles had 'switched off' a little too early. Didier had the lead. For the final part of the lap, he went defensive, placing his car on the tarmac in such a way as to deny Villeneuve a chance to return the favour. At the finish, 0.3 of a second separated the gladiators.

Body language, it was all in the body language. Upon his arrival back at the paddock, Gilles threw his gloves out of the cockpit. To the amazement of those assembled, he then stormed off to the Ferrari motorhome. 'You need to get another driver!' shouted an inchoate French Canadian, steam pouring from every pore of his body. Gilles was angry, but who with? Didier? The team? Himself?

Having removed his helmet in typical uber-cool-Pironi fashion while steering his car home on the parade lap, the winner arrived back in the paddock beaming. The media already smelt blood. Pironi had duped his team-mate! Treachery! Betrayal! The pro-

Villeneuve faction of the media were already writing their stories. Initially, the runner-up refused to accompany his team-mate on the podium. Some minutes later, first and second appeared together side by side on the celebration platform, their expressions a world apart. As a jubilant though typically measured Didier sprayed the champagne, Gilles' demeanour indeed told its own story. Convinced he had been cheated out of a rightful victory, he declined to join Didier and third-placed Michele Alboreto on a victory lap of the circuit in the motorcade. Villeneuve left the circuit post-haste.

Reflecting on the race a day, later Gilles' fury was still obvious. He recalled the moment he had taken back the lead on the penultimate lap: 'I was really persuaded that we were going to stop there, but no. He came back at the last moment when I was not looking at my rear-view mirror.' When the Canadian declared his intention never to speak to his partner again, the press went into meltdown. The French driver had cheated his unsuspecting team-mate out of certain victory. It's war!

Didier's take was, as might be expected, far more circumspect. Expressing his surprise at his team-mate's fury, he went on to mention certain problems that had afflicted the 126C2's turbo-boost pressures, adding, 'I understand his bitterness. Back home, I watched several times the running of this race and everything seems normal. To say that I made a few dangerous attacks, that I did not meet certain guidelines ... I did not; Gilles has no reason to hate me, except that I finished ahead of him.'

Villeneuve, meanwhile, described how his partner had 'stolen' his victory. Worse, he went on to outline what he termed the team's – specifically Piccinini's – 'endorsement' of Didier's actions. From his home in Monte Carlo where he had immediately retreated, he also brought up the subject of team orders, a perennially thorny issue in the sport of Formula 1. Gilles reminded the media how once upon a time he had 'obeyed' team orders himself. Had the press forgotten about the 1979 Italian Grand Prix in which he had dutifully sat behind his team-mate of the time Jody Scheckter? Here was an example of how a junior team-mate should behave, respectfully, obediently. On one level, it was a seductive argument: Gilles had indeed followed team orders that day to follow Jody home for a Ferrari 1-2. That much was true. However, there was the small question of context. At Monza 1979, victory for the South African would bring him the world championship and team orders – explicit orders – ensured that title. As of Imola 1982, Ferrari had acquired a grand total of just one point. The two situations were poles apart.

'I want to clarify immediately,' Didier went on to tell his *Auto Hebdo* readers, 'that no team orders dictated our efforts. At Ferrari, this kind of "recommendation" does not exist, except in special cases.' Monza 1979 was just the kind of 'special' case to which he was referring. Nonetheless, the media had a story. They also had a hero (Villeneuve) and a villain (Pironi). Further, some of the most prominent chroniclers of the race just happened to be (self-avowed) confidants of the French Canadian driver and could thus hardly be described as impartial. No matter. In the days, months and years since those remarkable events in the Italian principality, the views and opinions of a small band of partisan journalists have carried unquestionable authority. A passage from the respected motor racing journalist Christopher Hilton, writing decades after the event, typifies the 'official' version of events. The excerpt comes from a chapter tellingly entitled 'A Man Betrayed …'

> 'In his innocence Villeneuve imagined that, with only seven cars circulating… Pironi had decided to put on a show for the crowd. They'd duel. The crowd would love it but Pironi would pull over and let Villeneuve into the lead, obeying the tradition. It never crossed Villeneuve's thinking that Pironi would do anything else…' [38]

The use of emotive language such as 'innocence' and loaded phrases such as 'obeying tradition' and 'it never crossed Villeneuve's thinking' are fairly typical examples of the type of language used in the good v bad guy narrative perpetuated in the mainstream press.

In an effort to quell the furore which followed, Enzo Ferrari sought an interview with his drivers. Legend has it that after pressuring his wayward 'sons' into a perfunctory handshake, 'Il Vecchio' spoke individually with the boys, assuring each one in turn he had acted with perfect decorum! To Mr Ferrari, what mattered most was that his cars had won, that Ferrari the constructor had triumphed. Nevertheless, Maranello issued a statement 48 hours after the race in which it appeared the team sided with Villeneuve, but in which great pains were taken not to chastise Didier. Diplomacy, Ferrari style.

Opinion amongst their fellow drivers was also ambiguous. While agreeing team orders should be observed, there was also sympathy for the plight of a driver – any driver – forced to comply with a directive that ran counter to every competitive instinct. Ex-Ferrari F1 pilot and media pundit Andrea de Adamich summarises the paradox thus:

'When you are a racing driver fighting for a world championship and victories in general, against your team-mate and number one competitor and you see him in technical difficulties, it will be very difficult – nearly impossible – to respect an "order" to oblige you to slow down to remain behind him. Your brain is thinking: "If his car is in trouble maybe it's because he has driven it badly and now my car is performing better because I have driven it sympathetically – then why should I remain behind? No way!"'

De Adamich is alluding to the suggestion that during the closing stages of the race, Gilles' car may have been compromised in some way – a theory the Canadian was quick to dismiss. As interesting as this driver's perspective is, it is offered in the context where team orders exist. At Imola, there were no such orders. His comments regarding the psychological aspect are perhaps more revealing. San Marino was not the first and would not be the last time the question of team orders had raised its contentious head in recent times. One year previously, Carlos Reutemann had ignored Williams's orders to let his team-mate Alan Jones take the lead in the Brazilian Grand Prix. René Arnoux would do much the same when refusing to allow Alain Prost to take victory at the French GP later that summer. In both examples cited however, orders had been explicit – a major departure from Imola.

In the midst of this acrimony, the last thing Didier could have done with were complications in his private life. This, however, was 1982. Nothing could be taken for granted in this tumultuous year, in public nor private spheres. Just a few days prior to the race,

Didier and Catherine had arrived at Imola's Hotel Olympia as F1's golden couple, smiling, holding hands. During the race, Mrs Pironi had shouted herself hoarse cheering her man on to victory. Also cutting a stunning figure in the Imola paddock that weekend was another gorgeous blonde, Eleonora Vallone, daughter of the celebrated Italian actor, Raf. Voluptuous and brimming with youth and sensuality, this model-cum-journalist had naturally already caught Didier's eye. The pair had been photographed together at the previous year's race. Though hardly a secret in Ferrari circles, Didier and this bewitching young woman had been involved in some sort of on-off relationship since the start of his Ferrari career, possibly even earlier. In the aftermath of the race, rumours circulated that Didier and Eleonora had been spotted at the Royal Hotel Finni, Modena, to where they had fled, emerging a few days later when the fallout from the race had subsided.

Other reports suggested post-race, he had returned home to Geneva to seek sanctuary from a media intent on milking the story for all it was worth. Whether he did stay on at Imola en route home is impossible to say. Eleonora herself does not recall the specific episode, though she clearly remembers her affection for the Ferrari star: 'Didier was a very special man, maybe he could have even been the love of my life. He was the most caring, the gentlest lover I have ever known in my life.' Still a very beautiful woman in her late fifties, Vallone has carved out a niche in the aqua-aerobics industry. Much time has passed, but she fondly recalls her time with Didier. 'We used to have candlelit dinners together while Villeneuve played the piano!' she laughs. 'As you can imagine it was very intimate!' High-speed police chases and romantic threesomes – prior to Imola, Gilles and Didier had been the best of friends, sharing not only danger, but even, it transpires, romantic moments too.

That friendship was now well and truly finished. Things would never be the same again between the two men. Although they could never have known it, the clock was ticking. The 1982 San Marino Grand Prix had been a race like no other. Who but Didier Pironi could have been sat right at its very epicentre? Joined at the hip, drama and Didi. Led by a large contingent of journalists overwhelmingly sympathetic to Gilles, history would forever record the day's events to the eternal detriment of the French ace.

Twenty-one
Summertime blues

THERE was much time for reflection in the fortnight between the San Marino Grand Prix and the next race on the calendar in Belgium. Conventional wisdom suggests that Villeneuve spent the time wrestling with a profound sense of despair following his 'betrayal'. Certainly, the lay of the land had irrevocably shifted at Ferrari. However, the inner circle believed – hoped – it was a temporary rather than permanent feud.

'I spent a lot of time with Gilles after San Marino,' recalls Allan de la Plante. 'Sure, he was pissed, but more with the management than Pironi. He thought Ferrari should have handled the situation way better than they did. His attitude was, OK so the bastard got me, next time I'll get him.'

To this day, the behaviour of the Ferrari pit on that fateful Imola afternoon remains a mystery. In the wake of Forghieri's enforced absence from the Ferrari pit due to family matters, some commentators detected incompetence. Without their pit-lane maestro to guide them, the team had floundered. Forghieri would have known exactly what to do. Some pundits, on the other hand, discerned method in the apparent madness. In this version, Ferrari's deployment of those 'slow' signs, confusing and ambiguous in equal measure, had been deliberate, an act of political expediency. Rumours that Villeneuve would jump ship to either McLaren or Williams in 1983 had been circulating for some time. Joining the enemy! Intolerable! Had the Ferrari sands subtly shifted in Didier's favour? Anecdotal evidence suggests the factory were more than pleased with Didier's win. 'After so much bad luck, he deserved to win,' said one employee doorstepped at the factory gates.[39]

Speculation and intrigue. For the international sporting press, the 'feud' was heaven sent. While Gilles continued to profess his disbelief in the weeks leading up to the Belgian Grand Prix, Didier struck a more conciliatory tone. He understood his team-mate's anger, but hoped in time that the two men could resume their good relations. Notwithstanding, the press had their own ideas: 'It's war' declared *Autosport*, the UK's leading motorsport weekly. In his popular Formula 1 column in the same publication, Nigel Roebuck wrote a piece provocatively entitled 'Bad blood at Maranello'. Pure theatre. In the run up to Zolder, however, rather than the brooding Hamlet-figure portrayed in the media, Allan de la Plante found a friend focused on other priorities:

'Basically it was the same old Gilles – laughing, fooling around, happy-go-lucky. Was he obsessing over Pironi? You gotta be joking! All he could talk about was this goddam new helicopter. He never shut up about it!' This is a picture of Gilles rarely, if ever glimpsed during those post-Imola weeks. As such, it is a portrait that hardly fits a media narrative revolving around betrayal and despair. 'All this Ferrari civil war stuff made good copy,' nods de la Plante. 'The media boys were just trying to stir things up – I know because I saw them doing it.'

At Zolder, the two Ferrari pilots did not speak. Gilles was sticking to his vow, despite Didier's desire to put the episode behind them. It made for an unpleasant atmosphere in the team garage. The tension, the rancour, the bitterness, however, all faded into insignificance on the afternoon of Saturday, 8 May. Determined to end the day as Ferrari's fastest diver, minutes to go before the close of play, Villeneuve left the Ferrari pit for a final do or die effort to achieve this goal. He would not complete the lap.

Footage of the accident exists, captured by amateur cine, a few jerky, horrific seconds. To the left of frame, a red car bears down upon a white car as the cars approach a left-hander. The speed differential is stark. The Ferrari is flying. For a moment, both cars disappear out of frame. We pick up on the white car again

– the March of German veteran Jochen Mass. At the edge of the frame, the red car is glimpsed at an unholy angle. Contact has been made. The camera tracks the white car. Seconds later, the red car plummets into view, an aeroplane crumpling like paper as it passes through the sound barrier, its pilot having been catapulted into the catch fencing at frightening velocity. Over to the right, the pilot's body lying like a discarded marionette, broken. Gilles Villeneuve would die from his injuries later that evening in Leuven hospital.

Death has always been a part of Formula 1 life. However, this, this felt different. In his short career, the French Canadian had won a legion of admirers. Villeneuve's exploits had taken on a life of their own. The man from Quebec was idolised in Italy, his native Canada and beyond. Ferrari was stunned. F1 was stunned. The air still ringing with accusations of duplicity and treachery in the fallout from Imola, Didier's emotions that day can be guessed. It hardly needed stating, but the two men had not had the chance to make their peace. Now, they never would.

As his team-mate lay in his hospital bed somewhere between life and death that awful afternoon, Didier stood silently at the foot of his friend's bed, alone with his thoughts. Piccinini summed the mood up succinctly: 'Today Ferrari mourns a champion; tomorrow and always we treasure the memory of a true friend, a generous man.'

Silently and with moistened eyes, Ferrari personnel loaded up the trailers. Time to go home. Didier had rightly opted not to race. 'What saddens me even more,' said a shaken Frenchman, 'is that we ended divided, when we had always been united.' He also had some scathing criticism to lay at the door of the sport's overlords: 'Only three years ago where we cornered at 180kmh, now we reach 260kmh. One of the greatest risks we run is driving with miniskirts. If you break one, the car takes off and there is nothing the pilot can do. One can only hope for the best.' The effect in such circumstances, he likened to 'sitting on a bullet'. If anyone should know, then Didier should. Only days before Villeneuve's fatal accident, his 126C2 had flown off the Fiorano test circuit at high speed. More accidents. Ferrari – all the teams – were playing a dangerous game of Russian roulette.

Imelda records that from Zolder, Didier went straight to Geneva where he locked himself away from the world. Already, the first stirrings of an unpleasant insinuation was beginning to raise its ugly head: Pironi killed Villeneuve. Intent on beating his duplicitous French team-mate, in the grip of a black mood, Gilles had taken one risk too many that bleak Belgian day, so went the official narrative. The responsibility for the Canadian's death thus lay squarely on Pironi's shoulders. Grieving, Didier would head for the pontoon moored at the end of the garden and where he could forget himself on the glassy waters of Lake Geneva.

In the wake of sadness and loss, everybody it seemed had a theory regarding Zolder. Niki Lauda pointed the finger squarely at the hapless Mass. In the face of criticism, the Austrian qualified his position thus: 'What I meant was, I would have acted differently.' Prior to the Monaco Grand Prix, FISA's investigative committee concluded that, 'The cause of the accident is attributed to a lack of control by Villeneuve.' In reality, neither man was to blame. Both drivers had made a snap decision, the consequences of which could never have been foreseen. This body of evidence did little to prevent the media returning to their favoured account: Pironi's actions that day at Imola had directly led to his team-mate's death. As a narrative, it had obvious appeal. It also had the added bonus of tarnishing the name of Didier Pironi even further. Of the current F1 drivers, only Jacques Laffite attended Villeneuve's funeral held in the small Canadian town of his childhood. With emotions still running high, family members intimated that Didier's presence might cause more harm than good.

Still, the show had to go on. Ferrari headed to Monte Carlo with heavy hearts, but determined not to let the wheels fall off their season. A race of attrition, first the Renaults and then the Brabham expired while holding the lead. With one lap to run, Didier found himself with an unexpected lead. The drama was not over yet. Entering the dimness of Loews tunnel, the 126C2 slowed. The car had run out of fuel! Didier coasted along. Fortunately, the race was all but over. Classified in second place, for the first time that year Didier announced himself as a possible world championship contender.

Attention meanwhile turned to the vacant Ferrari seat. Even as Gilles' widow Joann met with Enzo Ferrari, the team was assessing the claims of a dozen candidates. Even the names of Reutemann and Jones had been floated. It did not take long, however, for the names of Marc Surer and Patrick Tambay to emerge as favourites, the latter having been suggested by Didier. Planning even further ahead, Mr Ferrari had asked his French lieutenant for a preference in partners for 1983 and beyond. Didier had nominated his old friend René Arnoux. It was an interesting choice. Back in 1977, it had been the man from Grenoble who had taken the honours in European Formula 2. Didier had played second fiddle. By nominating the man who had previously been a nemesis, was Didier wishing to settle a few old scores? Possibly. Perhaps more importantly, as well as rivals, he and Arnoux were good friends. After the events of recent weeks, a harmonious camp was not to be taken lightly.

Ultimately, Tambay secured the seat. For the US-based driver it was a Formula 1 lifeline. A fast, neat driver, Didier must, however, have felt confident that he could contain the ex-McLaren and Theodore man.

A trip to Detroit in early June focused the mind back to matters of track safety. In his role as president of the GPDA, Didier headed a group of drivers calling for the banning of miniskirts, that part of the chassis responsible for creating the suction that glued the cars to the tarmac. As for the hastily built circuit in downtown Detroit, Didier was less than enthusiastic. 'It's a trap,' declared the Frenchman in relation to the many holes and bumps littering the course. 'We should pack up and leave now.' Ferrari were off the pace in the concrete jungle. In the event, third place was a more than satisfactory conclusion. Though fast and reliable, the 126C2 was not performing well at every circuit. In this respect it was not quite the equal of the Renault, which seemed at home on just about any circuit, fast or slow.

One week later the circus moved north to Montreal. A month had passed since the death of Villeneuve and Canada was still mourning one of its favourite sons. Ignoring the whistles and jeers of certain sections of the grandstand, a solemn Didier dedicated his first pole position in scarlet to the memory of the fallen Ferrari warrior.

'This is my first pole position at Ferrari, and it gives me great joy achieving it at the circuit named after the man who was not only my partner, but also my friend. I dedicate this achievement, because I know if he was still among us, it is he who would have obtained the best time.' A heartfelt tribute, Didier's words helped to allay some of the ill feeling circulating around Montreal's environs. But not everybody was in the mood to forgive. Later, he ignored the accusation of 'murderer' spat from the lips of a certain journalist who passed by the hospitality tent where he and Piccinini happened to be in discussion.

At the green light on Sunday, the Ferrari stalled. The 126C2 was going nowhere. His car now a sitting duck, all Didier could do was wave his left hand about in an attempt to warn his fellow drivers of his predicament. 'I closed my eyes, placed my hands firmly on the steering wheel and waited for the shock,' recalled Didier. 'Seconds seemed so long. I heard the cars pass, pass, pass ... then nothing more. I relaxed. And suddenly the shock.'[40]

While older hands like Rosberg and Lauda avoided the Ferrari, arriving from the back row of the grid, Riccardo Paletti, a young Italian driver in only his second Grand Prix, had no such luck. With cars diving left and right in a desperate effort to avoid the red obstacle, the unsighted Osella driver ploughed into the Ferrari's rear end. The impact was brutal. The Italian rookie sustained serious chest injuries. Two days short of his 26th birthday, Paletti would later succumb to those injuries. His car a write-off, Didier had somehow survived another major incident without as much as a scratch.

Was he leading a charmed life? It seemed that way. Meanwhile chaos ensued. The Osella burst into a ball of flames. Ambulances and medical vehicles swamped the starting grid, lights flashing, sirens wailing. Soon the Italian car was lost in a plume of thick white smoke. Didier was just one of many people on the scene attempting to aid the tragic young man, to no avail. Peering into the cockpit, a scene of horror met his eyes. It would take rescuers over 20 minutes to extract Paletti from the wreckage of his machine. Though he could hardly have known it, Didier was witnessing a dress rehearsal of events that would overtake him in just four weeks' time at Hockenheim. Omens. Portents. The signs had always been there, through child and adulthood. Didier chose to ignore them ...

When the race restarted Ferrari 28 slipped steadily down the field. The spare car into which he had switched was not in the sweet spot and besides, his heart was no longer in it. First Gilles, now the Osella rookie. Didier at its epicentre, 1982 was shaping into a quite ghastly season. Carnage. No other word for it.

Back in Europe, Ferrari's development showed no sign of easing up. Modifications to the suspension, gearbox and air-cooling system yielded some promising times at Paul Ricard. New recruit Patrick Tambay impressed too. The team were going flat out, continuing to test long into the warm summer evenings. At a little after 7pm on the evening of 17 June, Didier was flying down the main straight when he ploughed into the barriers at an estimated 185mph. Miraculously, he escaped this crash with mild concussion and a cracked rib. The 126C2, however, was not so lucky. 'I gave it a good blast, certainly the most violent of my career and the cockpit has stood up well,' Didier told readers of his *Auto Hebdo* column. 'I do not know for what reason, we have not yet ascertained why, but I don't think the monocoque is even recoverable.' He was pushing the limits, but for how much longer could he expect to flirt with disaster?

Upheaval was never far away that long, hot summer. At the end of June, his three-month marriage to Catherine apparently ended – with Didier you never could tell. 'I am stunned and do not understand,' writes Imelda. 'Didier's looks and behaviour tell me "no questions". The only explanation I can obtain is laconic. He left without anything he tells me. I await clarification …' Something had happened to shatter the golden couple's harmony, but what? Didier was not saying, neither was his bride. 'Catherine's silence on the matter is impenetrable,' notes Madame Pironi, whose bewilderment is obvious. It seems that upon his return to Geneva, Didier had made a discovery that radically altered his attitude towards his wife, profound enough for him to immediately abandon their marriage. Extracting information from Didier was never an easy task at the best of times. Turning detective, Imelda began her investigations. They led her to a conclusion she could hardly believe, the possible involvement of a third party, *un anonyme pilot*. Domestic dramas aside, just weeks after the acrimonious events described above, Catherine would be seen in the Zandvoort paddock, fresh and vivacious, oozing glamour ...

Complicated. Never more apt was the term than when applied to Didier's private life. Some time in early summer, the paparazzi snapped him on the pavement of a busy Parisian boulevard smooching the female driver of a car against which he knelt. The mystery woman was none other than Véronique Jannot, one of France's leading actresses.

In mid-June Didier attended a ceremony at the Monza circuit near Milan to commemorate the life of his late team-mate. Observers at the beautiful garden in front of the Royal Villa were shocked to see the cool, phlegmatic Frenchman break down in tears upon presenting a rose to the memory of his fallen colleague. Roses had been a favourite of Gilles. In happier times they had been a favourite gift to give Joann. 'Didier's tears surprised me,' wrote *Rombo*'s Mario Manini, 'as he has never been one to publicly display his emotions.' True, but that summer Didier was riding an emotional rollercoaster. Villeneuve's death had been hard enough, but now his nights were also haunted by visions of that horrific Montreal accident, the fire, the lights, the chaos.

Finally, all the anguish, sorrow and regret bottled up inside had broken through. The Frenchman was still weeping at the ceremony's end. 'Who actually is Didier Pironi?' asked Manini in the same article. 'I think nobody knows him too deeply.' That same old question attempting to unravel 'a silent form', which, in the words of the poet, 'dost tease us out of thought.'[41]

As the heat of summer enveloped the continent, back on the racetrack Ferrari finally began to flex their muscles. Joined by Tambay in his first outing for the Scuderia, Didier won the Dutch Grand Prix on 3 July in fine style. Although unable to match the Renaults in qualifying, within five laps car number 28 calmly overtook first Arnoux and then Prost. Thereafter, he simply disappeared into the sand dunes. Still aching from his Paul Ricard shunt two weeks earlier, he had declined the offer of a pain-killing injection prior to the start of the race. When you're winning, he would later say, you don't feel pain. So impressed was *Grand Prix International*, its chief writer compared the effortless manner of Didier's victory to the many wins achieved by the legendary Jim

Clark. High praise indeed. Talk turned to the world championship. Victory had brought him to within one point of current leader, John Watson. Meanwhile, Tambay had performed with some promise on his race debut. Patrick drove a solid race, even if he never really troubled his high-flying compatriot. With the coming of summer, it was as if the shy, diffident French pilot had metamorphosed into a potential F1 superstar.

Finishing runner-up at the British Grand Prix two weeks later took Didier to the top of the F1 table for the first time in his career:

Pironi	35 pts
Watson	30 pts
Lauda	24 pts
Rosberg	21 pts

When he had realised it was the Cosworth-powered cars that held all the aces around the Brands Hatch circuit this particular day, Didier had wisely settled for a points finish. He was driving like a champion. Now he was thinking like one. Second place behind Lauda was therefore a more than satisfactory outcome. Moreover, with Tambay taking third place, Ferrari consolidated their place behind McLaren in the constructors' race. Summer of 1982, Didier and Ferrari were making giant strides. Like a butterfly born to dazzle for but a few days, Didier's time in the sun, basking at the top of the F1 summit, would last the briefest of moments.

Twenty-two

Hockenheim

FOR one magical moment in July of 1982, life seemed to offer myriad possibilities to the French cavalier. The 126C2 was finally proving to be a very competitive machine, proof of which had been evident enough in Holland. Furthermore, Didier was leading the world championship and was now a strong favourite to achieve his dream of becoming France's first Formula 1 world champion. Although events at Imola, Zolder and Montreal would disturb his karma through 1982 and beyond, the pain was gradually diminishing. Life went on. Intricate and tangled to a quite exceptional degree, his private life was also about to take an interesting detour. As a heatwave settled over La Republic, professional and private spheres finally settling, Didi could have been forgiven for thinking that the worst was over.

Ever since he had watched her performance in the film *Le Toubib* alongside Alain Delon, Didier had been intrigued by Véronique Jannot, a 25-year-old actress and singer well known to French audiences. With her distinctive short, strawberry blonde hair, petite frame and almost boyish look, Jannot could not have been any more different to the likes of Vallone and Bleynie. Nonetheless, something clicked. As he later told *L'Automobile* magazine,[42] his interest had been further heightened upon reading an interview Jannot had given to a celebrity magazine. The actress, he had instantly felt, possessed an 'original and engaging personality'. In 1982 she was starring in the popular television soap opera *Pause-*

café where her role as a cheery, indefatigable social worker had endeared her to an entire nation, Didier included. 1982 had also seen the release of one of her biggest hits, the haunting *J'Ai fait l'amour avec la mer* (I made love to the sea), a great favourite of Didier's. He decided he had to meet this vivacious young girl.

In her memoir, Jannot recalls receiving a call out of the blue one day from the Ferrari superstar. Would she like to accompany him on a charity assignment for his sponsors Haribo? Véronique accepted. It would be the start of a whirlwind romance of unsurpassed intensity. In the days that followed the charity event Didier called several times from Modena where testing of the 126C2 continued. Movie star and F1 driver arranged to go for dinner: 'Our eyes met and never once dropped,' recalled Jannot. 'I knew something had happened. It was the beginning of the summer of 1982.' The couple became inseparable. Theirs was a romance straight from the pages of fiction. Together they went on walks, drives and moonlit boat rides, where they gazed up in wonder at the vast expanse of stars, silent, indescribably happy.

Shortly after their first meeting, the couple accepted an invitation to speak to *L'Automobile* magazine. The location chosen for the interview was an equestrian centre near Toulon. Didier and Véronique enjoyed the experience immensely; horse riding, lunching and chatting, the young lovers giggled, blissfully happy in the first flushes of love. The interview was a regular feature of the magazine, in which stars from different vocations met to share experiences of their professions. When approached to take part, Didier had nominated Véronique as his choice to compare notes: the actor and the racer. He asked her about life as an actress: stage fright, improvising and suchlike. In a similar vein, she asked him about fear and the F1 driver; had he ever known real fear? Their affair in its infancy, the lovers' eyes sparkled. Ahead stretched endless summer days and nights.

Véronique was delighted to accept an invitation to Paul Ricard to watch her hero perform at the French Grand Prix on 25 July. It was their first public outing as a couple. The waiflike actress took up a place in the Ferrari garage, from where she had a ringside view of her hero taking the fight to the mighty Renault team. It was a bakingly hot weekend on this part of France's Mediterranean coast. Practice days were hot and humid. If Ferrari personnel were shocked to find one of France's most familiar faces hanging around the garage, they did not betray it. Catherine had disappeared. In her place now stood Véronique. One beautiful woman had supplanted another. All in a day's work for the dashing French lieutenant on course to be crowned champion of the world. At the height of their powers, tanned and content in one another's presence, France's newest celebrity couple exuded well-being.

Although he now led the world championship, some sections of the Italian and French media were less than impressed. Didier, they said, was driving like an 'accountant', his eyes fixed a little too firmly on racking up points. Win or bust; some sectors of the media seemed to prefer this all or nothing approach even if it meant compromising points finishes. Had the Frenchman lost his bottle? 'It is not true I have softened,' said Didier, stung by the criticism. 'The fact is that in some races it is impossible to win at all costs.' The critics remained unconvinced.

On a blisteringly hot race afternoon, the Ferraris had no answer to the Renault turbo and in particular the French car's Michelin tyres. In qualifying the Italian squad had been almost 1.5 seconds off Arnoux's pole-winning time, superiority the yellow and white cars maintained in the race. Didier and Patrick finished a well-beaten third and fourth. Four points for Didier, however, increased his lead over Watson to nine. The world championship was within touching distance. The media, however, was not happy. 'The public,' declared an influential and widely read Italian magazine, 'tend to snub the driver who takes to the track with an abacus.' Similarly, a popular French motorsport title editorialised with a scathing headline entitled, 'Pironi's fear of winning.' The same article then went on to joke that the driver of car number 28 had been enjoying a 'nap' on what had admittedly been a somnolent Provençal afternoon. But these half-serious critiques failed to account for his team-mate's similarly lacklustre performance. Patrick had finished a further half a minute behind his team leader. If Didi had been dozing, Patrick must have been in a coma! Since the events of Imola and Zolder, the knives had been out for the Frenchman. Now, they were being sharpened. After standing for 'La Marseillaise' with the feuding Renault drivers, Didier headed straight for his motorhome. Washed and showered, he reappeared in the paddock laconic and relaxed, in the immortal words of Mr Roebuck, 'mocking the razzmatazz around him with that faintly mocking smile...'[43]

Inseparable, Didier and Véronique next headed east along the coast. He was eager to take his new love to St Tropez, to share with her its air, its ambience, its magic. It was an enchanting time for both partners. Alain Prost and Tullio Abbate were also in town. Didier joined the men down at the port for some powerboat fun and frolics. His love of these big, powerful boats had long been known. An infinite stretch of sea, a warm, benign sun, and the sheer thrill of bouncing atop St Tropez's turquoise waters in one of these 'sea monsters' – this was Didier's world, his playground.

It was not all play though. Didier continued to work hard as GPDA president. Under his stewardship, the drivers had recently voted for a ban on the dreaded skirts, responsible for so many accidents and incidents over the past four years. In that calm, authoritative way of his, he was also organising and then explaining the merits of various insurance packages tailored to the needs of his fellow drivers. Six months ago he had sworn to improve the safety of his chosen profession. He was determined to do just that. While his heart was full of joy that summer of wonder, his attaché case was stuffed full with any number of legal documents and files.

From southern France the lovers made their way to Heidelberg in the south-western corner of Germany. A strong result at Hockenheim, venue for the German Grand Prix, would all but seal the 1982 world championship in Didier's favour. Indeed, Ferrari were fancied to do well at the high-speed circuit which snakes its way through acres of densely packed pine forests. Formula 1's glamour couple arrived in Heidelberg in carefree mood. While Didier was excelling himself in the 126C2, his new beau watched her knight with admiration: 'I'm in love with my helmeted hero,' wrote Jannot in her autobiography. 'I am full of a happiness so intense that I almost hurt.'[44]

The man who haunted himself, the Ferrari ace went off the circuit during Friday's session at almost the same spot that 24 hours later would be the scene of such mayhem. Portents and omens – always, everywhere. Not that the skirmish upset Didier's rhythm.

When he ended up easily fastest at close of play, all bets for the championship were off. Practice times revealed a driver at the very top of his game. He was almost a full second faster than his nearest challenger:

Pironi	1'47.947
Prost	1'48.890
Arnoux	1'49.256
Piquet	1'49.415
Tambay	1'49.570

Saturday brought atrocious weather conditions to the Baden-Württemberg region of Germany. Didier and Véronique left the Holiday Inn hotel just before 9am. Despite the cold, grey weather, the couple laughed and smiled on the short drive to the circuit.

Grim morning notwithstanding, by 10am the qualifying session was ready to begin. Perhaps not surprisingly the majority of drivers opted to stay in the relative warmth and security of the team garages. With the skies darkening and rain starting to increase in both frequency and magnitude, improving on Friday's time was clearly not on the agenda. With a wet race on Sunday a distinct possibility, there was much work to do testing out wet configurations. Somewhat reluctantly, a handful of cars ventured out of the pits, among them Ferrari number 28. As expected, lap times were substantially slower than the previous day. The Hockenheim circuit was getting wetter by the minute. Undaunted, Didier exited the team garage to drive what would be the last four laps of his Grand Prix career. He would later say the car had given him a great feeling, wet track notwithstanding. The howl of the frantic V6 engine reverberated around the eerily quiet grandstands. The Frenchman was not holding back. Lapping five seconds faster than his team-mate, Didier was brimming with confidence. Time to start another lap, his fourth.

Blasting out of the chicane, he was catching a slower car hand over fist. Derek Daly was circulating some seven or eight seconds slower than the car with the prancing horse insignia. The Williams pulled off the racing line; its Irish driver had seen the rapidly approaching Ferrari and was now courteously moving over to allow the faster car past. At least that is how it looked from the cockpit of the number 28 car …

A Formula 1 racing car turned aeroplane, the 126C2 soared into the cheerless German skies. Didier's fate now lay in the lap of higher powers. The Ferrari climbed higher, 30 metres up, above the forests of pine that typify this part of the circuit. 'It's over,' thought Didier. The accident he had feared for so long, the accident he had been warning about for so long, had been avoiding even longer, had finally arrived.

Daly had not been alone on the circuit at the moment the Ferrari had arrived on his tail. An idling Alain Prost had been in front of the British car. The Irishman had actually not even seen the red car bearing down upon him. Derek had simply been trying to pass the Renault. Didier had assumed the Irish driver was simply being polite, observing F1 etiquette. Here then was a scenario with all the hallmarks of a misunderstanding. The Williams moved to the right. A wall of thick spray now presented itself. Trusting in himself and his God, Didier accelerated hard into the mist. It happened instantaneously, a single second, no more, the contact between the cars' tyres – Ferrari front and Renault back – and then the springboard effect as the red car launched into orbit. A ghostly spectre, the Renault had materialised out of nowhere. Nothing to be done. Time stood still. In the cockpit of his car, Didier closed his eyes and waited for the end.

Crashing to earth, the Ferrari performed a series of sickening somersaults. Alain Prost, meanwhile, could only watch in horror: 'I felt a violent shock; I saw a car pass me overhead, as if taking off. A real bullet that flew 30 metres into the sky.' Whereas Gilles had been flung out of his chariot after the harnesses had snapped, Didier was spared a similar fate. His safety belt held firm, at least part of it. As it tumbled along the saturated tarmac, the 126C2 disintegrated into pieces like a broken biscuit. The accursed car eventually came to rest 300 metres from the point of impact. An air crash scene. Surely, nobody could survive an accident of this violence.

Nelson Piquet quickly arrived on the scene, then Mansell and Cheever. Rain was now mercilessly bucketing down upon the actors below. It was a little before 10.30am. In the mangled wreckage, the pilot moved his head, which in itself seemed hard to believe. 'Get me out of here!' Didier screamed first in French and then English. With 190 litres of fuel on board, the risk of fire was all too real. Perhaps the words of the Paul Ricard sage echoed through his mind: 'You will never become world champion ... You will die in an accident by fire ...' Upon removing his friend's helmet, the Brazilian recoiled. The blonde, freckled face he knew so well had drained of colour, and now, as blood oozed from his nose, resembled something grotesque, alien. 'Get me out of here!' Nelson glanced at the remains of the car. What he saw next made his blood run cold: a bone protruding from a bloody gash on the leg of his friend. Thankfully, the emergency services swiftly arrived on the scene. Dazed, Nelson drifted away. Having vacated his smashed Renault, and unable to stomach the sight of his colleague's suffering, Alain Prost headed straight back to the garages.

Didier had sustained a catalogue of injuries: multiple fractures to both legs including the tibia and fibula bones in the right ankle as well as to the humerus bone in his left arm. His nose had also been broken. On top of which he had suffered severe bruising to the head (haematoma). Blood loss was profound. Worryingly, the pilot's system had also gone into shock, a common reaction to major trauma and a potentially fatal situation if not treated immediately. Early reports of a brain injury thankfully proved to be nothing more than the product of speculation.

Her heart thumping, Véronique ran along the track. She had to get to Didier; she had to. The Ferrari pit had received news of the incident the moment it had happened. As she approached the scene of the crash, the actress spied the wreckage and the debris strewn hundreds of yards around the track. *Oh my Didier! My love!* Stopping her in her tracks, the stewards blocked the distraught girl's path to her lover. She fought. She screamed. However, there was nothing to be done. The emergency services were already on the scene. Shaken to her core, the sobbing young woman allowed herself to be ushered back to the pits.

In the remains of his cockpit, Didier remained conscious. Deep in shock, he watched the chaos around him unfold in monochrome vision. It was as if he was watching a black and white movie – a movie from hell. When a member of the medical corps mentioned the need for amputation, he snapped out of his stupor:

'No! Please! Don't take my legs!' begged Didier.

Meanwhile, Professor Sid Watkins, F1's official doctor, arrived. Before him a mess of human bone and tissue. It did not look good, but the doc promised the hysterical driver he would do all that he could to save his legs. Heavily sedated, Didier would drift in and out of consciousness over the next hour.

When Marco Piccinini arrived on the scene, one look told him a great career had ended. The dream was over. A deeply religious man, Marco tried to make sense of the carnage before him. It was not easy. Why? Why should this happen, and happen now? Life was unfathomable, that much he accepted. It was also unfair, brutally so.

Back in the Ferrari pit Véronique was inconsolable. The lovers had spent a matter of weeks together, just a handful of summer days in which to discover the essence of one another. Now, the man she had fallen so deeply in love with, the man in whom she had discerned so many hidden depths, that same man lay mangled on the hard, grey bitumen of a German racetrack, doctors struggling to save his life, torrential rain mocking his agony. It was unjust, intolerable, senseless.

It was life.

After 25 minutes, the rescuers freed the pilot from his prison. Nearby a helicopter waited to fly him to the nearby University of Heidelberg hospital, which just happened to be Germany's leading centre for road traffic trauma. Later he would say he had felt no pain, not until his stretcher knocked inadvertently into the 'copter's door causing him to cry out. Up into the dark, grey sky the helicopter went leaving a scene of utter desolation on the ground below.

Michele Alboreto returned to the Tyrrell garage fighting back tears. He and Didier had always got along well since they had appeared on Italian TV together. An emotional, sensitive man, Michele had seen enough. All he could think about was getting over to the hospital. So when burly team boss Ken Tyrrell ordered him back on track, Michele let his boss know his feelings in no uncertain terms:

'I have a friend in hospital right now! And you ask me to get in the car! You are not serious!'

'You must get in the car straight away, to get over the shock,' reasoned Tyrrell, who had seen more than his fair share of motor racing tragedies over the years.

'No! I can't. I'm shocked by what has happened and by the insecurity of these cars,' replied a visibly shaken driver. 'I just want to know how Pironi is.'

'At least do a few laps …'

'No. You drive if you want.' With that, Michele headed off in the direction of Heidelberg. Ligier driver Eddie Cheever wept in the team motorhome. Arriving within seconds of the crash, Didier's old rival from European Formula 2 had witnessed the aftermath in all its grisly horror. 'I saw Pironi's right foot,' choked the American. 'It didn't seem to belong to either leg.' Jacques Laffite was also despondent. When Guy Ligier invited his drivers to reacquaint themselves with their car, Jacques responded by offering his overalls to his boss.

At Heidelberg a medical team led by consultant surgeon Dr Mischowski awaited the helicopter. At 11.30am, the stricken driver was transferred to the operating theatre after blood and respiratory functions had been checked. The priority was saving the right leg. Before entering theatre, Didier caught sight of Piccinini who, along with Véronique, Alboreto, Lauda and Cheever, haunted the hospital corridors.

During the next hours, conflicting reports of the intervention would emerge. Initially, it seemed likely that at least one leg – the right – would require amputation.

'Marco, please be careful how you tell my mother,' whispered Didier as the medical team prepared him for surgery. 'She has a bad heart, and the shock …'

Didier had crashed exactly 13 weeks to the very day since Villeneuve's fatal accident at Zolder.

One thousand kilometres south of Heidelberg, the Pironi-Dolhem clan were entertaining part of their extended Italian family in the St Tropez villa. Noon, and the party stood around the pool basking in the Mediterranean sunshine. Leaving her guests, Imelda returned indoors to answer the telephone.

'Mrs Pironi! It's Marco.'

'Marco? Oh, how are you Marco?'

'Didier has had a big accident. He has broken both legs. He is in hospital, but he is OK. Mrs Pironi?'

Imelda's eyes had fallen on the TV screen where a programme had been interrupted by a news flash: 'Champion injured at Hockenheim.' Face contorted, ghostly, eyes closed and blood flowing from his nostrils, notwithstanding, mother recognised son immediately. Imelda watched the screen aghast. Didier! My Didier!

'Marco! You are not telling me the truth!'

'Madame, I swear to you! It was Didier who asked me to warn you.'

An hour later, an anxious family party took off from Nice in a private jet put at their disposal by a family friend. The group, which included Catherine and her brother, arrived at the hospital early that evening fearing the worst. Dr Mischowski's team had just finished a gruelling five-and-a-half-hour operation to save the right leg. In the recovery room Véronique tenderly watched over her lover, an angel of mercy. At this stage, it was difficult to tell whether the operation had been a success. If the attempt to reconnect the vital arteries and stimulate blood flow to the limb failed, the threat of amputation would not only become probable but unavoidable.

Meanwhile the party from Nice had arrived. When Piccinini gently suggested that girlfriend make way for wife, Véronique broke down. The thought of leaving her man in this, his hour of need, was unbearable to her. After some persuasion, she left the fallen hero moments before the official Mrs Pironi and Imelda entered dressed in the sterile white hospital-issue gowns and masks. The risk of infection was high and would be for several days. Gangrene was just one of many potential hazards.

'Mum ...'

'He is calm, relaxed, almost smiling,' records Imelda. 'His eyelids, round black eyes, bring out the blue of his eyeballs. He's hot, shirtless, muscular, tanned, blonde hair as in battle. It is reassuring.'

After aunt Ilva and 'uncle' Louis and José had looked in, Marco showed Catherine into the room. Didier looked serenely at the woman with whom he had exchanged wedding vows just months before. His clear blue eyes welling up, he addressed himself to his wife: 'You see, the good Lord has punished me!' Catherine burst into tears. The woman who had once so dazzled him understood the meaning well, even if those around did not. Piccinini escorted her out of the room. Didier intimated that he did not wish to see his wife again. The young woman would leave her superstar racer and shortly after fall into the arms of another superstar, Alain Delon, for whom she had carried a torch since meeting the actor at the age of 18. Didier and Catherine were over, at least officially …

Professor Mischowski ushered the family, minus Mrs Pironi, into his office:

'Didier's legs are crushed,' announced the surgeon gravely. 'The right poses a very big problem in terms of circulation – the veins are cut. In a first response, I re-connected as I could. A piece of tibia in his right leg is missing. I intend to re-operate tonight.' At this point, the name of another surgeon cropped up. As the world's leading authority in orthopaedic surgical techniques, Paris-based Dr Emile Letournel seemed an obvious choice to seek counsel from at this point. Mischowski agreed. Holidaying in Barcarès in the south of France, Emmanuel agreed to help all he could. The eminent surgeons spent some time discussing the Pironi case and all its many complications via telephone. Letournel promised also to come to Heidelberg himself in a few days. It was just past 11pm when Mischowski finally removed his surgical apparel for the final time that day. In the intensive care unit, the patient was sleeping soundly. The doctor had done all he could.

By morning the prognosis looked better. To the delight of Imelda and Véronique, who arrived later that Sunday afternoon, Didier greeted them with a smile.

'Look! My toes!' Didier seemed almost delirious with joy to find his foot still attached to his leg. Since the moment of the accident, he had feared losing at least one of his lower limbs, maybe both. Under the circumstances, his euphoria was understandable. However, his ordeal was not over yet. The possibility of infection was high. Added to which, there was the very sinister risk of a necrosis developing, the condition that results in death of tissue which has been starved of blood supply. Didier was not out of the woods yet, not by a long way. Nonetheless, Mischowski struck an optimistic note on the morning after:

'Pironi passed a fairly quiet night,' announced the doctor, 'and there are encouraging signs, because he moved the toes of his right foot, a clear sign that the circulation is good.' Although it seemed a world away and hardly important, Patrick Tambay had just won the German Grand Prix and now, along with several other drivers, anxiously awaited news at the hospital. 'There is no Prost,' remarks Imelda.

Under such tragic circumstances it would be normal practice for a team to withdraw its cars as a mark of respect. Didier had however insisted that Patrick be allowed to start the race. With four races of the season left to run, Ferrari's new recruit might just be able to take enough points away from the likes of Watson or Rosberg to enable his team leader to cling on to his world championship lead. It was a long shot. It was Didier's best and only shot. By winning in Germany, Patrick had suggested he might be able to do just as much: protect his team-mate's championship.

Five days after the accident, on 12 August Dr Mischowski entered the room in high spirits, bottle of champagne in hand. 'We've won! We've won! It's moving!' Circulation had resumed its usual course. Thanks to the swift actions of Sid Watkins on that foul Hockenheim morning, and later the skill of the Heidelberg medical team, the pilot's legs had been saved. The family celebrated with a gala dinner. Didier immediately declared his intention to return to Formula 1.

Twenty-three
A love of infinite spaces

FOR Véronique Jannot the weekend of 7–8 August seemed hallucinatory, a bad dream from which she must surely wake. It broke her heart to see Didier lying in bed beneath a multitude of drips and pipes. She wanted to be strong, for his sake. It was not easy. In the days following the crash, when the threat of amputation had still hung heavily in the air, the actress never once left her hero's side. The Heidelberg staff even erected a temporary bed to enable her to do just that. She had arrived in Germany a young, carefree girl, madly in love, stood on the brink of a great adventure.

Days later, those hopes and dreams had been shattered beyond all recognition.

On 13 August, Professor Letournel arrived at the clinic having flown in from Perpignan in the private plane belonging to Didier's good friend, McLaren part-owner Mansour Ojjeh. Glasses resting on his forehead, he inspected the patient's wounds at length. It was an anxious time for Didier and Véronique. They waited patiently for the verdict of this kindly and jovial man. Eventually, the professor declared himself satisfied.

'Next week you come to Choisy. Then I will operate! With what has already been done, I think I can keep the mobility of your ankles.'

A ray of hope. Didier was overjoyed. With his ankles restored there would be nothing to prevent him returning to his former life, the life that had been so cruelly ripped away from him so recently. And Formula 1? Perhaps. The young lovers dared to hope.

True to his word, almost two weeks after first arriving at the Heidelberg clinic, an air ambulance transferred Didier to the Clinique Porte de la Choisy in central Paris, the hospital where Emile occupied the position of head of the department for orthopaedic surgery. Didier was installed on the sixth floor of the hospital in room 626, the room he would call home for the next three and a half months. Letournel ordered a bed too for Véronique. This little room overlooking the southern edge of central Paris, claustrophobic, anodyne, mundane, became the couple's world, both a sanctuary and a prison. On late summer afternoons, the hum of traffic from the nearby Boulevard Périphérique – the four-lane highway that encircles central Paris – would filter up into the room. On such afternoons, hot and languid, the couple longed to fly. Oh how they longed to fly.

Thus began a doctor–patient relationship that the professor would readily confess gave him many a sleepless night that summer of 1982 and beyond. Didier's was a tricky case, one of the most complex he had yet encountered in his long and distinguished career. Although he had broken both legs, the right presented a particular problem. Added to the multiple fractures and the constant battle against infection from pseudomonas – a virulent microbe – Letournel and his team faced an even greater problem, one that would test even the celebrated surgeon's skills to the limit: 17cm of bone was missing from the right tibia (shinbone), lost somewhere on the Hockenheim circuit. Understanding the complex mechanisms of the human skeletal system and its inter-relationships, in order to get Didier mobile again, the doctor knew he had a single option. The Papineau technique is a process whereby the bone is gradually built back up, piece by little piece. Over time, the body knits these bone fragments into a new tibia. In order to facilitate this painstaking process, a fixator or metal rod is used to preserve the length of leg during the healing process.

'The treatment is very long, the patient must understand and accept it,' explains Francine, Letournel's long-term partner who bore witness to the professor's agonising over the case and who came to call the ex-Ferrari ace a friend. 'In the case of Didier, several grafts were necessary because the infection did not respond to antibiotics. That is, the grafts were eaten by the infection that persisted.'

Disappointments became a frequent occurrence of life in room 626. That autumn the stricken driver was riding an emotional rollercoaster where moments of wild optimism were just as quickly followed by periods of introspection. 'Every time a transplant failed,' remembers Francine, 'the prof and Didier looked at one another. Eventually Didier would say, "OK, we start again."'

His angel sat faithfully at his side, never wavering in her devotion. Didier endured a never-ending cycle of assessments, general anaesthetics and operations over the months that followed. Some of them, like the one that took place on 26 August, lasted for up to 14 hours. It was a pivotal intervention, one of many to come. Prior to the start of the procedure, the medics discovered that the ulna of the right arm was also broken, overlooked in the haste to treat his other more serious injuries. To cap an unnerving day, sometime into the procedure the patient awoke! Didier could clearly hear the professor delivering one of his celebrated running commentaries. By moving his humerus, the patient alerted the surgeon, who duly administered more anaesthetic. Later, when he came round, Didier was able to recount the professor's monologue almost word for word!

Such marathon sessions on the operating table were not without consequence. Didier would arrive back from theatre blue in the face, shivering uncontrollably. At such times Véronique would hold him tightly, describing the warm, golden beaches they would one day visit together when this nightmare finally came to an end. In the meantime, while the nurses tended to Didier's medical needs, Véronique focused on his personal needs: washing, shaving, cleaning and feeding the man she adored; above all else, being there for him: 'Didier was everything to me. He was my passion, my love, my child.'[45] Sometimes she would push her man around the hospital floors in his wheelchair, the couple squealing with laughter as Didier played the role of pilot. Days became weeks became months.

The arrival every day at lunch and dinnertime of Imelda and Ilva bearing home-cooked delicacies helped to relieve the monotony. An Italian boy at heart, Didier always loved his momma's (and aunt's) food. In addition, there, amid the porcelain plates presenting their delicious wares, always a single orchid, Didier's flower. 'He really appreciates these moments,' observes Imelda, 'that bring him pleasure, relaxation, a family flavour. He shares these feasts with his love, Véronique.' Visits from his F1 colleagues also helped raise his spirits. Needless to say, occasionally the situation got on top of him and hope would turn to despair. With Véronique's help, he soon snapped out of such gloomy moods. A constant stream of telephone calls from friends and associates also helped divert attention away from his predicament. Didier was especially delighted when Enzo Ferrari telephoned one day and promised him a place back with the Scuderia upon his recovery. Thus the hours passed, slowly. Time seemed to come to a standstill in room 626 that summer.

Watching the remaining Grands Prix from his bed, Didier kept a keen eye on the Formula 1 championship battle. Thanks to his consistency, Keke Rosberg was edging closer to Didier's 39 points. Victory in the Swiss Grand Prix on 29 August saw the Finnish driver finally overhaul his rival in the table, 42–39. Winning the world championship from a hospital bed had always been a forlorn hope. Nevertheless, it was another downwards dip on the Pironi rollercoaster. Good and bad days, he had his share of both.

Into this milieu one day, stepped Jean Cau. The journalist had been sent by *Paris Match* to write a story about the tragedy that had befallen France's celebrity couple. Arriving at Choisy, Cau immediately sensed the delicacy of the situation before him. 'We do not know how to approach this story – a story of love,' he mused in the introductory paragraph to his front-page scoop, 'Pironi: Sauve par l'amour' (Pironi: saved by love)[46]. 'We are afraid of being indiscreet, rude, awkward …' Reservations aside, there was huge appetite for a story so tragic, Shakespeare himself might have composed it. Didier's plight had touched people around the world, proof of which could be found in the stack of cards and letters delivered daily to the hospital from all four corners of the globe. One such letter arrived from Argentina. The writer – a member of the Argentinian rugby team that had crashed in the Andes – urged him to not give up hope. Other letters arrived from fans expressing their sadness. From Vienna, a young Austrian girl was so moved by his plight she sent the driver drawings she had sketched of him and the 126C2. Touched by the simplicity of such gestures, Didier ensured he replied to every letter.

Among the many packages sent, a couple of paperbacks arrived, thrillers, sent by 'the woman of your life' but one too embarrassed to visit in person. Didier understood the subtext perfectly.

Cau's piece perfectly captured the emotion contained within the four walls of room 626 that unforgettable summer. Noting Jannot's presence in the sickroom, he described the exact moment he clasped eyes on the actress: 'She was there and did not have time to escape, like a deer, this gentle animal which she resembles.' Clearly smitten by his 'deer', Cau's attention turned to the medical paraphernalia on show:

'But what are these weird little tubes that Didier has at the end of his feet? She tells me it's "suction drains" and it sucks traces of infection that might occur in the legs. What a nurse we have here! And he [Didier] looks at her in the corner with the full happiness of an absolutely infinite tenderness.'

Cau continues his piece in the same delicate, almost reverent tone. What emerges is a fascinating window into Didier's world at this time. The *Paris Match* writer notes how the couple clasp hands throughout the interview, afraid almost to let go of one another:

'Where did you find this gem?' 'On the Castellet circuit', replies Didier, 'She agreed to come and never left ... Eight days later, at Hockenheim, I had (he smiles) a traffic accident ...' Cau is spellbound, overwhelmed by the tenderness he his privy to: 'I listen to this extraordinary poem they recite in low voices, this song of life, where love is born and death conquered. They will go to the sun, they told me, when Didier recovers.'

Interest in the couple indeed reached fever pitch. Not only were the mailbags full, but a constant stream of guests made their way to Choisy that autumn. Much to Letournel's chagrin, racing drivers, actors and politicians joined a queue of international journalists eager for a scoop. All arrived at room 626 to pay homage to the fallen hero. On one occasion, Piero Lardi Ferrari arrived with Marco Piccinini. They presented Didier with a beautiful sculpture of a rearing horse, the emblem of Ferrari.

Inscribed in marble underneath were the following words: 'a Didier vero Campione Mondiale 1982' (to Didier the true 1982 world champion). Flattered as he was to receive this trophy, as ever Didier remained pragmatic:

'I have often read that I am the moral 1982 world champion. This means absolutely nothing. We play according to precise rules. The world champion is he who accumulates more points than his opponents. The rest is literature!'

When *GEO* asked Didier to compose a piece for the December edition of their social science magazine, he readily agreed to produce some 'literature' of his own. In the piece, written from his Paris sickbed, the pilot pens an extraordinary composition, part biography, part daydream, the result of which is a metaphysical journey through time and space. As an insight into his emotional state at this time it is well worth quoting in detail. Written in the first person, a narrative unfolds that is as compelling as it is poignant.[47] It begins:

'Wet, this autumn evening! It rains on Paris. The last visitors have left. Professor Letournel shouted that he thought my room, between two operations, was noisier than the winning team's garage at the finish of the 24 Hours of Le Mans! Draconian instructions: ten minutes per visitor. Tomorrow, small passage on the operating table. Like insect bites, I do not count them. My gaze comes to rest on the model of the Ferrari, placed on my radiator, between two piles of books. I close my eyes. I dream ... '

Staring at the model car, Didier enters a trance-like state from where the reader is taken on an astonishing journey into the realms of fancy and whimsy. Projecting himself into a future time when he is free of the physical torments that assail his body, his reverie takes him to Italy, to Ferrari:

'I'm in Maranello, near Turin, on Ferrari's private test track. We are in April or May 1983 ... I recognise the bald silhouette of Ballentani, my chief mechanic ...' Didier's friend and colleague is preparing the new Ferrari. On seeing the machine, the writer's heart skips a beat: 'That car is mine. In a few minutes, I will slip behind its wheel. Am I unconscious, or mad, to feel this violent urge to drive a Formula 1 car only nine months after so closely brushing death, and even closer to the amputation of my two legs?'

Interspersed into this surreal, introspective dreamscape, the author reveals tantalising glimpses into his own nature and essence: 'I think I am a sentimental boy, extraordinarily attached to life and all that it brings. I love orchids, astronomy, the sea. Whenever today I enter a greenhouse, I have the same pleasure as at the age of 15. As a child, the catechism did not bring me the expected answers on the creation of the world, so one day I decided to immerse myself in a book of astronomy. The taste for infinite spaces remained with me.'

Didier goes on to reveal his 'weakness for solitude in nature' and following in the footsteps of Peterson, Depailler and Villeneuve, a fatalistic conviction that one day he will similarly 'hurt himself'.

Just as revealing is the scenario he conjures up to describe the reunion with his faithful crew: 'In a joyful ruckus, the entire Ferrari team from Maranello welcomes me. They look as happy to see me as I do to find them. I catch Ballentani's eye. He smiles at me. I'm warm in the heart.' In the midst of these celebrations in which the team welcomes home its prodigal son, the writer senses the Ferrari engineers are wary, reluctant even. The team is worried about his legs, worried if he will be able to perform to the level he did before the accident. Didier dismisses their concerns, 'Come on guys, forget my legs – don't be afraid!' Evidently, returning to the fold will present its own problems. Not least convincing a sceptical team – Formula 1 itself – of his physical well-being.

He observes the team lovingly preparing the red chariot. 'She's beautiful, is she not?' asks Tomaini, the chief engineer. 'She's ready for you.' Didier slips into the cockpit once more:

'Hello to you, old accomplice! My eyes caress the dials, unconsciously note the temperature of water and oil, stop at the pressure indicator of the turbo. My hands play with the steering wheel, the buttons, the gearshift.' Reacquainted with his Ferrari all the doubts vanish both internal and external. The pilot has returned to his spiritual home, whole again. Although still haunted by the events of Hockenheim, Didier has the strength to face his demons. What follows is a vivid description of the accident in which the author recounts his thoughts that grim morning. He recalls, for example, the sensation of flying through the air, the ground coming ever closer: 'Fear? No. I did not have time. No pinch in the heart, no cold sweat, no anxiety. The certainty, simply, that I was going to die …'

Nothing can stop him pursuing his dream, not even memories of the horrific accident. He is ready to start all over again; ready to conquer the world once more. It is a goal that gets him through the long days and even longer nights in the clinic. It is also a way to cope with the physical and spiritual pain, and he clings to it, tenaciously so. In reality, the satisfactory reconstruction of his legs, in particular that troublesome right tibia and ankle, would take far longer to achieve than he might have hoped as winter 1982 set in. Ahead lay a prolonged and not to mention painful rehabilitation programme. On top of this, the process of grafting had only just begun; many more general anaesthetics would follow, many more highs and lows. Didier might have been leaving Choisy in time for Christmas, but he would return many times over the months and years that followed. Even so, by December that year a small landmark had been reached: with the aid of crutches he was now able to stand up. Thus, on 3 December he was discharged from Choisy under strict instructions from the professor how he should adapt himself to incapacitation. The hospital marked the occasion by holding a small party in his room from where Didier went home to Neuilly.

Before the end of the year, he had journeyed to Italy to meet Enzo Ferrari and the team, an arduous proposition for one in his condition. He still considered himself a Ferrari driver and always would. While at Maranello he visited the factory and discussed F1's new regulations for 1983 that he had helped create. He loved being back among his old friends again. Ferrari was where he felt he belonged.

A hellish year was finally over. In the sheer scale of its acrimony and tragedy, 1982 had been an unprecedented year in F1 history. A year that had begun in the calm, untroubled waters of the Caribbean, the promise of glory ahead, the promise too of happiness and fulfilment, had finished in destruction and despair. Didier had effectively been one race away from triumph. Had he clinched the title in Germany or elsewhere his lifetime ambition would have been fulfilled; he would have quit the sport at the height of his powers. He never had intended hanging round F1 forever.

Life had a multitude of experiences to offer and Didier Pironi, bon viveur, astronomer, philosopher, had only just embarked on his investigations

The *GEO* article ends with the driver sat in the cockpit of his Ferrari. This is where he belongs. Peace at last. Serenity. All too quickly, it is time to return to the present, to Paris and to the routine of the sickroom, to the pain and uncertainty: 'I open my eyes. A blurred image of Formula 1 becomes clear: the model of the Ferrari is again in front of me, on the radiator of the clinic ... A dream? No. Next spring, in Maranello ... It's called hope. It's called life ...'

Twenty-four
The long road back

FREE of his sick bed, Didier next headed to Chamonix where Véronique was filming the movie, *Thieves After Dark*. Didier arrived on crutches, his right foot entombed in a cast. When his lover had hesitated to leave the side of his bed to join the film set, Didier had insisted she go. His devoted nurse had a life of her own, as well he knew. In between takes, the young couple frolicked in the snow, glad to be in one another's arms once more.

In spring, they made an appearance together on an edition of *Le Grand Éxchiquier* (The Great Chessboard), a popular TV magazine programme hosted by Jacques Chancel. They spoke about the accident of course, about their hopes and fears. There were also trips to film and theatre premieres. On the surface, everything appeared as before; they laughed and loved, but it was not the same, not any more. In the period between Choisy and the resumption of their life together, the ground had somehow imperceptibly shifted. Differences that had hitherto been hidden or ignored came to the surface. Even before their first anniversary approached, the couple had agreed to separate. From the moment Didier had crashed that Hockenheim day, there had been an inevitability as regards how this great romance would end. The pressure had been enormous, on both parties. Releasing that pressure could only lead to one place.

'Every minute of my life was devoted to Didier,' recalled Jannot in her autobiography. 'He never left my heart or my mind.

Whatever I did, he was in me. It was a permanent emotional charge. It ended up being exhausting.'[48]

Had the couple burned themselves out, compelled by fate to live as a single entity too soon? Had the very strength of their feelings consumed that same passion? They had certainly shared an experience of profound intensity in which there had been no time to catch so much as a single breath. Distance had afforded the opportunity to take a step back, to pause, reconsider. If the lovers were a little jaded, it is easy to see why. Between the four walls of room 626 – their room – emotionally they had lived the equivalent of a lifetime. Furthermore, Didier faced a long and painful convalescence. Véronique, meanwhile, had a career to pursue.

Not that there was time to mope, at least not for Didier. Invitations to events flooded in. He had always cultivated excellent relations with his sponsors Haribo and Candy and continued to do so. Business occupied a considerable amount of his time too, both the family construction company, but more so the St Tropez powerboat sales and rental venture, Euronautique. Much time was invested working with Lloyds of London on a bespoke insurance policy for racing drivers, from F1 to rally and junior ranks. He also invested in a string of health clubs and a timber yard. An avid collector of all things Ferrari, he devoted time and energy to his fleet of cars which included several models: a Daytona, a Berlinetta Boxer, a Dino 246, the 308 GTB and the jewel in his crown, a rare GTO rumoured to be one of only a handful in existence. Business concluded, he liked nothing more than to dine at the Tong Yen, a favourite restaurant located on the Champs-Élysées. Just six months after that horrific day in Germany, paradoxically Didier found himself busier than ever. When he had said that F1 was not the start and end of his world, he had not been kidding.

Before the accident he had been prepared to walk away from F1 as a champion. He could see no reason, he professed, to carry on once he had achieved this goal. Things had however changed, radically so. His career as well as legs shattered into fragments, he vowed to return to F1 – to claim the prize that had been ripped from his grasp so unjustly and so brutally, but only, he stressed, if he was 100%. Better to stop right now than come back a shadow of his former self. Didier was never going to be an also-ran.

Thus, throughout 1983 he formulated a plan to return to the sport if not by the end of the year, then in 1984. There was talk also of a Ferrari 'B' team. Certainly, Didier was aiming to be on the starting grid in '84. Between twice-weekly visits to Professor Letournel's clinic, he embarked on a punishing schedule of physiotherapy and gym sessions. A special fitness room was even commissioned at the castle. A relationship begun in the consulting rooms and operating theatres of Choisy, developed into a genuine friendship. Emile and Francine would share the patient's joys as well as his disappointments over the course of the next five years.

As president of the GPDA, he was still very much involved with the evolution of Formula 1 safety. One of his commitments involved visiting circuits around the world such as that proposed by Fuengirola in Spain, checking and advising on safety provision. Back in October, then newly crowned champion Keke Rosberg had visited Choisy in company with Jean-Marie Balestre whereupon Didier had congratulated the Finnish driver on his achievement. The three men had gone on to talk at length about the sport's safety issues. Although too late to help his own case, Didier derived great satisfaction from changes to the F1 regulations in 1983, not least the banning of skirts. The man who had campaigned so tirelessly to improve the safety of his sport was the same one upon whom its full wrath had fallen. The irony was not lost on him.

A journey to Stuttgart in April to collect a new Mercedes afforded an opportunity to express his gratitude to the team who had saved his legs that catastrophic August day in '82. Driving back from the factory he realised he was within reach of Heidelberg. A whim, a chance to exorcise some ghosts, Didier soon found himself at the clinic car park. Oddly, his recollections of the hospital did not pertain to his own confinement 12 months previously, but rather to those when he had attended the aftermath of Depailler's fatal crash in 1980.

Professor Mischowski was delighted and shocked to see his former patient hobbling into his office on crutches. The two men renewed a friendship born in adversity.

'For me your two ankles were locked for life,' confessed the doctor. 'There was no question of you ever driving again, just the hope that maybe you would one day walk.' Didier was happy to have proved the oracle wrong. The doctor inspected the limbs he had come to know so intimately the previous summer. Letournel had worked wonders, he had to admit. The doctor declared himself 'flabbergasted'.

'By the way, how did you get here today?' asked the professor as the two men parted. 'Why,' replied Didier with a broad grin, 'I drove …' Mischowski refused to believe him. It was a joke, surely.

'This is the day I think,' declared Didier, 'that I celebrated my true resurrection.' This habit of popping up unexpectedly manifested itself once again when Didier ventured to Vienna one day to meet the young girl whose letter had touched him so deeply in his Choisy sickroom. 'There was a knock on the door one afternoon,' recalls the girl, now in her fifties and still resident in the Austrian capital. 'I opened the door and there was Didier Pironi smiling back at me! I could not believe it! I think he thought I was going to leave him standing there on the doorstep! Thankfully, my mother and father invited him into our home. I was completely stunned. He limped into the house on his crutch and later showed us the scars on his leg, explaining about all his operations. We had tea together. It was a day I will never forget!'

Throughout 1983, he was back and forth from room 626. More grafts. More pain. In early June, from the now familiar surroundings of his Choisy sickroom, he watched Yannick Noah triumph in the French Open tennis final. Any hopes of a quick return to Formula 1 were fading fast. Later that summer he learned of an accident involving Philippe Paoli, a promising young driver who had himself won the Pilot-Elf competition in 1981. The young man had sustained a catalogue of injuries in a race at Albi. By all accounts doctors at the local hospital had just about given up hope of him ever walking again when a phone call arrived from Paris:

'You aren't going nowhere in Albi hospital – would you like to join me here in Paris where my friend Professor Letournel works magic?' Philippe agreed. The two men went back a long way.

'We met in 1972 for the Pilot-Elf final in Paul Ricard,' recalls Paoli. 'I was only 12, but I remember perfectly this beautiful sunny day and this young blonde guy who easily won the contest on the 3.3km circuit.' After Jean-Pierre Jarier had flown him to Paris, 24 hours later, the injured driver was lying on the Choisy operating table. There, the professor indeed worked his magic on the driver's knee, leg and vertebrae, thus enabling him to compete in the final rounds of the European and French F3 championships.

'I left the hospital way before Didier,' continues Philippe, 'then I purchased a nice Montblanc fountain pen as a gift for what he did for me, and got it engraved on the pin part "Didier Pironi". A few years later, as he was talking business with my father, he mentioned that his house had been broken into and everything had been stolen. Then he said I don't give a damn for what they took, the only thing that pisses me off, is that they took Philippe's pen.'

Summer 1983, and Paris was wilting under a heatwave. Didier would spend six long weeks in his old room that August stripped to the waist, lean, tanned, blonde, a picture of health and virility. Indeed, had it not been for the heavy bandaging of his right leg and the ever present fixator, you would never have known the dark recesses he had only recently visited. It was a delicate stage of his recuperation. If these latest grafts held, it would represent a major landmark on the road to recovery: he would, for the first time in 12 months, be able to place his full weight on to the cursed right foot. From here, the aim was to resume jogging and tennis. By the end of the year, he hoped to be functioning something approximating to 'normal'. Moreover, there was always Ferrari's promise to furnish him with a car upon his recovery. The thought consoled him through some dark days, a glint of hope at the end of a long, dark tunnel. In fact, admission to Choisy that summer had been his idea and his alone, a way of driving his recuperation forward.

Sport-Auto magazine encountered an exhilarated Didier brimming with hope following this pivotal moment in his treatment: 'I saw my first X-rays. They are great! My bones really look like bones. Nevertheless, this graft, very delicate, requires doubling of daily irrigation.' The report notes Didier's 'eyes shining with confidence'.

On 7 August, exactly one year to the day since his accident, he reappeared in the Formula 1 paddock to spectate at the German Grand Prix, hobbling on his crutches, but otherwise his usual serene self. No, he shrugged, time and place were merely a matter of coincidence. It was the first time he had been fit enough to attend a Grand Prix. He spent the day conducting interview after interview, answering the sort of questions the BBC's *Grand Prix* programme put to him: *would he be returning to F1 and if so, when?* Escaping the media's attention, he managed to lunch with old rivals Arnoux and Jabouille. Perhaps he really believed Formula 1 was getting closer. If so, he would be sorely disappointed. Far from coming to an end, his convalescence was just beginning. Indeed, not until January of 1986 would he finally be able to walk without crutches.

One winter evening Didier returned to the clinic where bad news awaited: the August transplant had failed for a third time. Even Didier's optimism failed him momentarily. Waiting to drive him home, Imelda notes how it was the first and only time that he almost gave in to despair. 'Jaw clenched', Didier sunk into the passenger seat, throwing his crutches into the back of the vehicle:

'He looks me in the eye. I see in the headlights the shine of tears in his eyes: "Mom, what will I become?" This pathetic moment lasted only the space of a flash. He sits up, grabs the steering wheel angrily and says, "Let's go! We will spend the weekend in Magny-Cours!" And he began to whistle.'

Realisation was sinking in. His convalescence was clearly going to last a lot longer than he had anticipated. Perhaps for the first time he began to question his own self-belief, the certitude that had kept him going this past year. Was his Formula 1 career now over? Anger and frustration exhausted, it was only natural perhaps to view the ordeal as part of some wider purpose or as part of a grander scheme. Why else destroy a dream so wilfully? Why else destroy a trajectory so perfect? Didier began alluding to a new-found sense of perception and enlightenment. He spoke of turning defeat into victory.

'I feel more serene, more modest too. My relationships with others have gained in depth. I am more focused on them. Small everyday matters are less important.' He went on to articulate in *Ciné Revue* how the accident had been the catalyst for a deeper appreciation of the universe and his place therein: 'To some extent, my accident made me realise I brought something to the public! At the hospital, I was surprised to receive daily hundreds of very sincere letters. Driving very fast in a racing car is not necessarily a very noble aim. Bring something into someone's life, be an example for the handicapped or those who doubt or cease to hope, that's something wonderful.'[49]

'Brave' and 'courageous' were words often used in conjunction with this quest for self-fulfilment, terms which Didier would invariably scoff at. In August of 1982 he had faced a stark choice: a quick fix or a long and painful rehabilitation. While the former would have been the easier option, the result would have removed the possibility of the ankle ever being strong enough to pilot an F1 car. Didier had chosen the long and painful road – purposely so.

The desire to return to competition burned as strong as ever. Rumours of a guest appearance at the Nürburgring champions' race scheduled in May of 1984 proved to be just that: rumours. Mercedes had been very keen for Didier to join in the fun, driving one of their iconic 190E saloons against Senna, Prost, Lauda *et al*, but the right leg was still not anywhere near full operating capacity. Reluctantly, Didier declined the invitation. In the event, he watched from the sidelines. That year he would become a familiar sight in the garages of F1, a somewhat tragic figure propped up on crutches, forever on the fringes, so close but so far from the world he craved to be part of again.

'My goal,' he maintained, 'has remained the one announced as soon as I knew that I could walk normally: I want to drive in Formula 1. I'm doing the impossible to achieve this goal which has become the only one in my life.'[50]

Do what they might, this mercurial family could seemingly not avoid misfortune. Entertaining a group of friends one evening that included the photographer Emmanuel Zurini, Didier answered a telephone call. 'I was cooking pasta for 12 fellows at his beautiful house close to Rambouillet,' recalls Zurini, 'when the telephone rang announcing that his mother and aunt [José's mother] had had a big car crash on the way to their south French residence. His reaction was, "I leave you this place Manou – please take care of our guests. I go south by car." It was 10pm!'

Imelda and Ilva had been driving from Toulon to St Tropez when they had been involved in a serious road traffic accident. For the second time in recent history, the younger of the sisters escaped serious injury. Ilva was not so lucky. The accident had occurred near the small, private airport of Le Mole, some ten minutes from their ultimate destination. José, Imelda and Didier had lost a beloved mother, sister and aunt respectively.

Around this time – summer 1984 – he had become reacquainted with Catherine Goux, the petite young woman he had known during his earlier racing days. In the time that had passed since their last contact, both partners had never stopped believing that one day they would resume their relationship. The years in between had merely been an interim, a period of separation to sow wild seeds, to grow emotionally and spiritually, to ultimately enhance the moment of reunion. The couple moved to 'Souvigny', a rambling property located in the forest of Rambouillet, accessible only to those of an adventurous nature. Here they created their own version of paradise. Dinner parties such as the one Zurini attended were a common occurrence in this fairy-tale setting. Establishing a Japanese garden allowed the couple to indulge their love of exotic plants, while upon the estate's ornamental lake a noble knight rowed and wooed his lady. They had waited a long while for this – a decade and more. The Souvigny pleasure dome allowed them to satiate a deep physical desire, a craving for one another that had been held in abeyance for a decade.

By her own admission, Catherine had been a 'zombie' when Didier suddenly reappeared in her life one day in June 1984. Plagued by illness, she had withered away latterly. A telephone chat that went on for hours brought the star cross'd lovers together again. Didier took 'the woman of his life' to the Tong Yen, where he taught her how to eat again, spoon feeding the gaunt young woman with infinite patience. Vitality restored, it would soon be Catherine feeding Didier. Later on, she would sometimes ask him to wait five minutes while she got ready, to which he, anxious to be off, would always joke: 'I've been waiting 30 years, no more!'

The couple's thoughts turned to family. Catherine already had a son from a previous relationship whom Didier readily adopted, and he had always treated José's three children as if his own. Nonetheless, at 32 years of age the time, he thought, was ripe to have a family of his own. Easier said than done. The reunited lovers were about to embark on yet another long and difficult quest.

Twenty-five
Limbo

FORMULA 1 in the mid-eighties had become the domain of just one man: Alain Prost. Didier's old sparring partner had risen to the top of the F1 tree, winning Grands Prix as he pleased. Didier had no choice but to watch his old adversary close in on the ambition he himself had so dearly cherished: the honour of becoming France's first Formula 1 world champion. If Didier envied his old rival his success, he never showed it. That it was Prost's Renault that had acted as launch pad to his red rocket that foul Hockenheim morning, was just another example of the perverse kind of coincidences that had dogged him throughout his life. Thinking back to that grim morning, one or two people wondered why his compatriot had even been out on circuit in the first place.

'What the hell was he [Prost] doing out there going so bloody slowly anyway?' growled one driver. 'He had no right to be on that track.' What-ifs. Whys. Wherefores. Yet more: had the Renault been displaying its rear hazard light as required? Later, Didier would allude to a distinct impression that the Renault had dramatically slowed in the moments before contact ... If his reaction to his countryman's run of success was something less than ecstatic he was, after all, only human.

In the meantime, he got his kicks in the usual way: bikes, cars, boats and planes. Professor Letournel and Francine, by now great friends, accepted an invitation to Souvigny that year. Emile was more than a little disconcerted to see the full range of his charge's 'toys'. As spring 1985 dawned, Didier might have been walking again, but the professor was acutely aware of the precariousness of his patient's condition.

'With Didier the notion of risk was not the same as for an ordinary patient,' recalls Francine. 'We were in our room one morning when suddenly we heard the noise of a motorcycle. Professor Letournel rushed to the window. Didier was not riding a motorcycle, oh no. He was not on two wheels, but on a quad bike! He was rearing up in front of the window on both rear wheels!'

Being physician to Didier Pironi was not an easy job. Quad bikes aside, there were always those powerboats. After experiencing Didier's boat for himself at that year's Monaco GP, a white-faced Professor Letournel prohibited his patient from piloting the boat in a standing position. The prof – more accurately his legs – had felt the 'shock' when accompanying his patient for a spin on *Masha*. As he stood tentatively behind the pilot observing his dexterity, the boat bumping, banging and bouncing from one wave to another, the doctor experienced first-hand the bruising after-effects produced by these vessels. Such consistently rigid impacts could hardly help his friend's rehabilitation. Subsequently, Didier had a seat adapted to allow him to pilot in a reclining position. Returning to St Tropez harbour, patient and doctor found the harbour had just closed. Large gates blocked their access to the dock. Pas de problem! Emile and Francine watched in disbelief as Didier scrambled over the 2.5-metre-high gates in order to procure the keys.

The quayside at Cogolin had become somewhat of a second home since the Hockenheim crash. Hiring and selling high-end powerboats to the rich and famous, the market into which Didier and José had tapped was a lucrative one. By 1985, Euronautique employed over 40 people. The company had recently moved to a new site in Canoubiers just east of St Tropez, providing 5,000 square metres of workshop in two hangars for a maximum capacity of 300 boats. Despite run-ins with screen legend Brigitte Bardot who complained that the expansion of the company would spoil the area's peace and tranquillity, and whose famous La Madrague villa stood close by, the company was going from strength to strength.

Less contentious pursuits included playing pool with old friends such as Jean-Louis Schlesser up at the villa or tending the lavish gardens of its terraces. He had also carved out somewhat of a niche test-driving commercial cars. During January, Didier clocked up 60 miles driving a Saab 900 turbo around the icy streets of Paris. In a typically concise report written for *L'Équipe*, while he was less than enthusiastic about the vehicle's handling, its four-cylinder, two-litre engine made a more favourable impression on the ex-Grand Prix star: 'The flexibility and low-end torque is remarkable, the available power is worthy of the best modern sports cars and has nothing to envy from Mercedes' 2.3-litre, 16-valve model.'[51] Life was busier than ever. Had he so wished he could have settled for a life of comfort, road-testing cars, running his various enterprises and after dipping his toe as an F1 commentator/pundit, perhaps developing a media career.

But no, he had only one goal: to win the Formula 1 world championship; to exorcise the ghost of Saturday, 7 August 1982.

With this aim in mind, in late summer '85 he stepped back into a Formula 1 cockpit for the first time since that fateful day. Didier sampled a 1982 Williams – ironically the car in which Rosberg had 'stolen' his title – at a private Parisian circuit belonging to the entrepreneur and classic car collector Jack Setton. A watershed moment. He came away from the top-secret test with mixed emotions. On the one hand, he had set a new circuit record, beating times set by drivers such as Tambay and Cheever, cause for great optimism. In doing so, however, he could hardly ignore the stiffness and pain from his right leg and ankle. Clearly, he still had the speed. Nevertheless, would his compromised right limb allow him to operate at maximum capacity ever again? Almost three years after Hockenheim, his recovery was still not yet complete. As reality checks go, it was a sobering moment.

Formula 1 then was out of the question, at least in the short term. It may or may not have been of significance, but over in Maranello, Enzo Ferrari had not of late mentioned the promise made in the aftermath of the crash, that a Ferrari F1 seat awaited him. Furthermore, in the three years since Hockenheim, F1 had moved on. Arnoux and Tambay had both left Ferrari; neither man would win a Grand Prix again. Prost and McLaren were riding high. A new phenomenon had burst on to the scene – a driver who went by the handle Senna.

Driven by an urge to compete, perhaps it was only inevitable that this compulsion should manifest itself in some other way. Didier was not unfamiliar with the world of offshore powerboat racing, and the huge four-tonne 'sea monsters' that contested Class I races, the offshore equivalent to F1. In May of 1985, he helped organise an event between St Tropez and Monaco, a race counting towards the European championships. From here, it was but a short step to enter the fray himself. He certainly knew his way around a powerboat. Having imported Abbate and Lamborghini to France for several years, Didier had made many contacts in this glamorous and exclusive sport that attracted not only the wealthy but royalty too. Besides, powerboating was fun. It set the pulse racing. 'There are many similarities between driving these machines and those in Formula 1,' he explained in an interview. There was, however, a crucial difference. With powerboating you got a different 'feeling', not the same feeling as F1, rather 'being on edge, always on the razor's edge'.[52]

In some ways 1985 was becoming a transitional year, one in which Didier's affiliation shifted slightly from road to sea. The prospect of competing in F1 seemed a distant prospect whereas joining the ranks of offshore racing seemed entirely realistic. He was certainly spending more time in the boatyard, more time out at sea. Gradually, he slipped away from his duties with the GPDA. He did, however, continue his frequent trips to Italy, but in summer 1985 the destination was more likely to be the ports of Lavagna or Chiavari, boating strongholds both, rather than Modena, home of Scuderia Ferrari. On one occasion, the Lavagna port authority refused him entry to dock. The noise of his Lamborghini engines had apparently not met with the approval of the port's resident boaters the previous year!

When he telephoned rising French F1 star Philippe Streiff to congratulate him on his third-place finish at the 1985 Australian Grand Prix, the conversation turned to powerboats. The Ligier driver was a fellow boating enthusiast. During the exchange, Streiff mentioned his intention to attend the offshore world championships to be held in Florida later that month. Didier liked the sound of that. Sure enough, in November he and Catherine flew out to the States. The contingent of French journalists gathered at Key West to cover the event did a double take when who should come limping up the quayside, but the ex-Formula 1 star. Popping up out of the blue, a Pironi speciality.

FISA press secretary and Streiff's manager Gilles Gaignault was among the French media contingent and just as surprised as anyone at the identity of the man hobbling along the quayside. 'We arrived in Miami from Los Angeles after a long season which had started back in January, and here we find … Didier Pironi!'

The world championships took place that year in Key West, the hedonistic island that lies at the southernmost tip of the Florida straits, the haunt of Hemingway, Tennessee Williams and others. Here Didier met father and son team Jean-Pierre and Stephane Fruitier, France's sole representative in a sport dominated by Italians and to a lesser extent Americans. Fruitier had made a fortune in fruit and vegetable wholesale and was typical of the wealthy enthusiasts attracted to offshore racing. Bearing the convoluted but commercially valuable name *Rocky le Juice de fruit Fraises*, Fruitier's boat fascinated Didier. Over the obligatory Cuba libres, talk soon turned to plans for 1986.

One evening Didier and Philippe contrived to get on the wrong side of local law enforcement. Dining in an Italian restaurant the boys had parked their cars outside the establishment, illegally as it transpired. Requested to rectify the situation, the French aces simply reversed their cars up the road, only to find themselves promptly arrested for committing a traffic violation. It took several minutes for Gaignault and the party to realise what had happened. Didi and Philippe were released from jail a few hours later.

A timely reminder that offshore racing had a dark as well as glamorous side came home during the week. The pilots of the 38-foot boat *Still Crazy* crashed fatally during one event off the coast. Travelling at 90mph, the boat had flipped on a wave, crashing into a nearby vessel. The boat's two American pilots were killed instantly. Offshore racing had teeth. It could bite just as hard as Formula 1, harder in fact.

No matter, Didier's plans for 1986 had crystallised: he would form an entirely French team with the aim of becoming offshore world champion within three years. It was an ambitious project. Not only would he be taking on a core group of battle-hardened Italian pilots and teams in a sport they rightly considered a speciality, but he would also need to secure considerable financial support in order to compete at the top level, Class I. It was just as well that he loved a challenge. In offshore racing, he had found one.

Didier returned from America with renewed purpose. He discussed his vision with José who, despite his preference for aviation, was similarly enthused. That winter the brothers worked hard on two key fronts: financial and technical. By early 1986 they had put together a package that fused the genius of Bruno Abbate's design skills with the precision engineering of Lamborghini whose pair of 12-valve fuel-injected engines delivered in excess of 750hp each! With Fruitier and lone French wolf, the Parisian-based owner of Ecole Supérieure de Tourisme (EST) Roger Berthault combining forces with Leader, France now had a triple assault team aiming for offshore glory. It seemed somehow fitting that into this world populated by a mix of dilettantes, wealthy enthusiasts, and royalty such as Princess Caroline of Monaco's husband, Stefano Casiraghi, should enter Didier Pironi, ex-Ferrari F1 superstar. That was offshore racing in the eighties: random, eclectic, affluent. With running costs of a full season's offshore estimated at anything up to $1.5 million, Didier turned to his old friends at Elf for funding.

The 1986 offshore programme began in April in the Spanish port of Villanueva, visited Monaco, St Tropez and Venice on successive weekends in May, hit Argentario and Porto Cervo in June, before homing in on Viareggio in July, Öregrund (Sweden), Poole and Cowes in August and finished its peripatetic tour on the island of Guernsey in September. It would be a tough baptism. Italian aces such as Renato Della Valle and Dario Spelta were not going to permit a French newbie to muscle in on their territory without a ferocious fight. So it proved. A mixture of inexperience and poor mechanical reliability blighted Leader's season. Pironi and Fruitier managed fourth place at Cowes, but little else that year. As learning curves went, offshore racing was as deep as it was steep.

Meanwhile back on the racetrack, there were developments too. In July, veteran of over 170 Grands Prix, Jacques Laffite broke both legs in a crash during the British Grand Prix. On hearing the news, Didier immediately attempted to contact his friend, Letournel. Several hours and phone calls later he finally tracked the professor down to New Zealand where he was delivering a seminar. A surprised prof (*How on earth did you find me?*) agreed to accept Laffite as a patient. Didier had just secured for his old team-mate the services of the best physician in the business. Jacques' accident added an extra layer of spice to the month of August when Didier was scheduled to dip a toe into the F1 melting pot once more. Guy Ligier's team now had a vacancy ...

And so, late on a sultry August afternoon, Didier landed his helicopter at the Paul Ricard circuit as a battalion of journalists and photographers scrambled to get the story and the picture. Pironi was back to drive an F1, well an AGS, more specifically a jazzed-up 1983 Renault RE40 with a Motori Moderni engine together with white paint job.

Fuelling speculation of a return to the sport, Didier had agreed to drive Henri Julien's new, but chronically under-financed F1 car on its maiden voyage. Was this then the moment of his rebirth? If so, then in Paul Ricard, venue of his original 'birth' in '72, he could not have chosen a symbolically more appropriate venue for his resurrection. If he looked a little heavier than in times past, nobody cared that much. Hell, the guy had undergone over 30 major surgeries these past years and spent more time in than out of hospital. The sun dipping below the Provençal mountains, he completed 70 untroubled laps. A solid performance. On vacating the cockpit he cried, 'I've not changed!' Evidently, the driver felt he had just crossed a huge psychological barrier.

In some quarters, it was felt the AGS test had been a stunt, a way of gaining press coverage for the fledgling team. That might have been the team's motive, but Didier's it was not. Already, the Brabham and Ferrari F1 teams had contacted him regarding test driver roles in 1987. He was not interested. 'I am in contact with several teams,' he told the media, 'but when I return it will be only if I find a competitive car, capable of winning and to allow me to win the world title.' All or nothing for Didier, it always had been.

When he accepted a test for Ligier-Renault later that same month, an imminent return to F1 seemed certain. Guy and

Didi knew each other of old of course. Memories of that single, blistering 1980 season were still fresh in some minds. With Renault also involved, the omens looked good. There was however a snag. Physical concerns aside, Didier was rumoured to have received a substantial insurance payment following Hockenheim. A return to the sport would therefore, it was strongly suggested, invalidate that claim. Didier might be forced to repay the money. Returning to F1 was not going to be easy on any level. Nevertheless, on a cloudy Burgundy afternoon in late August, he wriggled into the cockpit of the Ligier JS27 at the Dijon-Prenois circuit. Nerves? Watching his methodical preparations, you would not necessarily have thought so. Inside, the heart must surely have been beating a little faster than usual. While the AGS test had been nothing more than a run-out, this was the moment of truth. Four years of blood, guts and determination rested on the outcome of the next few hours. Was he about to make the most improbable F1 comeback in the history of the sport? Those gathered at the circuit crossed their fingers. Everybody was rooting for him. The Loto-sponsored car roared out on to the Dijon circuit ...

In the pits, the team anxiously recorded the lap times. Was he on the pace? Did he still have it? Ligier and the boys hoped so. As the car threaded through the super-fast Combe and Pouas corners to enter the long pit straight for another lap, shoulders relaxed, one or two personnel smiled contentedly to themselves. The blue car was flying! Demonstrating all his old panache the little prince of speed was rediscovering his mojo out there, vanquishing the doubt-demons that had plagued him these last four years. Back again, the Pironi swagger. Forty nostalgic laps later, he had recorded a best time of 1'05.50. To put that into context, Alain Prost held the circuit record with a time of 1'05.25. More significantly, he had beaten Arnoux's time from the previous test albeit using softer tyres. He *still* had it.

As impressive as the test had been Didier remained typically measured in his reaction: 'I didn't really drive hard,' he told the assembled media, 'because I didn't want to damage the car Guy had kindly let me try.' He spoke too about the 'pleasure' of driving a car no longer running with skirts and the corresponding 'delicacy' now required. He ended the day on a cautiously optimistic note:

'I now feel confident I can compete again at the top level.' Pironi was back in the game.

Inexplicably, following this impressive run, Guy Ligier prevaricated. It all depended on the progress of Laffite, now in the capable hands of Letournel. Didier was nonplussed. After four years away from the sport, only a blind man (or Guy) could not appreciate the extent of his achievement that Dijon afternoon. In reality, the prospect of a Ligier seat in F1's midfield held little appeal. Despite a brief upturn in form in 1986, the French cavaliers had been falling down the F1 grid for some years and would continue to do so.

One man who did seem to appreciate his efforts was McLaren's Ron Dennis, a long-time admirer of the Frenchman. Rumours circulated in the French media that Marlboro France were keen to get Didier into the Woking team as partner to Prost in '87. Following Keke Rosberg's retirement at the end of 1986, McLaren were in the market for a stop-gap driver before the arrival of Ayrton Senna in 1988. Didier fitted that bill. A berth with McLaren would thrust him back to the front of the F1 grid if even for a single season. Alain Prost, however, allegedly vetoed the move. 'Didier was furious,' says Catherine Goux, 'absolutely furious ...'

A door had closed. If the rumours were true, for reasons best known to himself, Prost had denied his friend the chance of an F1 lifeline. In the event, Dennis eventually signed Swedish journeyman Stefan Johansson, but not until the 1987 season had almost begun. Pironi and McLaren would have been huge news, a horror story that had ended happily ever after. Had Didier rejoined the F1 circuit in 1987, his offshore career – at least as a competitor – would likely have ended right there. Alas, it was not to be.

Many years have passed, but today, 30 years on, there is a certain name of a multiple Formula 1 world champion that is never mentioned in a certain household, ever.

Twenty-six

The habit of perfection

'HE WAS, Didier, a perfectionist, you know?' The words are those of Philippe Lecouffle, the childhood friend whose family had run Europe's premier orchid farm just down the road from the Boissy castle and where Didier had first fallen in love with these exotic flowers. 'He always wanted to be the best he could, to be perfect.' His rehabilitation was a perfect example of this disposition. In order to avoid ankylosis – stiffening and immobility of joints – in choosing the Papineau technique, he had opted for a process that required unusually high levels of patience, determination and faith. Not once had he baulked, not even when faced with a long and painful series of bone grafts and equally painful physiotherapy schedule. To reach his goal, he had to suffer. Didier fully accepted the situation. If that is what it took to claim his world championship, then so be it.

In fact, the process only ended in 1987, almost five years after it had begun. Remarkably, in all this time he never once saw his wounds. Professor Letournel judged it best not to traumatise his patients more than necessary.

'Didier saw his wounds and his surgical "history" only in '87 when the bone was reconstituted,' recalls Francine. 'Professor Letournel showed him all the slides of the evolution of his leg during a weekend that we spent at his house. I can tell you that there was too much silence after the projection of the slides.' A quick check online into case histories reveals the grisly reality

233

entailed with the Papineau method. It is not for the faint-hearted.

This same will to achieve nothing more than the best surfaced in his new pursuit. His F1 prospects having seemingly stalled, Didier focused his energies back to offshore. His first season in this exotic sport had yielded little in terms of tangible success. Yes, he had accumulated experience, some of it painful – as four cracked ribs from an early-season accident in Barcelona had attested. No question, in 1986 Leader had under-performed. Offshore was a tougher nut to crack than he could ever have expected.

Undeterred, he set out to create a powerboat like no other. This boat would be a monohull built in fibre-reinforced polymers (FRP) and powered by Lamborghini petrol engines. Didier being Didier, he wanted this boat, his concept, his baby, to be unique. Weight reduction became the Holy Grail; the lighter the boat, the faster it would go. Didier was seeking a 20% reduction compared to conventional crafts, a potential game-changer. Sourcing a company that could or indeed wanted to work to this exacting brief became somewhat of an obsession. Didier's research had led to the kind of moulding techniques usually deployed in the aerospace industry. As ever, he was pushing the boundaries. Designing a run-of-the-mill boat would have been a pointless exercise. Along with Jean-Claude Guénard, he worked assiduously on a design the pair knew had the potential to revolutionise offshore racing. Was there any other kind? Guénard himself had an impressive track record not only as a competitor, but also in a variety of technical capacities. Like his childhood pal, the ex-Renault F1 technical director loved the thrill of high-speed competition in whichever way it came, bikes, cars or boats. Kindred spirits, Didi and GueGue.

All well and good, but revolutions do not come easily or cheaply. The project needed a significant cash injection. Step forward Philippe Midy. A keen sailor himself, the Midial food group of which he was CEO had already sponsored the efforts of round-the-world yachtsman Olivier de Kersauson in his trimaran *Poulain Midial*. Conquering oceans and seas appealed to a notion Midy held that an association with endeavour could only enhance brand value.[53]

Didier's research eventually led him to the naval architect Xavier Joubert and his design practice in La Rochelle. Specialising in the design of sailing yachts, Joubert readily accepted this intriguing project. His manufacturing and research company ACX, based in Brest, boasted a state-of-the-art FRP composites workshop and had established a solid reputation in the study and manufacture of high-performance structures utilising carbon and Kevlar. ACX had the technology. A major piece of the jigsaw had thus fallen into place. Had he not been a racing driver, Didier could surely have forged a successful career in project management.

Joubert and his team got to work. From concept to reality, Didier awaited the progress of the various stages of production like an expectant father. Creation of this superlight hull went thus: once the composite mixture of carbon fibres, Kevlar and epoxy resin had been laid in the moulds, they would be pressed together by suction and baked to a temperature approaching 150°C, within an autoclave or big oven, to compact the materials into one homogeneous mass and once cooled and trimmed, the two halves would be joined.

Approximately 9,000 man-hours later, the monohull and deck assembly emerged from the workshop to make the southwards journey to St Tropez for final touches and a rigorous programme of testing.

In the meantime, Didier had been in conversation with Midy with regards to baptising the boat. From among Midial's many brands, the businessman and Didier chose to christen their flagship boat after the company's famous pastry brand. Thus did the new 41ft, 3,000kg composite monohull race boat powered by twin V12 Lamborghini engines take to the water as *Colibri* or 'hummingbird' as it translates in English.

The next task was to put together a crew. Racing these beasts required the efforts of three distinct components, namely throttle, steering and navigation. With Didier on the helm (steering) and Guénard on throttle, navigation duties fell to Bernard Giroux, F1 commentator for French TV channel TF1. Giroux had a taste for adventure. A double winner of the Paris–Dakar rally – most recently alongside Ari Vatanen – he had also participated in the Rouen 24-hour and Paris 6-hour races with distinction. Didier's kind of guy then – fearless, brave and up for a challenge. When TV commitments absented him, his place was taken by Pierre

'Pom' Harnois, another member of this close-knit circle of French daredevils and petrol heads.

Colibri was officially launched in May to a media fanfare. It was a bright, sunny afternoon when she was unveiled in St Tropez. Immaculate in their matching team blazers, Didier and the Leader crew toasted the future. Thirteen races in the European Championship lay ahead beginning in Villanueva in Spain in April, ending in Guernsey in September, plus the three-race World Championships in Key West in November.

'Looking and going like a bullet,' was *Powerboating International*'s assessment of *Colibri* in the opening Villanueva race, its reporter sounding a note of caution, however, when observing the craft 'rolling all the way ...'[54] The boat was already gaining a reputation for instability. In the event, a sixth-place finish was a more than satisfactory way to start a season.

Forty-five boats lined up at Monte Carlo harbour for the next round in early June, most of them Class I. Didier joined a field of competitors that included ex-Ferrari F1 and Le Mans legend Jacky Ickx, ex-tennis star Adriano Panatta, Casiraghi and a raft of Italian champions. Although not F1, offshore undeniably had a certain cachet all its own. Didier's conversion to a sport that was every bit as glamorous and just as dangerous – more so – than its automotive counterpart, is easy to understand. Certainly, the offshore course was every bit as challenging as that facing its four-wheeled cousins. Starting at the Monaco yacht club in front of the famous harbour, the 136-mile course skirted Nice en route to Cape Ampello in Italian waters before heading back to the Principality, a circuit repeated three times and lasting around two hours. Formula 1 of the seas, they called it. This was Didi's new world.

The Monaco F1 Grand Prix and offshore race coinciding this Côte d'Azur weekend, *Rombo* magazine asked Didier to compare his current world with that of his old one. A journalist was thus despatched to accompany him into both hemispheres, past and future. In the section dealing with motorsport, the magazine alluded to the moment the French ace arrived in the Ferrari paddock. On chancing upon the 158s of current drivers Michele Alboreto (27) and Stefan Johansson (28), Didier cast a wistful eye over the scarlet cars. Was there the faintest hint of sorrow in those deep blue eyes? Perhaps. On the day after the Grand Prix, *Rombo* then accompanied him on *Colibri*. Noting a subtle change in his demeanour, the magazine commented that, 'He has only just lost that sad look of 24 hours before, when he observed with nostalgia in his eyes and heart, the Ferrari F1 cars at the Monte Carlo pits.' Talk turned to the current F1 scene, and the pre-eminence of Prost. The writer ended his piece with an observation as perceptive as it was poignant:

'Pironi then falls silent for a moment. And crouching on the hull looks away towards the sea. Perhaps the nostalgia that comes back or maybe the bitter thought that instead of Prost, in France and in the world, it could be him ...'

His Formula 1 career on hold, Didier threw himself into his quest to conquer offshore. He had no other choice. Blistering speed apart, a catalogue of technical gremlins had plagued *Colibri* and Monaco became another fruitless race to add to those in Cannes, St Tropez and Porto Cervo (Sardinia). Moreover, concerns regarding the boat's stability refused to go away. Some elements of the Italian media used a line from a popular song to describe her handling – *guarda come dondolo* – see how she rocks ... After six rounds of the 1987 championship, Didier only lay in tenth place in the standings, some way off the Italian pacesetters Gigi Radice and Antonio Giofreddi. Undaunted, he pressed on. His faith in his hummingbird never wavered.

It was not until the gala visited Sweden in early August that *Colibri* started to flex her muscles. Racing among the archipelagos of Öregrund, the boats encountered freezing rain, poor visibility and choppy seas at little more than zero temperatures. Cannes this was not. On race day, *Colibri* streaked into an early lead and held on for half the race. It could not and did not last. Didier recorded another non-finish. There was better news for Fruitier however, who managed third behind the rampant Italians. *Colibri* – Hummingbird – had been created in her master's image, speed to burn, but fragility to match. Should it all hold together, who could doubt that victory was nearby?

One week later in Norway on 15 August, *Colibri* duly scorched to her first Class I victory. The race took place in Arendal, a pretty little waterside town sheltered by a long island and featuring a racecourse that circled the surrounding fjords. Joined by Harnois as Giroux's replacement, Didier and Jean-Claude comfortably beat the best the Italians could throw at them. Abbate, Della Valle, Spelta and Gioffredi all trailed behind the red and white arrow's wake. Vive la Republique! France had finally arrived in offshore. Perhaps of more value than the winner's trophy was the congratulatory telegram sent by Enzo Ferrari. *Il Commendatore* was still following the progress of his French lieutenant, albeit from afar.

Before the next round of the championship in the marine town of Poole on the south-east coast of England, Didier was as busy as ever. A man always in demand, in early August he attended a party in Pamplona with his good friend Paul Belmondo, an aspiring driver and son of French movie legend Jean-Paul Belmondo. Wearing his Leader T-shirt, he was part of a large party dining al fresco. Belmondo junior and Didier liked to get around. In true Didier fashion, he also stopped off at Île de Porquerolles, a small holiday island just off France's Mediterranean coast where he dined with friends including the actor André Pousse. Didier arrived for the appointment via helicopter:

'He chose to land in the tightest possible space, surrounded with trees,' recalls a fellow guest. 'I just saw one small part of a branch fly off a tree. No pilot would have chosen the spot he chose. As he came down from his 'copter he was smiling at me, and I said to him: "Didier, you had plenty of space on the other side!" He replied in that calm, confident voice: "I was just trying something – it was quite tight …"'

Catherine's absence at his side during these events was for a very good reason: she was pregnant. After several unsuccessful past IVF treatments, in early June she had called the hospital with a good dose of trepidation to learn the outcome of their latest effort. What if this attempt – their fifth – failed?

'Madame, your test is positive…'

Expecting the worst, Catherine was already choking back tears. 'Pardon? Can it be true?

'Yes Madame, it is true. You are pregnant!'

Sobbing with happiness, Catherine flew upstairs. Going about his business in the couple's bedroom, Didier took his lover gently in his arms, 'Do not worry, we start again.'

'No!' whispered Catherine. 'This time, Didier, we won.'

Prevented from conceiving naturally due to Catherine's history of gynaecological problems, the couple had turned to Professor Zorn, a specialist in 'test-tube' technology. Given her catalogue of health issues, IVF was a path she might have rejected outright had it not been for her partner's desire to become a father. The prospect of twins thrilled the couple. 'Pink or blue?' Didier would often wonder which colour teddy bear to bring back from his offshore adventures. At night, he would place his head gently on Catherine's stomach, asking playfully, 'How are you today, my babies?'

August 1987 and the future appeared brighter than ever. Not only was *Colibri* fulfilling her potential, but a return to Formula 1 was a reality merely requiring a signature on a contract. On the Friday before leaving for the UK, Didier had met with his old friend and mentor Gérard Larrousse to discuss a sensational return to the ex-Renault chief's eponymous team. According to Larrousse, the deal had been done: Pironi would be back in F1 in 1988.

Twenty-seven

Thus ends this strange, eventful history[55]

IDIER headed to England in an optimistic frame of mind. The night before he left, he had kissed Catherine and the twins goodbye. As the helicopter had risen above the thatched roof of their Souvigny love nest, the lady of the manor could surely never have known it would be the last time she would glimpse her noble knight, the man in whose presence she claimed never to have any fear. Three days later, he would be back, winner of the Needles offshore race. They would resume their life together, planning for the twins, looking forward to a new phase of life. Didier had spent five years fighting doubt as well as pain. Catherine was no stranger to despair herself. After many trials and more than a few errors, fate had brought them back together. Happiness was within reach.

The *Colibri* crew arrived in England on Friday evening ahead of Sunday's race. Together with a small group of French journalists, they went for pizzas. The mood was relaxed – with one exception. During the evening, Bernard Giroux privately expressed reservations to a member of the media. He was concerned about Sunday's race, concerned about *Colibri*, about safety. To his media colleague Poivre d'Arvor he had fretted about the consequences of an accident at sea. If such an event occurred, how could the crew avoid the worst outcome? Giroux was wary. TV commitments now allowing, the presenter was back in the crew, replacing Harnois as navigator. However, he was not happy. Nor was his partner, singing star Jeane Manson, who had implored him to give up powerboating, a pursuit she considered highly risky and just plain irresponsible.

Indeed, Just Jaeckin remembers speaking to the presenter only days before the race in England. 'I was with Didier and Bernard in St Tropez the day before they left for England,' remembers Just. 'I went on the boat, but it was not so enjoyable for me. Bernard told me that the boat hurt his back and that he had had enough.' Giroux had promised the Isle of Wight would be his last race.

Saturday was scrutineering day. A maharajah sitting atop his prized elephant, Didier straddled *Colibri* as a lorry guided the gigantic craft into the quay in the heart of the town. Residents and holidaymakers alike could stroll past while these four-tonne beasts waited to be unleashed into the waters. The Royal Motor Yacht Club – the organisation hosting the event – set about checking the boat's technical specifications. A comprehensive checklist also included ascertaining provision of items such as life jackets, flares, radio, foghorns, torches etc.

At 6pm the competitors assembled on the quayside for the mandatory briefing in which race officials ran through various procedures for the following day's 170-mile event. Organisers also disclosed the positions of the fleet of observation and safety boats. The briefing ended with a meteorological forecast that suggested light winds of 3–4 mph for the morrow.

The crew rose early on Sunday morning. When Didier took the boat out for a final shakedown, a member of the French media took the place of Bernard Giroux, who seemed reluctant to even climb aboard the vessel. After poring over navigation maps, the TV man accompanied his team leader on a walk around the quay where they chatted to Stefano Casiraghi[56] and posed for photographs. A little while later Bernard bumped into his media colleague Gilles Klein:

'Bernard was standing by *Colibri* but he wasn't smiling,' recalls Klein. 'I thought it was not like him. I got a strange feeling about things. I said "Hey, what's up?" He looked serious.'

It was a relatively calm day in Poole harbour, one of the largest and shallowest enclosed harbours in the world. As is usually the way, the open sea was choppier, although visibility was good – about 15 miles. As the aroma of frying bacon diffused from the hospitality tents that lined the quayside, crews and officials buzzed around the boats. Once satisfied, craning into the harbour could begin. At what was an indecent hour for a Sunday or any other day, the roar of diesel engines filled the air. The monsters were seaborne.

From Poole the flotilla headed to the muster point just west of the holiday town of Bournemouth. A total of 57 boats took the start, from the Class I boats producing a fearsome 1,500–1,600hp, through Class II and III incorporating National Cruiser classes and the 1.3-litre class boats producing a relatively tiny 90hp. Named after the famous 30-metre chalk stacks that rise out of the sea at the western extremity of the Isle of Wight, the Needles offshore race comprised four circuits, starting with a short 24-mile inshore lap.

The main courses took the boats past the town of Christchurch to the southern tip of the New Forest at Milford on Sea. From here, the fleet skirted the Needles as it raced towards Atherfield Bell on the south-west end of the Isle of Wight. There followed a long, straight stretch back across to the town of Swanage before a sharp right turn back towards Christchurch to complete what was in effect a large triangle.

At 10.36am the Class I race started. The 'cigarettes' skimmed the waves, leaving their distinctive spidery white trails behind. From the start, *Colibri* battled for the lead with *Pinot de Pinot*, the mount of former world champion Renato Della Valle. It soon became a two-boat race. While *Colibri* handled the turns at the various buoys better, the Italian boat seemed to fare better in open stretches.

Following the action from above in two helicopters, the French media crew were witnessing a titanic scrap, which in order to keep up with necessitated a perilously low altitude. For Gilles Klein it was a completely new experience. The young photojournalist had been a late addition to the troop, only having accepted the commission the day before the race.

'I was in one of the helicopters shadowing *Colibri*. It was pretty hair-raising stuff – to keep up, we sometimes flew what seemed like just metres above the boat.'

Strange as it sounds, the powerboats shared the waters with the usual array of private and leisure craft out for a weekend cruise. While F1 cars do not share race circuits with Sunday drivers, offshore did just that. An accident waiting to happen? One cruiser thought so: 'It is a frightening sight to see powerboats racing towards you at 30-second intervals, in line astern, at speeds of over 100mph,' read a complaint to a local newspaper.

Given its many hazards, offshore racing had formulated its own mantra: safety first, racing second. Indeed, The Royal Motor Yacht Club had left nothing to chance, stringently following Union Internationale Motonautique (UIM) guidelines regarding race procedure and safety provision. A total of 43 safety and rescue craft were deployed along the route, 14 at turning marks. Two race doctors also stood by.

An hour into the race, *Colibri* had taken the lead. In doing so, she had allegedly infringed the course boundaries, a transgression that if confirmed would incur a ten-minute penalty.

From his helicopter vantage point, Klein had already noticed a small 'dot' on the horizon. A 90-metre bitumen tanker, the *Esso Avon* had left Southampton en route to Belfast via the Solent and had entered the Needles channel-shipping lane some minutes before. Depending on size, marine traffic has two available routes when approaching or departing from Southampton. Larger vessels – e.g. cruise and container ships – use the eastern channel that has the deeper draught, while smaller ones may take the western approach. Owned and operated by Esso Petroleum at just over 3,000 tonnes, the *Avon* was one of the smaller coastal tankers in its fleet. Travelling at better than 10 knots (12mph), the tanker was headed for the open waters of the English Channel.

While race control had not notified competitors of the *Avon*'s potential presence, they had warned them to expect a range of vessels to be in the vicinity. As to whether crews envisaged a craft with the oil tanker's dimension is a moot point. Similarly, the tanker captain was unaware of the offshore race. In the aftermath of what followed, questions were raised in certain parts of the media regarding the wisdom or lack of therein of these decisions. Conventional wisdom suggested that prior knowledge would not have altered the course of events to any great degree. Bottom line: safety first, racing second.

As *Colibri* and *Pinot de Pinot* rounded back into the Needles channel, they were now on the same trajectory as the tanker, albeit several hundred yards behind. North-west of the Needles, the tanker had passed an observation boat, *Blue Thunder*, whose two-man crew noted with concern, 'a large wash consisting of three or four waves on either side of the stern of the boat'.[57] Furthermore, they estimated the size of the wash to be 3–5 feet high, enough of a swell to shake their own craft 'quite violently'. Patrolling near a point known as Shingles Elbow, two minutes later – at around 11.40am – the crew next observed *Colibri* approach at high speed, chased by the Italian boat. To reach the next course marker necessitated crossing the tanker's wash from left to right, a diagonal change in direction invariably requiring a commensurate change in approach and speed. According to *Blue Thunder*, *Colibri* did neither. Riding first one wave, the French boat hit a second, but this time corkscrewed up into the air about 20 feet, flipping upside down, before crashing into the sea cockpit first. Observers estimated the speed to have been around 85–90mph, possibly higher. At these speeds, the sea effectively becomes concrete and just as unforgiving. *Pinot de Pinot* by contrast successfully negotiated the wash, leading some observers to point the finger of blame at *Colibri*'s unconventional design and moreover what they perceived as the crew's reckless approach to a dangerous situation.

Blue Thunder arrived on the scene within 30 seconds. Various other rescue craft arrived minutes later to be greeted by the disheartening sight of an upturned boat and a lifeless body lying face down, blood oozing into the sea. The crew of *Blue Thunder* pulled the motionless body aboard. There was no sign of a pulse. Nevertheless, the crew initiated resuscitation protocols.

Meanwhile, the crew of *Pinot de Pinot* arrived on the scene: 'After a short time the tops of three orange crash helmets appeared in the water,' recalled the boat's navigator and race director Tim Mellery-Pratt, 'and I realised their crash helmets had been torn off.'[58]

In line with established procedure, safety officer Geoff Warde immediately triggered a chain of events that resulted in HM Coastguard, Marine Police and a Search and Rescue (SAR) helicopter diving team scrambling to the scene. Warde recorded the time of the incident as 11.43. Within minutes, the SAR diver had recovered two more bodies from under the boat. 'There was a smell of fuel, there was a lot of fuel in the area, which could have been a hazard,' Sub-lieutenant Christian Crowther of the Royal Navy told local radio. He also noted the presence of several pleasure craft in the vicinity.[59]

The bodies were subsequently airlifted to Freshwater and thence to St Mary's Hospital, Newport, on the Isle of Wight. It fell to Pierre Harnois to identify the bodies of his friends and colleagues.

A stunned French photojournalist was following every twist from the press helicopter. 'I asked the pilot to follow SAR to wherever they went – a hospital,' recalls Gilles Klein, who happened to be a close friend of Giroux. Klein was anxious to gain further information. Instructing the pilot to hover in the hospital grounds, he jumped the remaining distance to the ground and proceeded to simply walk past the hastily arranged hospital security. 'I walked into a building and there I saw lying on the ground three bodies. I touched Bernard's neck. It was cold ...' Over on the mainland nobody was yet sure as to the extent of the men's injuries. Initial reports suggested it had been a nasty, but not fatal accident. Klein knew. Stunned by the day's events, the journalist made his way home with a reel of footage that would appear the next day in the international media.

It was time for official machinery to kick in. Various authorities were notified including the Isle of Wight coroner who then appointed a surveyor to carry out an inspection of *Colibri*, that had been impounded in a Lymington boatyard. The survey found the boat to have been technically sound. It also found that superficial damage might have been present before the accident. In other words, *Colibri* had come out of the accident virtually unscathed. Its electrically driven clock had stopped at precisely 11.42 and 20 seconds.

In the magical forest of Rambouillet it was a warm, motionless afternoon when the telephone ominously rang somewhere in the house. Not even a leaf stirred. Only the incessant noise of the phone had broken the lassitude. When she heard the voice of her de facto sister-in-law on the other end of the line, Catherine Goux instinctively knew she was about to hear the worst possible kind of news. Such was her reaction to Didier's death, friends feared not only for Catherine's health, but also for that of her unborn twins.

Pathologist Dr Neil Greenwood would record Didier's cause of death as drowning. The initial head injury had not in itself been fatal. Giroux, who had resolved to make the Needles trophy his final offshore race, died as a result of severe head and brain injuries. The two men found underneath the boat had been wearing safety harnesses and as such ignited a long-running debate in offshore racing in the face of accidents: to be thrown clear or remain strapped into the boat? Jean-Claude Guénard, Didier's childhood friend and soulmate, died from a serious chest injury. While the former pair had been trapped under the hull, the impact had flung Guénard clear. All three men had also lost their helmets in the crash, despite being fitted with chinstraps, prompting coroner Keith Chesterton to remark that he was 'disturbed' how two of the victims had suffered severe head injuries. He urged re-examination of helmet spec and design as a matter of priority.

Offshore went into a period of profound reflection. Renato Della Valle retired on the spot. One week later, several teams did not enter the Cowes–Torquay–Cowes race. In the wake of its worst tragedy, offshore took a long hard look at itself. Ever since that fateful day in the English Channel, offshore racing has never quite been the same sport.

Four days later, the remaining members of the family gathered in St Tropez for the funeral. Up at the villa nobody spoke. Imelda had lost a son, her only son, the boy she had proudly watched develop into a great sportsman, but more importantly a son who had remained devoted to his family. Words could not express her grief. Louis and José, father and brother-cousin were silent too, lost in their thoughts. Like everybody else, as well as feeling dazed, they were perplexed, angry, bitter, confounded – a cocktail of emotions. After everything Didier had been through these past years – fear, pain, doubt and latterly hope, the injustice seemed especially cruel, malicious almost.

Back in his early F1 days, Didier had witnessed the demise of several colleagues: 'Death? It's hard not to think about it,' he reflected in an interview of the time. 'Recent accidents have forced me to face certain truths. My disappearance would be unfortunate for my loved ones but they at least would know that I would die happy.'

Catherine Goux had also broached the subject on one occasion. Didier's view was emphatic: 'Death for me is the end of life. No more, no less. It is irreversibly the conclusion of every human being, of all life, whether vegetable or animal ... I do not believe in fate. One can meet death immediately or if you want to live safely, you get there. The moments that we live are probably more difficult to pass than when we die. Death will not be, a priori, a problem for me.'[60]

Late on a warm St Tropezian afternoon, the cortège made its sombre way to the chapel of Notre Dame de la Queste, a serene location a little under two kilometres from the village of Grimaud. Hundreds if not thousands of people lined the way. Resting on the coffin, a single orchid, Didi's flower. Within the chapel's cool, baroque interior, mourners from the world of motorsport and beyond joined the family to bid farewell to the blonde hero whose life had been such an incredible rollercoaster of triumph and tragedy.

Too fragile to walk, Catherine – his last and greatest love – attended the service in a wheelchair amid fears for a pregnancy that was now as delicate as it had once been improbable. Sat further back, with their cherished memories, some of the women who had loved him: the other Catherine, Véronique, Agnes.

'Our wings are burned in the sun of glory,' remarked Father Vinceleu in his homily. 'Even when one lives with a star in the head, one meets his destiny one day.' Didier had met his fate – a wave off the English Channel that had tossed his hummingbird high into the air rendering her wingless, helpless.

Didier Joseph Louis Pironi was laid to rest in the Cemetery of Grimaud. Though a Parisian through and through, this chimeric landscape of verdant hills, medieval villages and shaded villas had always had a special place in his heart. Not too far away from his final resting place, out beyond the harbours and the quays along which he used to haunt, a huge expanse of sea, the deep, dark Mediterranean, that infinite space which he loved so much.

'You had that moment,' Catherine would later write to her lost love, 'through which you always said it would not be difficult to pass ...'[61]

Twenty-eight
Forever 28

OUR story is not quite over. There is time for one final chapter, and in a story rich in coincidence, what better number for that final chapter than 28, the number of his Ferrari, Didi's number?

Shortly after the funeral, Catherine admitted herself into the Université de Paris Baudelocque clinic. Room 10 became her sanctuary. A history of gynaecological problems compounding her bereavement, she spent the next five months of her pregnancy confined within the pale pink walls of this one room. To hang on to her precious cargo, she faced the fight of her life.

Never was that fight so fragile than during the winter of 1987. Under the care of Professor Zorn, the progress of herself and the unborn twins was evaluated daily. In January, at the seven-and-a-half-month point in her pregnancy, temperature falling alarmingly, Catherine was rushed to theatre where surgeons performed an emergency caesarean. On 6 January she gave birth to twin boys who were immediately transferred to an incubation unit in intensive care. Here the twins' body temperatures could be maintained and monitored and the risk of infection minimised.

Eventually the danger period passed. The French media descended on the hospital. Happiness tinged with sadness, for even as the proud mother posed with her newborn babies, she acutely felt the lack of her partner's presence. Snuggled up in the warmth of their Souvigny bed Didier and Catherine had, as expectant parents do, often speculated about their babies; would the twins be boys or girls, or one of each sex? If boys, would they follow in their father's footsteps, on the race circuits? For a career Didier preferred, he said, astronomy over racing. That last summer had been a time of great joy. Didier would joke about how he had struggled for so long to create one baby, and now had succeeded in creating two at once!

In a gesture of reconciliation, the exhausted, but proud new mother, christened her babies Didier and Gilles. Time finally to lay the ghosts of Imola '82 to rest.

Cocooned in her hospital room, Catherine now realised she had another fight on her hands, weak as she felt. Pironi or Goux? Which name would the twins bear? Catherine had no doubts in her mind, but the law had different ideas. Didier had died before he could claim paternity, a necessary requirement in test-tube conception where the right is not automatically recognised. As things stood, the twins would therefore bear their mother's name. It would take recourse to the courts in order for in vitro fertilisation to be recognised as an act of paternity, thus allowing the twins to take the name of their father. Finally, after over six months of legal wrangling, the court of Nanterre granted the right to acknowledge Didier as father to the twins. Didier and Gilles would carry their father's name. As the first case of its kind where babies conceived in vitro while the father was alive were born after his death, 'the Pironi case' set a legal precedent.

Catherine returned to Souvigny, the 'little island'. As she coped with the demands of motherhood, she began to write *Lettre à Didier*, a long, tender epistle to her vanished partner conceived through an overwhelming need 'to talk to him, tell him how I loved him, tell him how he made me happy'. Part lament, part eulogy, as well as a final adieu, it is also an opportunity to say all the things she wanted but never had the chance to express. An object lesson in lyrical intimacy, the letter is not only therapeutic, but is also a testament to grief and yearning.

Souvigny became a shrine to lost love. Sometimes Catherine would daydream the sound of helicopter blades or the revving of the tricycle and imagine them followed soon after by her lover's familiar greeting and smile. Her 'man-too-fast' was there, an absent presence. Notwithstanding the company of her three sons, emptiness and solitude filled the days. Catherine vowed to carry on living in the once enchanted woods that had now lost all their lustre. Just a few years into the future, however, the palace-turned-mausoleum would mysteriously burn to the ground. While the twins slumbered one evening, a fire started in the nursery that raged through the property's thatched roof and its oak beams consuming everything, sparing nothing. Souvigny was reduced to ashes, a dream charred. 'The Pironi curse,' whispered the French media. End of one life, start of another. Catherine and the children left for Metz, the town of her childhood.

Tragedy did not end there. Since the death of his protégé, in addition to running Leader, José had started flying commercially for a private company. On 16 April, he was flying a party of five from Paris (Le Bourget) to Montpelier where they were due to attend an offshore event in company with Pierre Harnois. The party, which included sponsors and employees, stopped off at Roanne, a small town roughly equidistant between the two cities, and where they enjoyed a leisurely meal washed down with a good quantity of wine. At 17.40, the Mitsubishi Marquise took off once more. Fifteen minutes later, it crashed in a ball of flames into a field near St Just, killing all six people on board. José had survived Didier by just eight months. Once again, the family gathered in Grimaud, this time to inter the older of the maverick brother-cousins. José was duly laid to rest next to his younger sibling in the family plot where his mother Ilva rested. The inscription upon the joint grave of the daredevil brother-cousins reads, 'between the stars and the sea'.

Now in his seventies and suffering from dementia, Louis would often ask after his two sons. Any amount of reassurance would fail to allay his distress. Nursed by Imelda, the dejected old gentleman was living out his days in the comfort of the St Tropez villa, scene of so many joyous occasions. At the invitation of Catherine, Imelda would later join her grandsons in Metz. It was a supreme gesture of compassion. The old lady had lost everyone and everything she ever cared about; all she had left were the twins:

'This unexpected gift from heaven is my only reason for living.' They are my happiness, my pride,' concludes her memoir. 'I have the privilege to live with them and their mother. I watch them, trying to repress the pain that assails me when the implacable reality is clear: for them, their dad will be forever a beautiful memory.'

Today the twins live in Paris and Oxford respectively. Didier works in finance while Gilles works for the Mercedes F1 team. Unassuming, measured, softly spoken and scrupulously polite, these young men have inherited several of their father's characteristics, though a career change to astronomy seems, for the present at least, unlikely. After convincing herself that no man could ever fill the place of her lost knight, Catherine did eventually find another partner. Nowadays she lives quietly in a London suburb. As for the castle at Boissy, along with the splendid St Tropez villa, the grand old house was eventually lost to creditors as the once great company floundered into bankruptcy.

And so, inevitably, we arrive back where we started, at the question that has tantalised so many people: *Who was Didier Pironi?* Have we then moved any closer in our quest to unravel the identity of this enigma, a blonde Icarus who flew too close to the sun on one occasion too many?

'Your love of life was written on your face, apparent within the least of your actions,' writes Catherine Goux in her letter. 'Flames dancing in the intensity of your blue eyes that had me hooked the first time I saw you on a circuit.'[62] Emmanuel Zurini remembers a man who 'loved good food, nice girls, great cars, aeroplanes, helicopters. He loved spending good times with his friends. In fact, he was just a normal guy! I miss him a lot ...' Convivial, precocious, enigmatic, mysterious, elusive, he was all these things and more.

In his Boissy youth, the teenage Didier had admired a certain Henri de la Ferme, a local man who eked a living doing whatever he could do to make ends meet. Selling his vegetables and haunting the local cafés, his was an unpretentious existence, free of artifice and materialism. Though he lived in a splendid castle himself, the teenager found himself inexplicably drawn to this man and the modesty of his existence. Is that what he truly longed for: Simplicity? Obscurity? An ordinary life? More questions yet.

The last word goes to Philippe Paoli, family friend and fellow patient at Porte de la Choisy, who perhaps sums up the essence of Didier most eloquently of all:

'He had a soft voice, looked shy, but had the inflexible will to reach his objectives. Nothing looked serious to him, but he took everything seriously! Nobody or nothing could have stopped him!' The memory of the blonde hussar wooing the great and good of the Pilot-Elf jury that glorious day still clear in his mind, Paoli makes this final, perceptive analogy that might finally help solve the riddle of Didier Pironi:

> 'Didier always made a strange impression on me. He was for me "the man who wasn't there". As with everyone, he was a simple passenger on earth, but he was "passing" faster than anyone, crossing life like a Knight Templar who has a mission to complete. This is who he was, the Templar on his horse who is dedicated to fight to his death for an ideal, no matter what he was doing, it was how he was doing it that mattered.'

Notes

1 Using migrant Italian labour, in May 1924 construction of France's first motor racing circuit had begun on Autodrome de Linas-Montlhéry, 30 kilometres south of Paris.

2 Since arriving in France, Imelda was also known as 'Eliane'. Henceforth, we use her birth name Imelda.

3 Long after they had gone their separate ways, one member of the 'gang of three' would serve a lengthy prison sentence for his part in a robbery in which a part-time policeman was killed. Didier might have indeed had a close escape.

4 Didier would briefly allude to this curious incident in an interview in *Automobile* magazine, no. 12, 1978.

5 Winner in 1971, Tambay had triumphed with a combined time of 15'23.7.

6 About £290,000 in 2017.

7 Mange was another member of this drama to suffer an untimely end when, in 2009, he was attacked at the premises of his garage business by a disgruntled customer. Mange died of his injuries.

8 Camus, M. (2004) *La Fleche Brisee*, p.30, Editions du Palmier.

9 *Sport-Auto*, no. 182, January 1978.

10 *Motorsport*, July 1977, p.84.

11 Opert gave up motorsport altogether in 1983 when French driver Olivier Chandon of Moet-Chandon champagne fame drowned in one of his cars following an accident at the Florida motorway.

12 Hamilton, M. (2002) *Ken Tyrrell: The Authorised Biography*, p.216, Willow.

13 The medical term for excessive sweating is hyperhidrosis. It is a condition in which the body generates unnaturally high levels of perspiration. The amount of sweat produced is rarely, if ever, correlated with the actual extent of physical effort. Thus, in the worst cases, even when completing mundane tasks, sufferers can find themselves drenched in sweat.

14 *Grand Prix*, 'Didier Pironi' by Nigel Roebuck.

15 *La Fleche Brisee*, p.46.

16 *Motorsport*, March 1980, p.354.

17 *Autocar*: 1980 F1 review, p.15.

18 Fédération Internationale du Sport Automobile, the former governing body of motorsport.

19 Formula One Constructors' Association, the largely British-based group of chassis builders including Lotus, McLaren,

Tyrrell, Brabham and Williams, whose interests at the time were represented by Bernie Ecclestone.

20 *Grand Prix International*, no.21, page 53.

21 *Motorsport*, July 1997, p.97.

22 *Grand Prix International*, no.29, April 1981, p.32.

23 The bike still survives to this day, kept under lock and key by Didier's nephews.

24 *Sport-Auto*, January 1981, p. 23.

25 *Grand Prix International*, no.29, April 1981, p.35.

26 Looking as immaculate as the day it was first manufactured, a private collector bought the car for the sum of CHF 43,651 at a Swiss auction in 2005.

27 Hunt drove in a total of 92 Grands Prix between 1973 and 1979.

28 The top six times were: Piquet 1'08.4, Pironi 1'08.8, Rosberg 1'10.2, Reutemann 1'10.3, Arnoux 1'11.9, Prost 1'12.8.

29 Arnoux's pole position time of 1'06.3 at the 1982 event compares to Jabouille's pole time in the 1980 event of 1'10.0.

30 The Fédération Internationale de l'Automobile, overseer of motoring organisations worldwide.

31 The international image agency Getty images own the rights to the surviving wedding photographs.

32 At one point Balestre hinted at disqualification not only for Piquet and Rosberg, but also for Watson, Mansell, Alboreto and Winklehock, second, third, fourth and fifth respectively in Brazil. Had he carried out this threat, Didier's sixth place would have become second place. The extra five points would have given him a total of 44 at season's end – the same as Rosberg's final total.

33 Franco Gozzi, Enzo Ferrari's private secretary, confirmed that such a meeting did indeed take place.

34 *Profondo Rosso,'Gli ultimi giorni di Gilles'*. Leo Turrini, 2011.

35 Either way, Gilles' case does not improve; by overtaking his team-mate a few laps after his error, it was in fact the French Canadian driver who ignored the 'slow' signs and who therefore first 'disobeyed' team orders.

36 *Auto Hebdo*, no.315.

37 *Gilles Villeneuve: The Life of the Legendary Racing Driver*, p.305.

38 *1982: The inside story of an astonishing Grand Prix season*, p.42.

39 *La Stampa*, 27 April 1982.

40 *La Flèche Brisée*, p.86.

41 John Keats, 'Ode on a Grecian Urn'.

42 *L'Automobile* 435, September 1982.

43 'Didier Pironi' in *Grand Prix* (1981).

44 *Trouver Le Chemin*, p.106.

45 Ibid, p.112.

46 *Paris Match*, no.1745, 5 November 1982.

47 *GEO*, December 1982, No.46.

48 *Trouver Le Chemin*, p.114.

49 *Cine Revue*, 24 May 1984.

50 *La Stampa*, 10 May 1984.

51 *L'Equipe*, January 1985.

52 *Seven Days*, June 1985.

53 When he met an untimely end in the Himalayas, Midy would become yet another casualty from the pool of characters associated with Didier and his story.

54 *Powerboating International*, June 1987.

55 The quote approximates to a line from Jacques' 'Seven ages of man' speech in William Shakespeare's *As You Like It*. The actual line reads: 'Last scene of all that ends this strange, eventful history.' Act II, sc. 7.

56 The powerboat accident, which would claim his life in Monaco in October 1990, Casiraghi had vowed, would be his last.

57 The 1987 Poole Bay Needles Trophy Offshore Powerboat Race Accident Report: Exhibit 2: Paul Wavell testimony.

58 The 1987 Poole Bay Needles Trophy Offshore Powerboat Race Accident Report: Exhibit 6: Tim Mellery-Pratt testimony.

59 In a strange twist of fate, Sub-lieutenant Crowther would die in an accident himself not long after the *Colibri* incident. On holiday in Calpe, Spain, the Royal Navy man bungee-jumped from the town's famous bridge, but had miscalculated the length of rope required. The unfortunate man died of his injuries.

60 *Lettre a Didier*, p.19.

61 Ibid. p.19.

62 Ibid. p.57.

Select Bibliography

Bamber, J. Hodges, D. Nye, D. & Roebuck, N. (1981) *Grand Prix*, (London: Joseph).

Camus, M., (2004) *Didier Pironi: La Flèche Brisée*, (Editions du Palmier)

Courtel, C., (1981) *Formule Renault*, (Editions du Palmier)

Donaldson, G., (1989) *Gilles Villeneuve: The Life of the Legendary Racing Driver*, (McClelland & Stewart)

Goux, C., (1988) *Lettre a Didier*, (Fillipacchi)

Hamilton, M., (2002) *Ken Tyrrell: The Authorised Biography*, (Willow)

Hilton, C., (2007) *1982: The Inside Story of the Sensational Grand Prix Season*, (J.H. Haynes and Co Ltd)

Jannot, V., (2006) *Trouver Le Chemin*, (J'ailu)

Pironi, I., (1995) *La Trajectoire Brisee*, (unpublished)

The Royal Motor Yacht Club, (1987) *The 1987 Poole Bay Needles Trophy Offshore Powerboat Race* (unpublished)